Adventures of a World-Traveling Scientist

Adventures of a World-Traveling Scientist

Seventeen Amazing Stories of Discovery and Exploration

Stanley Randolf, M.Sc.

Tasora

Tasora
5120 Cedar Lake Road
Minneapolis, MN 55416
(952) 345-4488
Distributed by Itasca Books
Printed in the U.S.A.

Cover design by Debbie Johnson and John Houlgate
Original cover photo by naufalmq/depositphotos.com [1]
Section separator design by Irina Zharkova, modified by Debbie Johnson

Publishers Note: These stories are either true chronologically as experienced by the author or expressed as a combination of related events in a different order from what the author experienced.
Disclaimer: Any connection to any person living or deceased is purely coincidental; the names in these stories have been changed.

Library of Congress Cataloging-in-Publication Data

Randolf, Stanley.
Adventures of a World-Traveling Scientist/Stanley Randolf
Summary: "Seventeen short stories of adventure spanning the globe. Includes adventures in sport fishing, hunting, hiking, culture-building, native cultures, native beliefs, aliens, travel, murder, healing, and safari-adventures.
ISBN 978-1-934690-93-2 (softcover)
1. Travel - Non-Fiction 2. Special Interest 3. Adventure – Non-Fiction
TRV001000

Printed in the United States of America

Dear Family of Mine...and my Reader-Family,

These stories were written specially for my family, but my editor said some other folks might like them, too, so here they are in a published book! I hope the rest of you readers enjoy them as much as I did writing them.

For all those hours, days, and months that I was away from home, traveling, this book uncovers exciting details I may have left out of our bedtime talks... my journal documents, notes, and photographs were used to recover many of the hidden truths. The lesson for you: Always make notes of your special experiences and take lots of pictures—details can get lost in your memories.

To Get You to Clean up Your Rooms, I Started My Story Career:

Remember "The Thompson Family?" Oh yeah, they were fiction for my benefit. Remember, they were those small people that lived between the upstairs and downstairs in our old house. They helped convince you to keep your rooms clean—if you didn't they would come out when you were asleep and steal your favorite toys!

Have Your Own Adventure

There's lots to explore and research from this book if you want to move mountains in your own life or change the world.... Just look for the hidden treasure in each story.

With Love and Hugs,

Stanley Randolf

P.S. My family knows my real name, this is a pen name to protect the confidentially of the relationships of those involved in the stories: the innocent, the guilty, and the hung-over.

Dedications

First and foremost, to Phyllis, my wife, award winning grandmother, avid book lover, puzzle-fixer in the broadest sense, and the love of my life. Then…

Jennifer, first daughter, skilled schoolteacher, French-fluent artist, understanding mother, lover of cats and the simple life.

Angela, second daughter, animal and travel lover, artist, mother of style and dedication. And, lap-dog Barrow's master!

Caroline, third daughter, dedicated mother, first class homemaker, book and movie aficionado, Christmas queen.

Jeffrey, only son, President of the probiotic company I founded, artist, great father, good fisherman, guitar-man.

Dylan, oldest grandson, big and strong, professional physical education coach in-the-making.

William, number-two grandson, tall and thin, can throw a curve ball, understands calculus and matrix math, will start a financial advisory business someday.

Charles, number-three grandson, master of ceramics and cats, can make anybody laugh, including me; his patented red-hair will catch some gal and they'll open an upscale restaurant someday.

Hannah, smart, cute, and independent. First granddaughter. This college gal is a star.

Carson, fourth grandson, my number one assistant, can out-fish the whole family, loves playing hockey and snowmobiling.

Courtney, second granddaughter, dancing queen, smoothie expert, dog lover, follows in her mother's footsteps.

Emily, third granddaughter, very special, independent and loving, I-Pad queen. Her dark hair and sparkling eyes pull you in close.

Coen, fifth grandson, energy-boy, Lego expert, artist in his father's footsteps—a junior Jedi.

Kylie, fourth granddaughter, shy and sweet, follows brother Coen close. The world will turn for her.

Allison, soon to be a year old, redefines cute, smiles at everyone, even Dylan.

Adventures of a World-Traveling Scientist
Contents

Author studying an ancient termite mound

1

Dreamtime in Australia

True-Life Adventure Down Under

Prologue:

In July of 2001 I was working with Adam Rody in Australia's Northern Territory (NT). Adam was an aquaculture specialist and together we were pioneering the use of biotechnology to purify water in aquaculture ponds. Improving the growth and health of tiger prawns—big shrimp—was our priority. After working together in Southeast Asia for a month, were ready for some serious R & R. Adam lived in Darwin, the capital of the NT, with his wife and three children.

Darwin was at the doorstep of the wild frontier in the Northern Territory, the home of eighteen-foot crocodiles, the most poisonous snakes in the world, giant monitor lizards, and big seabass called barramundi. A Great place for some rest and relaxation, provided you're prepared for adventure with surprises! Adam suggested we go into the bush and do a walkabout, some fishing, and look around.

Darwin, Australia, 2001

We were ready to make camp about two kilometers from the river—far enough to avoid saltwater crocs notorious for making dry land excursions. We were south of Darwin and eighty kilometers east of the Stuart Highway with the Roper River to the north and Aboriginal Arnhem Land further north. It was 4:00 p.m.

I was excited for whatever adventure was ahead but in most of my travels to unconventional places, I usually tried to be with someone who knew the ropes. Adam was an Ozzie who was a veteran in Oz. There was a strange vastness to the Outback up here, and once off the highway, we were totally alone in it.

"Did you bring any croc-repellent?" I asked Adam jokingly, not knowing if there was such a product.

"No mate, just V.B.—Victoria Bitter! The best beer in Australia," Adam replied.

"Did you hear my question over the road noise?" We had been bumping along on a dirt road since turning off the highway.

"Aye Mate. Croc-repellents are sold at bars in Darwin: Two parts lime vodka, one-part Irish whiskey, two shakes of orange bitters, and enough ice and ginger ale to fill the glass. Great on a hot day!"

I laughed. "You got me! Didn't have a clue such a drink existed."

"After three or four a bloke stops worrying about crocs."

"I'll keep that in mind if we make it back to Darwin."

"No worries, crocs won't come off the river this far. About a hundred meters is their maximum trek from water—when they do a walkabout," Adam assured me.

"What about that eighteen-footer that crossed the street in Darwin yesterday—not far from your house!" I asked him, knowing he lived quite some distance from open water. "A picture of the monster was on the front page of the *Top End Review*. Its head was the size of a foot-locker!" I challenged Adam.

"That was Mad Max, he lives in ditch water. He doesn't eat people, just pets—dogs and cats mainly. The sheriff has been after him," Adam said nonchalantly. "There are no ditches out here, just the river two kilometers that way." He pointed east.

"Just checking—I'll trust the aquaculture specialist."

"Good man," Adan replied. "No worries, she'll be apples."

"I take it you mean everything will be all right?" Trying to recall the Aussie slang.

"That's what I said mate, she'll be apples. You Yanks need to spice up your English; it's gone stale on yah."

"No problem, she'll be apples!" I replied. "Actually, it makes me think of an old girlfriend in college."

We drove to a clearing in the bush where four trees made a square, so camp was simple to set up. We strung a large tarp high between the four trees and put two cots under it.

"Simplicity in Oz," Adam declared.

"I wouldn't have expected anything less! After all, less than nothing is nothing," I said jokingly. Indeed, simplicity was to be applauded.

It was hot—I mean oven-hot—in the middle of the dry season in the Northern Territory. The angle of the sun was twelve degrees south, a scorching angle! Australia's Top End—nickname for the Northern Territory—was hotter than places on the equator because it didn't get cloud shielding. There was rarely a cloud around during the dry season. The leaves on the eucalyptus trees, called gum trees in Oz, had curled up to limit water loss. The long grass was dead, brown, and dusty. I went over to the water bag on Mitsy's grill and filled my tin cup with cool water. Mitsy was Adam's nickname for the Mitsubishi SUV—a "ute" in Australian.

"It's hotter than a goanna's gonads!" Adam declared, and tossed his cup over to me. We were sitting on a dead gum tree. Not another soul was anywhere near; both of us put a wet towel over our shoulders.

"Evaporation cooling works every time, mate. That wet canvas bag keeps the water jug cool. An old Aussie desert trick," Adam elaborated.

"And you can use ditch water on the outside of the bag…" I added, thinking of Mad Max.

Camp set, we took a drive to the river. There were endless gum and woollybutt trees interspaced with termite mounds. The termite mounds were the largest I've seen anywhere; clay castles, some over twelve feet high!

"Do you know the chemical formula for these mounds, Mr. Biochemist?" Adam asked me.

"I could guess but you tell me," I replied. We were having "driveabout" school in the vastness.

"Soil, termite saliva, and termite dung," Adam enlightened me.

"I would have guessed two, forgot the spit!"

"Hey Mate, you're starting to get your English right!" Adam grinned.

The termite mounds were everywhere—it was a metropolis of mounds. They were rust-colored and had stalagmite-like pinnacles at their tops. Some were round on top and looked like monks in hooded robes.

"Them termites are bloody important out here," Adam added. "They recycle dead leaves and other organics; the mounds are the result."

"I read the aborigines used the mounds for medicine. For diarrhea and headaches."

"The Abos are bush-smart," Adam said. "There are biochemical compounds in those mounds that even modern science doesn't know. The Abo's knowledge comes from forty thousand years of experience."

"Can you call them Abos?" I asked.

"Up here in the NT it's okay if they know you. Out east, like in Brisbane, no. You must call them Indigenous Australians (I.A.)! If you want to get an Abo up here bummed off, just call him an I.A."

"I'll just call them by their first names," I said.

"Right, it's best for you Yanks to do that."

"Mitsy kicked up clouds of brown dust around several wallabies that were keeping up with us. "Everything jumps in Australia," Adam said. "Red kangaroos jump the highest and farthest, then gray roos, then wallys. Even rats and mice jump here."

I laughed, "C'mon, not rodents, too!"

"Hey, mate, it's true—there are also jumping bugs and spiders!"

"Maybe the hot ground was the evolutionary force?" I suggested.

"You got it mate, they all evolved to keep their arses off the ground as much as possible—air cooled bums!"

"These wallys move fast," I noted. They jumped into our path then swerved away at the last second. Looking out, beyond them, were more trees and termite mounds.

When we got to the water we could see a large billabong—a lagoon that was part of the river. It was in front of us with the Roper River behind. We got out and carefully looked around, always a smart thing to do in croc country.

"It's snake country too!" Adam reminded me. On the drive from Darwin we had discussed several lethal, poisonous snakes that also R & R in the NT.

"I remember you said the taipans and browns were a big worry in river country?"

"Aye, both snakes can kill you in less than an hour if you don't get first aid and a shot of antivenom. The taipans are usually darker than the browns."

"What if one of us gets bit out here?" I asked him.

"The short answer is: don't get bit out here. But should it happen, I've got special compression bandages in the ute; they get put on immediately along with a splint. Then we speed to Katherine for a shot of antivenom. No tourniquet. No cutting. No sucking. Just a firm compression bandage. The keys to living another day are compression, immobilization and antivenom," Adam explained without kidding around.

"Amber-Fluid Time," Adam declared, as he reached into one of the coolers in the back of the ute and pulled out two cold bottles of Victoria Bitter. "V.B., the best beer in the world," he proclaimed, holding it up.

"I recall you said it was the best beer in Australia."

"Aye, just promoted it to the world."

"Okay, you've got the credentials to do that," I added, opening my bottle on Mitsy's door hinge. A cold beer was what I needed after the snake talk.

"Aussies say it's ripper. Cold beer is a ripper on a hot day." I was still a student of the Australian language and the teacher was drinking while teaching me.

We walked down to the river. I held the V.B. bottle to my forehead and the cold felt good. There was a slight odor of algae tempered by the dry air. It wasn't unpleasant. We drank V.B. while looking out over the water.

"See any croc snouts?" He asked.

"Nope, none I can see." I was using binoculars and scanning the water. It reminded me of scanning trees for leopards in Tanzania.

"Wait, look at that lizard!" I said, pointing to a white gum tree on the river bank. "He's halfway up the main trunk and at least seven feet long!" I handed the binoculars to Adam.

"I see it—don't need the binocs—it's a lace goanna, a real beaut." It was a big lizard in the monitor family—that much I knew. I had never seen one this size in any zoo. It was making a strange grunting sound, something between a huff and a grunt and kept turning its head, snapping at us. Truly a living dinosaur. It was dark gray with yellow bands every inch or so and had raptor eyes. It was not happy to see us.

"He's a bloody loud grunter; doesn't like us," Adam said. Just then it ran up the tree about six feet and circled around halfway so we only could see its tail. The tail was easily four feet long.

"It's a monitor lizard. There are twenty-five different species in Oz; this one can grow to three meters," Adam explained.

"That's over nine feet!" I was impressed. Great sighting. We could still hear it huff-grunting.

"They are vicious carnivores, one like this can eat a kangaroo!" Adam kept the facts coming. I watched the lizard stretch its neck around the tree looking to see if we were still around.

"Several years ago, a bloke attending to one at a tourist zoo near Sydney got a hand mangled; lost several fingers. He'd been feeding raw meat to lions and had meat odor on his hands when he went into the monitor's containment. He was lucky—it could have been worse," Adam said, while biting three fingers as a demonstration.

Looking out beyond the lizard, Adam was studying the water in the billabong. "There's current here. It's not stagnant." Many billabongs were stagnant lagoons choked with algae.

"Means it could hold barra." I was pleased at the possibility.

"Aye mate, big ones."

Barramundi are giant sea bass that, like salmon, can live in both fresh and saltwater. It was a superb fighting fish that could reach sixty pounds; the premier gamefish in the Northern Territory. Catching a barra was at the top of my wish list for the trip.

We looked up. . .stars were starting to show. "The dark will come fast now," Adam remarked. Let's go back to camp and boil some shrimp, we'll fish here tomorrow for barra."

"Sounds good." I realized I was hungry!

Back at camp, it didn't take long to get a roaring fire going. One match! We burned mostly gum-tree wood, and the leaves, which produced a sweet eucalyptus odor. The hot fire coupled with the heat of the day was a strange sensation. It promoted sweating to the point where I shivered on my backside when facing the fire. Sweat just poured out of me. It was my body's natural cooling system working overtime. I had taken my shirt off earlier—found it, soaked it in melted ice water from the cooler, and put it back on. This provided some assistance to the natural process.

Adam was getting the bag of frozen shrimp from the cooler—the esky as they call it in Australia. These were large tiger prawns from the aquafarm we had visited last week—about three pounds. The bag was pinched between two large slabs of ice that had held up well.

"Victoria Bitter again, lad?" I nodded in the affirmative. He grabbed two more bottles. "It tastes even better deeper in the Never-Never! I'll tell you more about that later."

Adam was a classic Aussie specimen. Born in Sydney forty-four years ago, he was six-foot two, lanky and slender with short black hair and he always wore a wide- brim hat. Usually a white Stetson for business and an old crumpled bush hat in the Outback. He spoke Australian-English well.

I grabbed a copper kettle from the gear cooler and wiped it clean with a paper towel. We had verbally rehearsed these things on the drive from Darwin.

"Add wine now?" I asked him.

"Aye," Adam replied.

I was proud of my ability to skillfully open both wine bottles with my Swiss Army knife! Remembering to tap on the knife after the cork screw was in to break the wax seal—both corks then came out with an easy pull. I poured the two bottles of Adelaide Pinot Noir into the kettle and set it next to the fire. We needed enough wine to fully cover the prawns.

"Drunken shrimp coming up," Adam declared, stoked with hungry excitement.

"Here's to the Never-Never." I took a drink of V.B.

"Good on ya," Adam said, raising his bottle. We both looked up at the stars while waiting for the wine to boil. "We have two slabs of V.B. in the esky," Adam reaffirmed. He didn't want me worrying about not having enough beer!

"Can you find the Southern Cross?" He asked.

"Yes, give me a minute…hold on…there it is." I pointed to it. Five bright stars forming a cross high in the sky with the two pointer stars below it. "I remember seeing it for the first time in Africa. It was a crystal-clear night in the dry-season in Kenya, just like here."

"It's not the big 'X' of dimmer stars you see up there to the right; tourists get confused," Adam explained. "It's the compact smaller cross—some say it looks more like a kite. The Abos say it's an eagle's foot print,"

"It's on your flag," I said.

"Right-on mate," Adam replied. "One way or another, a man needs to find the cross."

"How do you find due south using the cross?" I asked him, "I should remember."

"Imagine a line running from the top of the cross to the bottom and extend it down four and a half times. The line will slant down. Then drop a second imaginary line straight down to the horizon from the end of the first line—that's due south!" Adam explained while putting more wood on the fire. "Now don't forget." It was the four and a half I had forgotten.

While waiting on the wine to boil, we got the garlic bread out, nicely wrapped in foil, ready to heat. Adam put it near the fire.

"Thank Abbey for me; the bread will be great with the shrimp."

"I will mate, she's a good lass." Adam had been married to Abbey for twelve years, they had three youngsters.

When the wine boiled, Adam broke the large clump of frozen tiger shrimp apart, two or three at a time, then dropped them into the boiling wine. They sizzled in purple bubbles as the bush bathed in the enticing aroma.

"She'll be right in five minutes," Adam said in Australian. "The best drunken shrimp in Oz!"

"Maybe in the world!" I interjected. In Indonesia prawn farmers dump live shrimp into boiling wine. They jump around drunk for about two seconds.

We sat on the ground and ate the wine-flavored tiger prawns and garlic bread while drinking V.B. We didn't talk about business. There had been enough of that during the previous three weeks. We talked about our wives and kids and how lucky we were compared to some other men. Life was good!

"How many beers in a slab?" I was curious.

"Twenty-four, mate, twenty-four. We'll have enough."

It was a perfect meal. The large prawns were delicious, tasting more like lobster than shrimp. They had been grown in an aquafarm that took precautions to limit water pollution by using my company's probiotic products. With improved water quality, the probiotics (eco-friendly bacteria) allowed the shrimp to grow faster and larger on less feed. This natural biotechnology also improved the prawn's taste and texture.

Looking up, the Southern Cross was easy to find—I just had to know where to look. It was to the left of the tarp!

Not much preparation was required for sleeping. The tarp only covered a small area above us; otherwise it was open. The crackle of the fire burning down was the only sound. Both of us were in shorts and tee shirts, ready for the cots and already dressed for fishing tomorrow. It was 10:00 p.m.

It took me longer to get to sleep than Adam. I had to go get a pair of jeans from the truck and roll them up for a pillow. I had a small flashlight on the ground between the cots next to a half-finished bottle of V.B. I thought about how an eighteen-foot, saltwater crocodile could run at ten miles per hour. No worries, we were two kilometers from the river. Adam was out cold, lying flat on his back snoring.

I awoke suddenly at 3:00 a.m. to a strange sound. *Crocs? Where are they?* My heart was pounding. *It can't be crocs! Was I dreaming? What kind of sound am I hearing?* I wondered. There was an eerie whining sound, all around us. I fumbled for the flashlight—found it and turned it on. Green eyes were everywhere. Moving green eyes. "What in the Sam Hell..."

"Adam," I said in a loud whisper. "Adam!" I said again, louder. I reached over, spilling the beer, and shook him. He groaned.

"Adam, wake up! Look in the flashlight beam!" He shifted around, grunting, and finally looked out.

"What the hell are those green eyes?" I said, shaking him again to get him sitting up.

"Dingoes," he mumbled, "No worries." Then he fell back to sleep.

Now I knew what they were; the wild dogs of Australia. A pack of them. Maybe one wouldn't attack, but a pack? I could see better now; there were five of them whining—Like a pet dog waiting to be fed—and walking in a large circle around us, about ten meters away. Large brown dogs with long necks, just whining and walking in a circle. The dinner fire was out except for a few embers and some smoke. I could see their profiles in its glow, I turned the flashlight off.

I stood up and shouted "*Go!*" as loud as I could. Then again. And again. They appeared to back up some and widen their circle. I thought about my options. *If they attacked; they might assume Adam was dead and only attack me.* My brain was beyond fear, it had switched to fight mode. *Could I get to the truck? No. I would have to go through them to get to it. I had my Swiss Army Knife out and open. There was only one self-defense option, lie flat on the ground and hold the cot on top of me upside down. And shout like hell! Maybe jab at them with the knife while under the cot. The cot was my only defense.* My brain was working overtime.

With these thoughts in mind, back to reality, I decided to stay awake watching the dogs. At 4:30 a.m. they were still there, but farther back and not as organized. There was no way to get to the truck without going through them. I thought of yelling again but didn't...

"Good morning most wonderful Yank, good morning. Glad to see you're up, glad you're not in a rut, good morning most wonderful Yank, good morning." Adam was singing to me, repeating that damned fraternity song over and over; the one I had mistakenly sung to him in Malaysia once.

I sat straight up. Looked around. It was 8:00 a.m. and the sun was shining bright. I must have fallen asleep sometime after 4:30 a.m., the last time I checked my watch. I was still alive! No blood! No upside-down cot on top of me. Wow.

"We had visitors last night," Adam said. "They ate all the shrimp shells and garlic bread. Licked the copper kettle spotless and dropped it behind Mitsy. Smart dogs those Dingoes."

"There were five of them—a pack," I said.

"Right, didn't get a good count myself."

"You woke up for about five seconds!"

"No worries mate. They just wanted our dinner scraps."

"Last month wild dingoes on Frazer Island killed a nine-year old boy," I told him. "Didn't you read about that?"

"Aye, it was a rare exception. Those dogs were starving on the island. They'd been trying to eat seagulls."

"Maybe so, but tonight I'm sleeping in Mitsy!"

"No problem, you might be a bit cramped; she's a small ute. Let's have some brekkie! Abbey mixed up some pancake batter. You start the fire, and I'll make coffee and clean the frying pan." Adam was wide awake and moving fast—it took me awhile longer to revive.

After breakfast, we got ready to go fishing. Barra fishing! I rigged my spinning rod and reel with twenty-pound test monofilament line and a blue Rapala. These lures had been good to me in many places and with different fish; which color to use was usually a guess. "What pound test are you going to use?" I asked Adam.

"Don't know mate, whatever's wound around the Coke can."

"Coke can?"

"That's what us blokes use up here, same as the Abos."

"You're kidding, right?" I remembered now that when we left Darwin, the only fishing rod in the truck was mine.

"No kidding, mate. We bait up a hook on the end of the line, which is wound around the can, and tie a hollow gum-tree stick an arm's length above the hook so it floats. Then we let the current take it off the can. I hold a screwdriver in the hole on top of the can and the line spins off. We don't need any fancy fishing gadgets."

"What do you do if you catch a big one?"

"No worries; just pull him in slow and easy, winding the line back on the can. You can palm the bottom of the can to add drag if necessary. Up around Katherine it's common to see a line of blokes holding cans with screwdrivers along the river.

"What's your biggest barra?"

"Don't know for sure, maybe two or three kilos. We need to get one for dinner or we'll be eating Spam."

"Okay," I said, "it will be an education to watch you. I hope you could afford to bring along a spare coke can!" That got a good Aussie laugh out of him.

"How far out can you throw that thing?" he asked, pointing to my rod and reel.

"You'll see," I said. I was amazed a guy with a Master's Degree in Aquaculture Science would fish with a coke can. Nevertheless, we were both excited and ready to go fishing.

The wallabies followed us again on the drive to the billabong. Adam played with them by making slow S-turns through the bush while they jumped and accurately followed our turns.

While he drove, Adam gave me a lesson on what the aborigines call the Dreamtime: "We are in the third part of the Dreamtime now: 'Now' being the last several thousand years or so. The first part was the time before time. The second part was the creation events that made everything. Aussies and Yanks are recent mutants. Abos go back forty thousand years. They are the real deal, direct descendants of the first beings. And, I haven't told you yet, the Roper River is called the 'River of Dreaming' by the Abos."

"And I thought you just studied aquaculture; I'm impressed!"

"I had a professor friend who knew all about Abos," Adam said. "You're going to meet a very smart one named George in Katherine tomorrow, on our way back to Darwin. And it's okay to call him an Abo."

"I'll just call him George."

"No problem. He makes paintings on bark that tell stories of the Now Time. He'll want to hear about the dingoes—he might even play the didgeridoo for you!"

"That will give you a chance to hear more about the dingoes too," I said to Adam, smiling. "Five seconds wasn't exactly an accurate evaluation."

On the opposite shore of the billabong a large brolga—a red-headed stork-like bird—was eating a small yellow fish lying on the water. I immediately replaced the blue Rapala with a yellow one and started casting. I was on shore in an open area free of shore grass where there was plenty of room for both of us. Large numbers of lily pads were straight out about ten meters and there was enough space between them to cast a lure. It was easy to cast the Rapala. It was the same size and color as the fish the brolga was eating.

Adam was looking for something in the back of the ute while I fished. What are you looking for?" I shouted.

"Found it," he answered—bringing out a baseball bat!

"What's that for?" I said in amazement and then, instantly, I knew.

"Tell me that's not for hitting crocs. . ." I said.

"Sure is, mate. You just keep fishing and I'll stand guard for a bit. This is serious business. Keep looking for snouts!" Adam had a major-league Louisville Slugger in his hands! He stood to my left, ankle deep in the water, with his legs spread wide, bat on his shoulder. "Smacking them on the snout gets them to leave," he said. I never would have guessed.

I tried not to think about the bat or the crocs. I didn't want to eat Spam tonight! All we needed was a five or six-pound barramundi for dinner. But a bigger one would be a nice surprise. Fishing off shore was a disadvantage compared to being in a boat.

I was reeling in the Rapala and bringing in algae slime with every cast. It was just under the surface in front of the lily pads. Having the lure dive and run about a foot deep wasn't working. I noticed the brolga had moved and was now looking at another yellow minnow lying motionless on the surface. Quickly, he stabbed it with his bill and swallowed. An easy meal, no chase. That's all I had to see; I knew what to do.

There was an outcropping of dead wood off to my right, half in and half out of the water. "Adam, I'm moving to the right a few meters." I made a special effort to look for snakes around the wood that was on shore.

"I'll be right next to you," he said. It was obvious now that guarding me was his main mission, fishing was secondary. His Coke can rig was lying on shore.

I was casting by the dead wood about five meters out from it. When the lure hit the water, I didn't do anything; I let it float and go still. It was about half way out to the lily pads. Bass fishermen in Florida called this "dead-sticking." But twitching the lure periodically, moving it an inch or so, then back to still, was essential. More time still than moving was the key.

Just then Adam noticed a snout out in the water on the left. "Little one," he said. "Four-footer in your language, bout ten yards out. He's just watching us." I had been mixing English with metric measurements on the trip, so Adam's jab was in order.

I looked over my shoulder; the crocodile wasn't making much of a wake. "Should we move?" I looked at Adam.

"No worries, I can handle this croc if he gets close. Keep fishing."

I kept casting out beyond the dead wood, each time twitching the lure after it went still. I moved it about two inches per twitch. Got about twenty twitches per cast. More time was spent keeping the lure still than moving. I paused and looked back at the croc which had stopped moving about five meters away and was just looking at us. I could see its eyes and most of its head. *An ancient reptile from dinosaur times,* I thought.

With Adam in charge of the croc, I got my attention back to fishing. I slightly twitched the lure and let it go still again. Then repeated, just slightly moving it, then back to still. To a large predator fish, the lure looked like an easy meal, and it didn't snag algae fishing it this way! When the brolga ate the second yellow minnow, I recalled the fish was still alive but sluggish, alternating movement with dead stops. I tried my best to mimic that action.

The croc was stone still, it seemed to be waiting for something to happen. I decided to cast closer to the dead wood. Nothing. Then I tried casting ten meters out from the wood, right at the edge of the lily pads. I let the lure go still, then gave it just a very slight twitch by moving the rod tip.

Instantly, a large fish inhaled the lure, disrupting the calm with a huge splash. I pulled back hard on the rod to set the hook. The fish skyrocketed into the air, completely clearing water. It was a barra! I held the rod high and moved left. I had to keep the fish away from the wood. There were two treble hooks on the Rapala; the forward treble was in the corner of the fish's mouth—a "good hook" as fishermen say.

The fish didn't run; it stayed close to where it was hooked. It swam in a wide circle as I kept medium pressure on it. "No slack line" was the rule. She thrashed violently. It was a big, fat, female barramundi.

"Big barra!" Adam shouted.

"It's a nice one!" I yelled back. I brought the fish closer to us and kept it going in a small circle. The eight-foot rod was helping me control the fish. The reel's drag would give line and then hold. I reeled line in, keeping just enough pressure on the fish as it shook its head, mouth open, trying to throw the Rapala.

Just then the croc kicked its tail and moved toward the fish. "He's going after the barra!" Adam yelled. Both Adam and I were ankle-deep in the water and we could see the full croc now; much bigger than what his snout had predicted.

"He's a big, small-snout bugger!" Adam exclaimed as he held the bat like Pete Rose waiting for a low fastball.

When I got the barra in closer I could see the Rapala deep in her mouth—she had bitten it in half! It was made of balsa wood and could not hold up to her bite. But, thank the stars, the lure's through-wire construction had held one treble hook in place. The two halves of the lure's body were on the wire between the treble hooks. She was two meters in front of me, head shaking and tail splashing. Your mind operates on a different frequency when adrenaline pours into it; I finally realized this was, indeed, a big fish with a good-size crocodile chasing it. If I didn't act fast, it would be half of a big fish.

As I kept her moving in a tight circle, she rapidly opened and closed her mouth, instinctively trying to throw the lure. She was going wild in the shallow water. The croc came after the fish, snapping at its tail. Adam was now in the water knee-deep holding the bat higher.

"She's still green with fight, but I gotta horse her closer to shore before the croc gets her!" I shouted.

"I'll club the croc, you beach the fish!" Adam shouted back.

I pulled hard on the barra bringing her closer. The croc was right behind the fish. Adam smashed at the croc and missed. He tried again and missed the snout but hit its shoulder with a glancing blow as it twisted sideways. Now it was mad and coming at Adam. I pulled up on the rod to get the fish higher in the water. Adam, with a clear opening now, smashed the crocs snout. Its mouth, with all its teeth showing, snapped at the bat. Adam hit the croc again. At the same time, with a strong pull on the rod, I beached the fish—dropped the rod—and jumped on her. I grabbed tightly under the gill plate and quickly carried the fish off the beach up to the ute. I didn't want our dinner jumping back in the water and becoming croc food! Looking back, I could see Adam was okay and the croc was gone. We were both wet and somewhere between petrified and triumphant.

"She'll be apples!" Adam yelled from the water.

"No worries, all's well!" I hollered back. "It took both of us to catch this barra!"

"Hey mate, I had the easy part," Adam said, walking out of the water with the bat over his shoulder. "Nice barra!"

"Adam Rody, you *are* The Louisville Slugger!" I saluted him.

The fish was on the ground in front of us, shining silver-white in the sun with a perfectly back tail. She measured thirty-eight inches and weighed eighteen pounds.

"Good on ya mate! She'll make a great dinner tonight," Adam said before starting Mitsi. "The Spam is going back to Darwin."

The billabong was calm again. The brolga had flown away, the lace goanna had moved on, a crocodile had been fought, and a barramundi had been caught. A pleasant smell of eucalyptus filled the air.

We talked a lot about fishing while preparing dinner. We gutted the fish and put a tire iron through it lengthwise to hold it over the fire. Two slabs of termite-mound rock acted as yokes to hold it. Adam took charge and kept rotating the fish and sprinkling it with Aussie Outback Spice. The barra tasted great...

I slept in the back seat of Mitsy while Adam slept on his cot under the tarp. I was cramped all night and had a sore neck as Adam had predicted. No dingoes visited as far as we could tell. Adam had disposed of the barra carcass an adequate distance from camp. More than half the fish was bagged the night before and iced to take home to Darwin. Abbey and the kids would enjoy a couple of meals with dad.

It was another hot, dry-season day, but we didn't mind. We cleaned up the camp site, packed the gear in Mitsy, put on wet tee shirts, and headed out to the Stuart Highway. We were on the way to Katherine to see George.

"Mitsy's getting old," Adam said, "need to think about a new ute."

"She got us to a barra," I confirmed.

"That she did," Adam replied. We were going about fifty kilometers per hour on the dirt and she was shaking. Then suddenly, coming from behind us, two gray kangaroos cut us off.

They turned quickly to avoid hitting us, then jumped along parallel to the ute on my side. Their hind legs reached as high as the top of my window! I was astounded. They were playing with us; this wasn't their first rodeo with a ute. The larger of the two was right beside my window, taking about a two-second look at me before bounding high, then another look as it came back down. Then up and down again, giving me glances each time. I put my right thumb up out the window; the kangaroo appeared to sense the meaning.

"Both of their Z-shaped legs must jump together," Adam quickly explained, as he slowed down and made S-turns like he had for the wallabies. If the roos wanted to play, he could play, too! They weaved in and out for close to a mile until we could see the intersection with the Stuart Highway ahead in the distance. Then, suddenly, they both jumped right at us! I ducked down with hands on my head. They cleared the top of the truck completely, one in front of the other. I couldn't believe it! Adam stopped the truck and we jumped out to look for them. They were bounding out to the south, in the direction of Alice Springs. I was speechless. What a performance! Mitsy with her S-turns could not out-do the roos.

"Gray roos," Adam remarked. "They can jump three meters high! It's Australia, mate—great fun."

The town of Katherine was a hundred kilometers ahead. Traffic was light on the highway except for frequent road trains, large trucks pulling several trailers or more! These road-trains were the lifeblood of northern Australia. They carried oil and other materials south to Alice Springs; more than half-the-width-of-the- continent away. Going ninety kilometers per hour, we got to Katherine in just over an hour. Mitsy seemed to run better at higher speeds.

George was sitting on a bench in front of a gift shop on the main street. He couldn't be missed. He was a large aboriginal man—an elder with dark penetrating eyes, a large bushy mop of black hair streaked with gray, and a pure white beard. Dressed in a clean white shirt and short black pants, he was playing a deep, hollow melody on his didgeridoo. He stopped when he saw us.

"Hello Adam, my friend," he said in a rich baritone voice.

"George, my man, what's going on?" Adam replied with a smile. They slapped hands.

"Where is your marvelous, magnificent, white Stetson hat?" George asked, speaking slowly and clearly.

"Back in Darwin with Abbey and the kids. We've been camping in the bush so I've got my bush hat on." Fortunately, our tee shirts had dried and our hats hid our dusty hair. It was no secret we had been out in the bush and George knew it.

"I want you to meet Mr. Stanley Randolf, my Yank business partner from Minnesota."

"Minnesota," George said. "Land of ten-thousand lakes. Glad to meet you!" We slapped hands.

"That's right, but I believe half of them are frog ponds," I said. George laughed. I could tell right away he was a wise man.

George asked about my wife and family, listening intently when I introduced them with loving words, sorry I didn't have a photo with me. Adam stood by with a hand on my shoulder.

George closed his eyes and was silent for a minute or so while looking at Adam. Then said: "You have a good man for a business partner as does he with you."

The three of us paused for a few moments as several yellow birds flew over us.

"Yellow Fig Birds," George said. "They know me."

"So, tell me about your time in the bush. Tell it all," George politely requested.

Adam and I took turns telling George about the five dingoes, the eighteen-pound barra, the attacking croc, the brolga, the wallabies, the seven-foot goanna, and the playful gray kangaroos. And about the two of us camping under the stars by eucalyptus and woollybutt trees while admiring giant termite mounds. We told it all.

George looked directly at me, then at Adam. It was a deep, all-seeing look. He said nothing for several minutes while he concentrated on a pot of multi-colored flowers next to his bench. Then he spoke.

"You both have shared a special Dreamtime," he said after the pause. "You have experienced some great events in the bush. You must thank the divine half of the spirit world for allowing you this opportunity. And for protecting you! I'm happy there were no snakes in your story."

"He's spot-on mate," Adam interrupted. "George is always spot-on. There's two sides in the spirit world just like down here!"

George nodded at Adam then continued: "You are living in the Now Dreamtime. Not everyone will experience the events you told me about. Many have never seen a giant goanna or caught a barramundi. You have and more. You must share your experience through writings and stories, even pictures if you can draw or paint. We are here because we chose to be. The Divine Oneness planned it this way. We are here to experience this creation we call the universe. Keep doing what you are doing and share your journey through life for as long as you can.

"We are in the late third period of the Dreamtime. A period just before great changes will happen. Changes in the solar system and the natural order of things. Do you both understand?"

"Yes, George, I understand!"

Adam was nodding that he understood, too.

"May I ask you a question?" I was really moved by this man.

"Certainly," George replied. Just as he spoke a cool breeze came on us, cooling the heat of the day and ruffling the flowers in the pot next to George. Then the Fig Birds flew back over us. It gave me pause for a moment.

"George, where does our soul reside in the Dreamtime?"

"Your soul is an extension of the Divine Oneness! It has existed forever. Including the Time before Time."

"That is certainly something to ponder and discuss with my soul voice!"

"Absolutely, you must do this! And you must share your journey! Promise me." George looked right at me.

"I promise! Thank you for sharing your wisdom with us. I really appreciate your thoughts and words. I will do my best to share my experiences with others. I will take your advice and write them down."

Adam agreed, but he wasn't a writer or painter, so he said, "I will tell the story many times. And I will explain the Never-Never to Stan on our way to Darwin."

George looked at Adam and nodded his head, smiling. Then he looked at me and said, "This is excellent—*transcending!* It's a marvelous day in the Dreamtime. I'm happy you stopped to see me!

"Mr. Randolf, have a safe trip back to Minneapolis. Mr. Rody, my good friend, tell your family I love them. I will paint a picture on bark from the paperbark tree of what you have told me. I will show it to many visitors!" George looked at us again and smiled wisely, then played us a song on his didgeridoo.

Postscript:

I have had many opportunities to visit Australia. Each visit taught me something about The Land Down Under and its animals, plants and people. The Never-Never is a special frame of mind that exists deep in the wild bush; in this story we just touched its edges. We'll talk more about it in a future book.

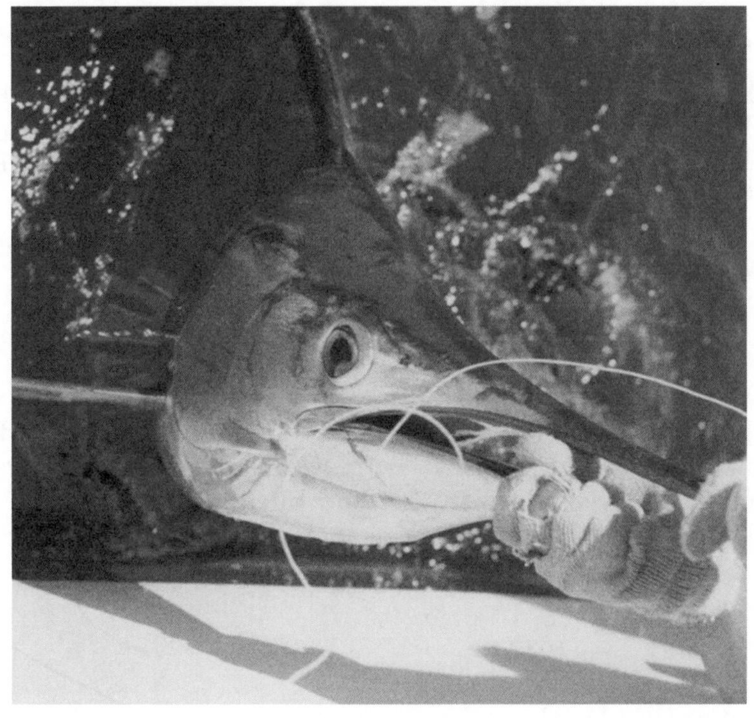

700 lb. Marlin caught by author using techniques discussed in story

2

The Soul of the Sea

The Challenge of Becoming a Man

The Caribbean Sea, east of Cuba, 1995

The old man stumbled up the steps from the galley onto the deck. It was 3:00 a.m. and the sea was calm. Dizzy and feeling like his head could explode, he chewed two more aspirin.

Radio Cubano was playing salsa music on the deck speaker as the lights of Havana disappeared behind the boat. They were drifting east in the Gulf Stream, with Cuba to the south. The old man couldn't find his portable VHF radio; he needed to make a distress call. *This is my worst headache ever!* he thought. He had to do something more, so he reached for his leather gloves lying on the deck and filled them with ice from the cooler. Then he laid flat on the gritty deck and put them on his head. He didn't want to wake the boy, who was collapsed on a bunk below with a swollen right arm.

"Grandpa, wake up," the boy said, his voice dry and strained. He trembled when he touched his grandfather.

"Grandpa, please wake up!" the boy pleaded. Kneeling, rocking on his knees, he touched his grandfather again. The old man lay motionless, half in the sun and half in the shade of the boat's canopy. It seemed a slow-motion spell had come over them, like in a dream. The boy wanted to wake up for just a moment, look around, check that everything was all right, and then go back to sleep, entering the dream at an earlier time when his grandfather was answering him. But he couldn't.

"Grandpa, wake up!" the boy tried to shout the words. "Please, wake up." His voice broke, words squeaked from his throat, sore from swallowing tears. Salt had crystallized on his cheeks along the paths of tears. It had been like this since dawn. The boy repeatedly beckoned his grandfather to wake up but got no response from the old man lying flat on his back with his eyes shut. They were alone and nobody could hear them. The boy knew this. He moved his grandfather completely into the sun so the old man would feel warm all over, kicking away the wet leather gloves and spilled bottle of aspirin.

Maybe the Soul of the Sea can hear me, the boy thought. The old man had often talked about the Soul of the Sea and how it could hear your thoughts. Maybe he should just think his grandfather awake, rather than shouting dry words. He tried this, then tried it again, concentrating on forming a loud thought. It didn't work. He began massaging the old man's hands, still rocking on his knees. He was indifferent to the boat's hard, gritty floor.

By mid-afternoon the sun was strong but not unbearable. The boy stopped talking to his grandfather and just stared at the sea, miles and miles of it in all directions. It was calm but flowing steadily, just like yesterday. Yesterday was easy to think about.

The homemade lure swam in the sea. When it hit the small waves, it splashed sideways, sending a yellow flash deep into the water. When a large swell lifted the sea behind it, the lure rose above the level of the boat, briefly, and then was pulled under as its broad lip caught the down-pouring sea. From below, viewed by the massive fish, it looked like a wounded tuna.

"Look boy, look behind the yellow lure." The old man pointed to the fish following the lure splashing in the boat's wake.

"It's a huge marlin, Grandpa!" the boy said excitedly. "She's after the lure." The boy knew large marlin were always females.

The marlin's tail and dorsal fin broke water behind the lure. The fish watched the lure swim and break on the small waves with instinctive concentration.

"Take it," the old man said. "My God, there's eight feet between the fins!" He could feel his heart pounding in his throat. His first action was to increase the speed of the lure.

"Watch close, Robby, watch her." The old man pushed the throttle forward; instantly the fish slashed at the lure with its bill, throwing it forward.

"Take it, don't play with it!" the old man barked. The fish slashed at the lure again and then, mouth open, engulfed it by turning its head sideways.

Whop! Whap! Whop! the heavy fishing rod buckled and flexed. The old man grabbed it from the gunnel as line screamed off the large reel. The boy screamed too. The old man held the rod high and pushed the drag lever forward, instantly increasing tension on the line. Immediately he pulled back hard on the rod once, then again, then one more time. The hook was set.

"She's on, we got her on!" he shouted as he reset the reel's drag to the fighting position.

The marlin felt the sting of the large hook as it pierced deep into the corner of her mouth. Instinctively, she bolted into the air vertically, flexing and gyrating in a rainbow of spray.

"Grandpa! She's huge!" the boy shouted, all 120 pounds of him sitting straight up in the fighting chair, wide-eyed with anticipation.

"Get ready Robby!" the old man bellowed, his heart pounding, holding the rod with both hands. Line racing out, he slammed the butt end into the swivel cup on the boy's chair. The fish, sensing beyond the sting of the hook-set, felt another strange sensation for the first time: resistance to its ability to swim. Crazy from this feeling, it flew into the air and somersaulted high above the water. Coming down, it flexed its its tail wildly, propelling itself twenty yards across the surface, slashing its bill and sending white spray everywhere.

"Hold the rod up, Robby—let her feel the rod!" Robby leaned forward, gripping the rod with all his strength, line racing out.

"Hold tight, I'm letting go," the old man said as he let go of the rod's midsection.

The boy had it. He'd promised his grandson a fish, and now the boy had a giant.

"I got it grandpa, I got it!" There were seven hundred yards of line left on the reel, fifty yards was out with the fish.

The marlin, full of rage, bolted into the air again. It was a colossal fish and all fifteen feet of her was out of the water. Flipping over, on her side, she re-entered the water in a splash that could engulf an elephant. The boy's arm muscles tightened as he gripped the rod. His young body, legs straight out pressing on the foot plate of the fighting chair, flooded with adrenaline.

"Bow the rod to the fish when she jumps!" the old man shouted. But the boy knew this and was lowering the rod before the old man finished his words.

"I know, Grandpa, so not to strain the line."

"Good boy, Robby. Good boy." The old man was infused with joy. The boy had paid attention to his instructions from the day before and from all the times when they just talked about marlin fishing. Now they were doing it.

The fish swam violently, bounding from the water in half-leaps, dolphin leaps, one after another. The boy could do nothing but fight to keep the rod up off the transom—the reel on the rod weighed nine pounds. Line raced off making a high-pitched zinging sound, sweet music to marlin fishermen.

"Let her run!" the old man shouted. "She's too green to pump." The boy pulled back on the rod slightly as line continued going out. Steering the boat from the back, the old man swung it around, putting the fish off the starboard corner of the transom. Immediately, he cranked in the two other rods that were still out.

"Look how purple she is, Grandpa!" The marlin was an iridescent purple with brilliant vertical stripes, a rare pattern for a blue marlin. If she got out too far, she could race across the water from left to right using one set of lateral muscles and then back, right to left, using the other set; always resting one set. Never tiring. Impossible to slow unless you got her turned toward the boat. To catch a marlin this size, she had to cooperate and swim toward you.

"She's a beauty, Robby. Keep the rod up! Don't crank while she's running." The fish had not slowed, not even slightly. It was straight back 150 yards. The old man ran the boat in reverse, slowly, just enough to allow the boy to stay even with the fish and get some line back. The sea was mostly calm, with occasional moderate swells, not a cloud in the sky. How pleased he was to get this fish on for the boy. He had caught many, but this was the first for the boy and it was a great one. He knew very well you could not fully appreciate this experience unless you were in it. No book or movie could duplicate the reality of it. You had to be there.

"She's pulling hard!" the boy shouted as he struggled to get the rod up to a forty-five-degree angle, only to have the fish pull it back, flat down, slamming it on the transom. The nine-pound reel was heavier than a gallon of milk, just lifting it and the rod, without a fish on, took effort.

The old man slowly changed the boat's direction by moving it forward at an angle to the fish, which was now three hundred yards out and jumping. Line gushed off the reel. *She's huge,* he thought to himself, *look at her from this distance!* He reached ahead of the boy and pushed the drag lever on the reel slightly forward, putting more resistance on the fish. The reel had 450 yards of line left on the spool.

"Don't move the drag," the old man instructed the boy. "I'll watch it for you." The drag setting was critical: too tight and the fish breaks the line, too loose the fish runs the line out. Either way you lose and the fish wins.

"I've never seen a fish this big!" the boy shouted as he pulled back on the rod to get it up, then cranked hard on its way down. This was the only way you could get line in. Pumping a big fish was a major challenge for a 120 pound, fourteen-year old. Often, turning the reel handle did not bring in line. The drag prevented the spool from taking line until the pressure from the fish eased.

"She's a giant, Robby! Gotta hold that rod up so she can feel it!" This was a thousand-pound-class blue marlin. The old man, stunned by its size, didn't want his surprise to spook the boy.

"I know, Grandpa. It's hard."

"It's supposed to be hard. Want help?"

"No! I can do it!" The boy lifted the rod back to forty-five degrees. He tried to crank in line, but the resistance was still too great. The reel handle turned, but the spool didn't rotate. The fish was off to the right now, taking out less line. At 350-yards away, the line curved out to the fish, allowing it to turn and feel less resistance.

"Crank fast now!" the old man shouted. He was behind the boy steering and could see the curve in the line. Robby cranked as fast as he could, his skinny right arm was a blur. He knew to use his left hand to guide the line back on the reel evenly, his legs clamped around the rod just above the swivel cup. The custom-built rod was made to handle large billfish; the reel was the best you could buy, the 130-pound test monofilament line had been freshly spooled last night. A length of double line preceded a heavy, fluorocarbon leader that held the lure. The old man knew there was no substitute for the best equipment.

"This is the hardest thing I've ever done." The boy was worried, straining to get the words out. "Can you increase the drag more?" The boy had reeled in the slack line and had gained about fifty yards on the fish. But now it was all tight again and the fish was pulling.

"I did before. Any more and the fish could break the line." The fish was swimming at the surface about three hundred yards out.

"It's hard to get line in again." Frustrated, the boy kept pumping and cranking.

"Yes, but you can do it," the old man said with football-coach confidence. His eye was on the amount of line on the reel. The boy lifted the rod back to a forty-five-degree angle with a grunt.

"She's getting out on us again," the boy said.

What incredible strength this fish has, the old man thought. "I'm going to move the boat toward her, reel in the slack line as soon as you can – keep it even!" He knew the boy would keep it even on the spool as he reeled in; he didn't have to tell him to do it. Of all his grandchildren, Robby was the most interested in sports and always did his best to follow instructions. He had learned this from his father who learned it from his Grandpa. He was old enough and determined enough to catch this fish.

"Grandpa. I want to catch this fish!"

"You must be tough to catch her—tougher than she is!"

"I'm tough!" the boy yelled as loud as he could.

"Yell that again!" the old man instructed. The boy yelled it again.

"Start cranking when I turn." As the boat swung around with its twin engines gushing water, the old man goosed it ahead to gain slack line, keeping it at an angle to the fish. The boy cranked fast with his right hand and guided line on the spool with his left hand.

"I'm getting line in!" the boy shouted.

"I see that. You're doing perfect!"

"I am." The boy said. He felt strong again and got back about seventy-five yards before the old man slowed the boat and put it in neutral. The fish was running below the surface now.

"Stay up girl!" the old man shouted. He didn't want her to sound. Big marlin can easily die of a heart attack if they sound suddenly during a fight. Then, being dead weight, they're impossible to pump up.

"She's taking line fast," the boy said. He held the rod up and it bucked and jolted him. His arms were numb from the isometric exercise of holding the rod high.

"She's going deep," the old man said, looking at the angle of the line. "Pump her up Robby!" The boy pulled back on the rod and then allowed it to go down flat on the transom. He got only ten cranks before the line became tight. Then another hard pull to get the rod up and then back down, quickly, to get another ten cranks. Each time, about nine feet of line came in. The boy's heart was pumping in his throat; more adrenaline flowed through him. He wanted to remember all of what was happening but it was hard to concentrate on anything but pulling the rod up with all his strength. *It's hard to think when you work this hard,* he thought. "I'm going to catch this fish!"

"You will! Keep pumping and reeling. Make her feel pressure," the old man said. The fish was sensing less resistance as it swam up. Suddenly, the boy could get line in.

"Reel as fast as you can! She's coming up."

The boy, feeling sore all over, cranked the reel. "I can do this!" he said confidently.

The old man didn't believe in a shoulder harness. He once saw a guide in a shoulder harness get pulled into the water by a marlin, right over the transom, when the line tangled on the reel. Better to lose a rod than a boy! Most men did not have the back for this. Without a harness the boy was safe, but handicapped. For a two hundred-pound fish, it wouldn't have been a problem. For this fish, it was.

"She's coming up, slower now," the boy grunted as he pulled back on the fishing rod. Suddenly, the fish jolted the rod and in a few seconds stripped off all the line the boy had retrieved. The rod throbbed hard and the boy knew, should he let go of it, it would be gone forever with the fish. He tightened his grip.

"She's big Robby. Big, big. Put your back into it!"

"How big, Grandpa?" The boy squeaked as he strained to pull back on the rod and restart the process of getting line back.

"One thousand pounds, maybe more," the old man said cautiously. He knew this was a huge blue marlin for the Atlantic and didn't want to alarm Robby who was already under enough stress.

"She's your biggest!' the boy said, huffing out words. It helped him to talk and not think about his sore arms.

"She's *your* biggest, Robby. This is your fish." The old man knew he had to maneuver the boat perfectly to give the boy odds on the fish.

The reality of it hit the boy. He was fighting a one thousand-pound fish on a thin line that was tied to a reel that was bolted to a rod that only he was holding. "I hope I have enough strength to catch this fish!" he shouted, his voice dry. The old man poured water into the boy's mouth but did not touch the rod or reel. This was truly the boy's fish to catch or lose, not his. The rod throbbed hard and more line raced off. The old man looked at the reel; about half the line was out with the fish. The fish was winning.

The great fish swam deep in the gulf-stream, resisting this strange pull she had never felt before. She knew nothing of such resistance to her ability to swim, until now. How to stop the pull, how to swim free again without resistance. Her primitive brain was electrified with synapses. Instinctively, she swam away from the pull in S-shaped swerves, lunging forward frequently, slashing her bill. On downward lunges, the fish accelerated up to seventy miles per hour.

The fish automatically obeyed primitive instructions from her brain; some were inherited, evolving by genetic selection over millions of years, and some came from her experience. Once, she had evaded attack by a great white shark by wounding it with her bill. Another time she escaped from a tuna fisherman's gill net by violently slashing her bill. Her bill was her weapon: four feet long, smooth on top and bottom, rasped on the sides. When in trouble, she slashed it back and forth. All that was required now was a moment of slack line, a loop of it, and one slash, a leader-cutting slash, and the strange resistance would be gone.

"Keep the rod up Robby, don't give her any slack." The old man could see the determination in the boy and it made him proud. With the fish running deep again, it had been over four hours since she had engulfed the lure. He knew the boy's determination was challenged by severe fatigue; he backed the boat to where the line entered the water, putting it over the fish. How fortunate and completely perfect it was to be having this experience with his grandson, he thought.

We've got to get this fish, he said to himself. "Pull back hard son, pump her up." The old man knew the boy could not overpower this fish. Maybe he himself could have in his younger days, in his thirties, but not the boy. The tackle was stronger than the boy. He would not be able to break it. But the fish could if given the opportunity.

Robby, arms tensed, pulled back hard. He was sweating, sore and tired, fighting to find the stamina he needed. With the rod, just a foot above the transom, the most he could lift it, he let it slam back down and cranked as many times as he could …

"Come up big fish!" the old man shouted. "Don't die deep on us." He opened a beer and gave the boy a drink of it, pouring it into his mouth, accidentally spilling some of it on the boy's face and shirt.

"Thanks a lot Grandpa," the boy said. "Mom will get mad if she finds out!"

"She won't unless you tell her."

"I won't." The cold beer seemed to stimulate him; it was something to taste other than water. He would have preferred a Pepsi.

"It's not as good as water for rehydration, but provides some necessary minerals," the old man explained.

Below, the fish responded again to the rod's pull by swimming toward the strange feeling, rather than away from it. The boy could pull the rod back and crank line in, lots of it. He repeated the process and pushed hard on the chair's footplate with both feet. Sweat poured off his face and down his arms. His back hurt. He knew the marlin could feel it too.

He was getting in line with every lift now, and there was a rhythm to it. It was a winning feeling; he was elated. Three hundred feet below the marlin continued to react. When it swam up, it felt less resistance, less of that strange pull. It swam up more.

The old man wiped the sweat from the boy's forehead. He envied the boy's strength and energy. "Whatever happens Robby, win or lose, you have fought a great fish. Remember this time; remember it well."

"I will grandpa. It's the hardest thing I've ever done," the boy repeated, straining less to get the words out. He kept pumping and cranking.

"Are we going to release her grandpa?"

"Yes, absolutely."

"We could keep her," the boy said as he pulled back, grunting again as the line tightened.

"She's too magnificent to keep," the old man said.

"But she's bigger than any marlin you ever caught."

"More reason to let her go."

"But how do we know when we've caught her?"

"When I can grab her bill, and hold her long enough to cut the leader close to her mouth. Then she's caught!" The old man had replaced the cadmium plated hook with a bronzed steel hook that rusted out much faster. But he had to remember to replace it frequently.

"Then she is caught and free at the same time," the boy said.

"That's right Robby, exactly right."

The old man knew it would be a miracle if he could grab her by the bill. A one thousand-pound fish! But he would try. If not, he would cut long on the leader, leaving a fifteen-foot trail of fluorocarbon. This could compromise the fish. He really didn't want to do that.

The line suddenly went slack. "Grandpa, she's gone, I can't feel her!" the boy screamed.

"Crank boy! Crank fast! She's not gone. She's coming up fast!" the old man shouted. The boy cranked the reel with electric intensity.

"Guide the line!" the old man yelled. "There's a football field of line out—you gotta get it on the reel fast!" The boy used his left hand to guide the line evenly and cranked hard with his right hand. He again became a blur of motion.

The fish rocketed out of the water, vertically, ten yards behind the boat. It flexed like a sheet of stainless steel, feeling no resistance, no sting. It cleared water by eight feet, arced, turned, and dove back bill first, smoothly, perfectly, without a splash. Before the boy and the old man could mentally register the spectacle of this unbelievable jump, the fish was up and out of the water again, head first, twisting in a wide spiral, then falling back on its side, hitting the water flat with a lightning crack and the splash of a breaching whale. The boy, bowed to the fish, cranked with all the speed his arm could produce; line poured onto the reel.

"Lower the rod!" the old man shouted; he could see the line was almost in.

"I can feel her again!" the boy yelled. "And she can feel me!"

By God, he's getting her in! the old man thought.

"Careful boy. Stay in the chair and I'll grab the leader when I can reach it." He leaned over the gunnel.

"Careful grandpa." The boy knew the danger: the fish could lunge and spear his grandfather with its bill. The old man had done this before—many times—but not with such a giant fish.

"Keep cranking Robby; I don't want her going under the boat." The fish was staying even with the reel's drag, it was straight down from the boat, about twenty feet deep.

"I'm getting all the line now, there's the leader!" the boy shouted.

"I see it!" the old man shouted back. The fish suddenly propelled itself into the side of the boat hard with a glancing blow, violently attacking it. A hundred gallons of water poured over the old man and the boy. The boy fell to the floor, and the old man hit his head hard on the cabin door as he was thrown back. *The fish was trying to kill the boat!* he thought, holding his head.

"Back in the chair!" the old man yelled as he stood back up. He had grabbed the fishing rod with one hand as it flew out of the swivel cup. One second more and it would have been gone with the fish. He slammed the butt of the rod back into the swivel cup on the chair. The boy leaped from the floor into the chair and grabbed hold of the rod. He screamed and cranked the reel—the fish felt the pull again.

"There she is!" The old man shouted. The fish, tail-walking alongside the boat, beat the sea into a white spray. *What amazing energy this fish has*. Unbelievable, the old man thought. His head was hurting.

"It's a tremendous fight, grandpa." The boy's words came out with a mouthful of saltwater. Saltwater dripped from twisted knots of blonde hair hanging in his face. He shook his head so he could see. The fish dove down thirty feet and streaked out to sea off the port side of the boat.

"Keep on her!" the old man shouted. Hoarse now from shouting, saltwater dripped from him, too. The boy pumped and cranked; he could not feel his arms. All his strength had been used against the strength of the fish. He had the leverage of the boat and good equipment; the fish had instinct and a dimensionless sea. In the pain of it and in the stress of it, it was the indescribable joy of living it that kept the boy in the fight. He was completely aware of the special significance of what was happening.

"Do you want me to take the rod?" The old man said, testing the boy.

"No," the boy squeaked, throat parched from swallowing saltwater. Stunned for a moment by it all, he quickly regained the rhythm of pumping and reeling.

"Good," the old man said. He could see the boy was gaining on the fish.

"She's coming in again!" the boy shouted, managing to find enough moisture for a loud shout. The old man watched for the leader, his gloved hand was ready to grab it …

"Duck!" the old man screamed as a blue flash came at him and the boy. The fish flew above the boat and over it, knocking the old man down and the boy out of the chair.

"She flew over us!" the boy screamed from the floor, engulfed in water. "Are you okay grandpa?"

"I'm okay, I think." His head hurt badly, worse than before. "Are you okay?" he asked Robby in a shaky voice.

"Yes! I'm okay!" The boy answered fast.

"Where's the fish?"

"On this side!" the boy yelled, belching saltwater. He got back in the chair and swiveled it, grabbing the rod and fighting the fish starboard. The fish had jumped over the width of the boat just forward of the transom. It landed in the water on the opposite side of the boat. Unbelievably, the rod was still in the swivel-cup on the chair. There had been enough slack line to compensate for the jump. Back in the water, the fish was taking line.

"Keep the rod low!" the old man shouted, surprised the fish was still on and that neither he nor the boy got speared. He couldn't believe the boy was back fishing.

The fish almost pulled the rod out of the boy's hands when it greyhounded out from starboard in a powerful run. The old man stood up, grabbed the wheel, put the boat in forward gear, and steered toward the fish. The fish dove deep again.

The big fish had amazing strength and stamina and had adjusted to the fight and restrictions on her swimming. She used different muscle groups in rotation and kept a deep and steady pace. Another hour went by. The boy would try to pump her up, gaining small lengths of line only to lose it back. The drag would give line, then hold steady. About one-third of the line capacity remained on the reel. The boy had somehow found enough reserve energy to keep fishing. The old man kept backing the boat to match the speed of the fish, watching the amount of line-out carefully. He never had a marlin maintain such a powerful deep pace for this long.

"She will swim deep forever," the boy said, dejectedly.

"No! She will come up again," the old man said. *But when?*—he thought to himself. "She will, just keep pumping her while I keep the line from running out." The old man steered the boat in reverse, slightly slower than the fish was taking line. Amazingly, the boy kept fishing.

The boy awoke from his daydream. His blistered hands and salty face made him look older today. He looked at his grandfather. The sight made him cry again. He loved his Grandpa.

He was just a skinny fourteen-year old boy. Yesterday's experience would mold his young life. He cried for it all, for the joy and the sorrow, and for the man who made it possible.

"Fish, great marlin fish!" the boy shouted. "I hate you!"

The boat's motor had died with his grandfather. The boy could not start it. He had tried all the things he could think of but nothing worked. He would try these again later… He found a wet cheese sandwich in the cooler, peeled the bread away and ate the cheese. He drank a beer, then looked at his grandfather, completely stiff and discolored. This was not his grandfather anymore. He understood this. This was the dead body that once held his grandfather. Now his grandfather was pure soul, and that soul still existed today as it did yesterday. It did not die. It could not die. The boy knew that his grandfather's soul held the experience of yesterday, and of many others, but they were gone now from this world.

"Fish, great marlin fish!" the boy shouted. "I love you." With tears flowing, he lifted his grandfather up to the transom, using all his strength, and eased him into the sea. He watched the body sink, gracefully and respectfully. The Soul of the Sea will provide safe harbor for his grandpa's soul, pleased by the love and rich experience it holds.

"Soul of the Sea, please guide my grandpa's soul!" the boy shouted—the words came out strong and clear. He was no longer a boy! He was a young man now.

He realized that the experience of yesterday only existed in his mind in this world. There were no photographs or witnesses. At first, this was a troubling thought. He knew he had to preserve the memory of it and those final moments when the fish came up for the last time. And the last words his grandfather spoke to him. This was too important to lose. It was something he must write down and tell others about. He would do these things after starting the boat.

The fish was fifty miles away, swimming deep in the gulfstream. She would eat deep today. A few inches of fluorocarbon leader hung from her mouth attached to a yellow lure. Right where it was when the old man cut it as he held the fish steady by her bill. It was almost like she let him do this. She stayed calm as the old man bent over the gunnel, watching him intently as he cut her loose. Then, feeling no resistance, no pressure, with her dorsal fin fully erect, she bolted out to sea. The short leader and the lure caused no pain or discomfort for the fish. Saltwater would rust the hook out soon.

Swimming without resistance she slashed her bill in a school of tuna, stabbing and wounding several. The giant blue marlin then swam around in a wide circle, rotating her eye sockets to keep focused on the wounded tuna. Then, timing her lunges perfectly, she ate ravenously. The cobalt blues and imperial indigoes of her vertical stripes were electrified with iridescence. She was alive and well. Thoughts of the strange pull and resistance of yesterday were gone. Only thoughts of today existed for this great fish.

Postscript:

This story was based on the author's true experience from several marlin fishing episodes where two standout: One, when I lost an eight hundred-pound blue marlin off Bimini in the Bahamas after a six-hour fight. The other, when I watched a young boy lose a bigger one out from Key West. With mine, the fish did fly over the boat, but when we got it back, the leader broke before the guide could grab it. On the boy's fish, it got off by attacking the boat and tangling the line at top of his rod. His father saved him by quickly unsnapping the boy's shoulder harness or he would have been gone with the fish. Now that I'm older, I do use a shoulder harness when marlin fishing, but always wear a lifejacket with a folding knife clipped to it.

Alaskan Kodiak Bear - full of pink salmon

3

Alaskan Moments

Big Fish, Big Bears, and the Mysterious Unknown

Kodiak Island, Alaska, 2004

"The largest king salmon on record was 126 pounds - from Alaska's Kenai River in 1949. It was caught in a fish trap," Ted reminded us.

It was fifty degrees on a windy August day in the Gulf of Alaska. We were trolling off Kodiak Island in the Shelikof Straight, rigged for Chinook or king salmon, the largest salmon species in the North Pacific. Ted, Dean, and I were on a charter boat hunting for big ones.

"The all-tackle record was a ninety-seven-pound beast, caught in the Kanai River in 1985," Dean informed us.

"It was caught in the morning by a guy named Les—forgot his last name. It laid in the bottom of his boat for seven hours while he kept fishing, then bounced around in his pickup truck for another two hours before getting weighed," Ted added.

"It was definitely a hundred-pounder," Dean insisted. "It would have been severely dehydrated after nine hours and would have lost at least five pounds, making it 102 pounds or more when caught."

"I saw a picture of him holding it; fat from head to tail and still bright with color after all those hours. The fish had a mammoth mouth—you could have put two footballs in it," I said, joining the discussion.

"Anderson. Les Anderson." Ted remembered the guy's name.

Ted, Dean, and I were not exactly fishermen like the old guys who sat on a rock with a cane-pole and worms. We were modern-day anglers always on the search for giant fish, only to set them free after catching them. It was hard to explain.

The *Hot Hooker* charter boat was pulling our custom lures that were ten inches long, flat, and bent like a banana. When pulled at six miles per hour, they pounded the rods with a tight pulse and dove twenty feet deep.

The sea, gray like the sky, was pounding too—rocking and rolling. A mix of seabirds, including two eagles, followed our wake hoping for wounded baitfish.

"There are fish at thirty feet, either kings or coho," the captain announced on the speaker. The two mates became alert, zipped up their yellow storm gear, and came out on deck. The big cabin cruiser was set up for fishing. Our lures pulsated vigorously—flashing metallic silver-blue except for the heads: Ted's was green, Dean's was pink, and mine yellow. We didn't use any outriggers or downriggers or flashers, just flat lines, one on each side of the boat and one straight out the back. We wanted the fish netted—not gaffed—so we could decide whether to keep or release it. This was not normal technique for the crew, but the captain was happy to accommodate. The three of us were big-fish purists and had specific techniques to follow.

Salmon limits in Alaska had become a complex issue, depending on the species and its size. The limit off Kodiak Island for king salmon was two per day with no annual limit. Six per day was the limit for all other salmon species. Our mission was for each man to take home twelve salmon to eat. And top priority was for one of us to catch a king over ninety-seven pounds!

The yellow-head lure interrupted our conversation with a nice hit. I lifted the rod quickly to set the hook and started reeling. The captain slowed the boat but kept it moving forward. I was standing in the starboard corner at the back of the boat; the Takota reel with sixty-pound monofilament line made controlling the fish easy. The fish came right in, splashing on the surface. Lars, the taller of the two mates, netted it. A glistening, chrome-blue, twelve-pound king; good eating size.

"Keep it," I said. Lars clubbed the fish and tossed it into a tub of ice.

"Now you can release them, unless it's a giant," Ted told me.

"Depends how large a giant. I would keep a world-record, anything else gets released," I said, grinning. I was happy to have broken the ice with the first fish.

"Look left!" Dean shouted. A huge humpback whale breached water close to the boat, then fell back in with a loud boom and a tail wave.

"I heard they average forty tons!" Ted remarked.

"He was following us, like the birds. These whales filter feed and when boats disturb a school of herring it improves their odds of gulping down a thousand at a time," Lars explained. We kept watching for another breach.

For the next two hours, the three of us caught twenty salmon in the ten-to-fifteen-pound range; mostly kings—three were coho. We kept a total of five kings, leaving room for a record fish. Two more whales breached and boomed. The birds were gone—too far from shore for them now.

We were trolling the northwest end of the Kodiak Archipelago, 290 miles southwest of Anchorage in the Gulf of Alaska. The fishing activity had slowed for over an hour when, suddenly, Dean's rod buckled!

"Dean's got a *Big Fish!*" I shouted. The captain slowed the boat; Ted and I quickly reeled our lines in. Dean's rod was bent in half and line was racing off the reel. He stood at the middle of the transom, held the rod high, and pulled back twice to set the hook. This was a big fish.

"Huge splash, straight behind the boat," Ted said, instinctively pointing at the fish fifty yards away.

"Hello, Dean!" I yelled. The captain slowed the boat down to a crawl. Dean started cranking, but only the reel handle turned; no line came in. More line raced off the reel.

"Dean, Dean, the fishing machine!" Ted repeated what a Wisconsin musky guide called Dean when fishing with him.

"He's at least sixty pounds," Lars said. "Nice king. Big salmon are strong, with super muscles; they can maintain full speed like a tuna or wahoo. Don't give him any slack."

"I got him good." Dean was serious. We could feel the determination he was broadcasting.

Excitedly, we watched Dean and the fish. It reminded me of a large wahoo I caught in the South Pacific—it just kept going and going. "Dean has got some serious business to take care of," I remarked. He glanced back at me smiling. Line was still racing off the reel as he kept the rod bent in an arc. The fish could feel the resistance!

The captain moved the boat slowly toward the fish, backing up. He could see that half of Dean's line was out. Dean kept pressure on the fish but could only get a few turns on the reel. The chrome-blue torpedo was accelerating. The captain backed up faster.

The sea was rough, it was a challenge to stand without holding onto something. Dean, from Texas, was short and stocky—rode bulls in rodeos in his younger days. He leaned against the transom and let the fish run, keeping his rod up. We were all cheering for him now.

Ted instructed Dean, in good humor: "This bull will take longer than eight seconds to beat!" In fact, many fishermen did call big king salmon bulls.

Dean looked back at Ted. "He's a bull of a fish, isn't he?

"I'm getting a little line in now." Dean pulled up on the rod, then down with it, reeling in line when the rod was down. Then he repeated this pumping action while his legs danced in tune with the waves. It did bear an analogy to riding bulls in rodeos. Catching a big fish in rough water was more difficult than in calm water.

"Strong bull," I said. "I'm watching you carefully, taking lessons."

Dean laughed without turning around. With serious determination, keeping constant pressure on the fish for forty minutes, he got the fish turned and coming to the boat. Now he could reel line in fast!

"Keep it?" Lars asked, standing next to Dean.

"No!" Dean said loudly. Ted squeezed in between them, taking pictures with his Nikon. The fish was swimming in a circle at the back of the boat.

"Let me tire him a bit more," Dean told Lars, loosening the reel's drag slightly. Their net was too small for this fish, and a gaff would kill it. This was a rare event for the mates; they usually kept such a fish—two men would lift it into the boat with a long gaff that penetrated deep into its flesh. Lars could see the substantial girth on the fish now.

The captain put the boat in neutral, shouting to the shorter mate to come take the wheel. "Keep us going slow against the sea," he told the boy, then came back and grabbed the net. Its handle was long enough to reach the water but the bag was too small. "No!" Dean shouted.

"Don't worry, I won't hurt the fish," the captain assured him. He could see the lure in the corner of its jaw. It was a "good hook" as anglers say, there was no way to just shake him off! "Bring him straight toward me," he told Dean. The fish had a huge mouth—you could have put a soccer ball in it. The captain was ready with the long-handle net while the fish was swimming around six feet below them. Dean kept him swimming in a tight circle. The captain leaned over the transom and put the bag of the net in the water away from the fish.

Dean was nervous about this—so were Ted and I. We knew what the captain was planning to do: he wasn't going to net the fish! At best, the net would hold one-third of the fish. We watched intently; Lars put on heavy rubber gloves in case he had to help. The captain controlled the net in the water, holding it by the end of the long handle. Dean kept the fish away from it at first—he knew what to do. He carefully redirected the fish to get its head pointed at the net, then pulled it slowly, head first. When the fish opened its mouth, the captain jammed the net into its jaw on top of the lure. The fish bit down and began twisting, biting and pulling on the net. The captain rotated the net's handle as the fish twisted.

"Look at the girth on this fish, it's almost a yard around!" Ted shouted as he clicked away with his Nikon. After a dozen twists by the fish, ripping and spraying seawater, the net snagged the lure, pulling it free. With the strange resistance gone, the fish became motionless, stunned momentarily as its large pectoral fins fanned rapidly to keep it vertical in the water. Then, after several seconds more, it flexed its lateral swimming muscles and bolted out to sea. Free and not hurt!

"By formula, that fish was forty-nine inches long with a thirty-four-inch girth; seventy-six pounds! Largest caught on the Hot Hooker this season!" The captain exclaimed, grinning big. He shook hands with Dean, who was happy the fish was released unharmed.

"There are two winners today: fisherman Dean and the monster bull salmon, a.k.a. Chinook, a.k.a. king!" I declared. The captain was happy that Dean was happy. We were all happy…

Some people can't appreciate the desire and ambition it takes to catch a huge fish with the intention of letting it go. Why do it? But catch-and-release fishing has parallels, like mountain climbing. Some climb a mountain to get to its top, then climb back down to where they started from. Why do it? Because doing such things require an integration of physical stamina, mental acuity, and strong will; a healthy calculus that enlivens the soul.

Back at the lodge in Kodiak, we relaxed in large comfortable pine-log chairs, warmed by a fireplace burning Alaskan hardwood in the center of the room.

"Want to try a special Manhattan?" I looked at Ted and Dean. Ted was a big guy, mid-fifties, smart on fishing, who owned a fishing lodge in northern Wisconsin. Both Dean and I had fished at Ted's lodge many times, but this was our first Alaskan outing together.

"What's the formula for those special Manhattans?" Ted asked, knowing I was a biochemist and had bartended my way through graduate school.

"Three parts Crown Royal whiskey and one-part Stock Vermouth, served over ice cubes made from Fiji Water." I had brought everything. Lynn, the lodge owner, boss, and chief cook, had made the ice cubes this morning.

"Can't say no to that." Ted was ready.

"That will make me put my beer down." Dean was already having a local brew.

I mixed the drinks in the lodge's kitchen with Lynn helping. She insisted that she carry the drinks over to us on a fancy wooden tray. "An Alutiiq Indian lady made this tray; it's a carving of a Chinook salmon. She was my best helper and she's gone now," Lynn explained sadly.

"Does this fish look familiar?" I asked Dean when Lynn showed him the tray after serving the drinks.

"That's a big bull!" Dean, the ex-bull rider exclaimed. Lynn looked puzzled until Ted explained Dean's history.

"Cheers!" I held my glass up, and the three of us drank the special nectar. Surrounding us in the lodge, on the high walls, were bear skins, moose heads, and the seven species of salmon found in Alaska. The Kodiak pelts were from large male bears with big heads, they defined ferocious. At sixteen-hundred pounds or more, Kodiaks were second only to polar bears in size; a subspecies of the grizzly bear but significantly larger due to their main diet—high-caloric salmon. There were 3,500 of these giant bears in the Kodiak Island Archipelago; about one per square mile.

"I propose a toast to Angler Dean." I lifted my Manhattan.

"I'll second that motion," Ted said. We all took another drink of the Crown Manhattans. Crown Royal was the smoothest of Canadian whiskeys and Stock Vermouth was a proprietary blend of spices in red wine. This vermouth synergized with the Crown creating a taste unique in the universe. . .

The conversation switched from fish to bears. "Weren't those bears something?" Dean said. After fishing, returning on the Hot Hooker, we had seen five Kodiaks catching salmon near the mouth of a small river. They were all in the water feeding on pink salmon. The salmon were feeding on insects trapped in a tidal pool—the bears were catching the fish easily.

"I was amazed to see them sorting fish, they only wanted females."

"And they only ate the roe!" Dean noted. The bears were so stuffed with salmon that they only selected females, pawed them out of the water, bit them open, ate out the roe, then left the rest of the fish uneaten. They couldn't get enough of the sweet salmon eggs! We studied them intently using our binoculars.

There was one gigantic male Kodiak bear (boar) that would put his head underwater so he could select the fattest female salmon. One of the female Kodiaks, half the size of the boar, was stomping on fish in shallow water, then grabbing the wounded. They paid no attention to us in the thirty-six-foot cabin cruiser.

There were eagles too—three of them. They would fly down and grab the carcasses of the dead fish with the bears chasing them. Shrieking, wings wide open to slow down, claws fully extended, they would confront a bear, aiming for its eyes. The bears backed off—fighting bald eagles wasn't worth the bother. This was not the eagles' first confrontation with bears!

So, our conversations went back and forth between big fish and big bears. It had been a good day. The soft, cushioned pine chairs with the warmth of the fire was a recipe for sleep.

"Well, boys, tomorrow's another day." Ted yawned. Our adjoining bedrooms were upstairs in the loft, complete with outside decks hosting the Milky Way. Dean and I had scheduled a floatplane for tomorrow to take us to a river on Kodiak Island where we could cast for salmon. Ted planned to stay back and visit other lodges—maybe buy one.

My room was in the middle between Ted's and Dean's, so the three of us went out on my deck to look at the stars before going to bed. It was calm now and stars were everywhere; the heart of the Milky Way was above us. Today's wind had cleared the sky. From Alaska, you could see the Milky Way at its best. The core of stars at its center exploded with white-brilliance on the northern horizon.

One-hundred billion stars were shining. All from one average galaxy—ours. Considering that the Hubble Telescope had found evidence of billions of other galaxies beyond what the naked eye could see, the thought of billions of galaxies, each containing billions of stars, humbled my mind, body, and spirit.

"Check out the satellite," Ted said, pointing northwest. Looking like a bright star, it was creeping slowly across the sky.

"How fast is it going?" Dean questioned. He was a retired airplane mechanic with an engineering degree, who often explained that becoming an engineer was something meaningful he needed to do after his bull-riding days—keeping passenger jets healthy fit the bill!

"About seventeen-thousand miles per hour," Ted declared. He was wide awake now.

I had taken college physics but couldn't recall the speed, either. Ted had been a high school physics teacher before becoming a lodge owner.

"That's a fast creep," I said. The satellite was moving a foot per minute at arm's length. I timed it with my watch. "I know it takes the space shuttle ninety minutes to orbit the earth."

"It's just above the Big Dipper," Dean remarked. We were facing north with the Big Dipper off to our left. Dean and I watched the satellite, appreciating its speed.

"Look over here!" Ted exclaimed. He was pointing east where it was darker. Dean and I turned and examined about half of the eastern sky—the lodge blocked the other half.

"What the hell are those?" Dean asked, showing some alarm. We saw three bright, satellite-like objects that could have doubled for moving stars. They were moving very fast, making full stops and sharp turns, going much faster than the satellite! I tried to time them using three fixed stars for reference.

"They're not satellites—too much velocity!" Ted deduced. The three of us watched the eastern sky, transfixed on the fast-moving, bright objects. They would dart about two feet at arm's length in two seconds, then instantly reverse direction, turn at right-angles, and go another two feet. They moved in triangular patterns. Dean estimated they were three-hundred miles high!

"UFO's." I had never seen one, and now three! Why couldn't they be closer? I wanted to know their shape. Was this part of a secret space program or from beyond?

Dean and I continued watching. Ted went to his room to get binoculars.

"They don't appear to be glowing balls of light or flashing orbs like in a sci-fi movie," Ted said, looking through his ten-power binoculars. "They look like moving stars, but no twinkle." He handed the binoculars to me.

"They're not quite as bright as the satellite, but definitely high enough to be in orbit," I reported. Except for their unbelievable speed and right-angle turns, they looked like super-speedy satellites.

After about twenty minutes they changed from making triangular patterns to pentagram patterns, taking up more sky, often stopping. We all three timed them separately, then I averaged the results as a multiple of seventeen-thousand miles per hour, the speed of the satellite.

"If that satellite is going seventeen-thousand miles per hour, these things are going sixty times faster!" I showed them the calculation. "Put a scientist, an engineer, and a retired physics teacher together and here's the bottom line: The objects are moving just over one-million miles per hour!"

"They're not ours; not from Earth!" Dean declared. His twenty years as a jet airplane mechanic spanning 707s to 747s qualified his deduction.

"Then what the hell are they doing, zipping around endlessly?" Ted questioned.

"Maybe they know we're watching them, so they're showing off over 'The Last Frontier,'" I said, attempting a sly grin.

"They did change from triangular patterns to pentagrams soon after we started observing them," Ted recalled.

"Reading our minds? That's crazier than saying they go one-million miles per hour!" Engineer Dean proclaimed. "The Crown Royal must have tilted our imaginations. We gotta bring Lynn into this to settle our confusion."

We watched them for two hours until 1:00 a.m. It was time to go to bed. The three of us were somewhere between stunned and dog tired.

The next morning, while Ted was lodge shopping, Dean and I were at thirty-five- hundred feet over Kodiak Island in Todd's Cessna. "I've been doing this for ten years," Todd said. "Never get tired of it." Todd was a skilled bush pilot, tough on safety.

"What's the horsepower on this Cessna-185?" Dean asked Todd.

"Three-hundred-thirty horsepower," Todd answered. It was a floatplane; six-seater. Smooth ride, but loud.

Todd landed next to a peninsula where Uganik Bay split and became the Uganik River about five miles in from the ocean. He idled the Cessna while we unloaded our gear and a large cooler. Then he shouted: "Be here at 4:30 or plan to spend the night! Good luck. Fish where I told you." He revved the engine and took off.

We started fishing from shore in Uganik bay before it narrowed into the river, which then ran east across Kodiak Island. Both trout and salmon spawned in the Uganik River. Todd had told us to start at the mouth, then follow the river upstream to where it opened into a lake, fish the lake, then come back and fish the mouth of the river again before pickup time.

We saw a sign: "Remote Area—No Services." We were in a place with fast rivers, wild bush, and moss-green mountains—no roads—unequivocally part of the Last Frontier.

It felt great to be casting lures. Trolling had its place, but this was true fishing for me! Dean was throwing a large, white, trout fly with a plastic float in front of it. The float kept the fly up and added weight for casting. Unlike yesterday's heavy gear, we were fishing today with medium-weight spinning tackle.

Dean got the first fish, his spinning rod bent in a sharp arc. The reel's drag sang as the fish jumped and splashed. It was an eight-pound dolly varden, a cousin of the rainbow trout.

I switched from a Rapala to a gold Panther Martin spinner and got the second fish ten minutes later, a twelve-pound coho salmon.

By noon we had our limit on ice in the cooler: two kings and two coho, gutted and ready for the grill. Bald eagles flew above, eyeing the heads and guts. It looked wild beyond where the river narrowed; we were ready to go find the lake.

We shouldered our rods and backpacks, left the cooler, and walked the old game trail upstream. The eagles flew down to the fish guts immediately after we left—one was already standing on the cooler with entrails hanging from its mouth.

We chewed on beef jerky as we walked, washing it down with a cold can of Coors. Neither of us could remember how many times we'd had such a nutritious lunch. Uncountable.

"Did we imagine those UFOs last night?" I asked Dean, who was behind me.

"I was going to ask you that; your Manhattans were potent but not mind- bending."

"I'm glad I wasn't alone when I saw them—that eliminated any self-doubt," I admitted.

"As an aeronautical engineer, it was an unsettling experience for me." Dean acknowledged. The technology to move that fast then turn and stop on a dime doesn't exist on Earth. At least not the Earth I come from!"

"We must tell Lynn about them. I'm curious if she's ever seen anything similar," I said.

We walked the narrow trail until we got to the lake, which was several hundred acres in size. Surprising us, there was a female Kodiak with two yearling cubs on the opposite shore.

"Good thing she's over there, not here," Dean declared while keeping his eyes on them.

"At least we're not going to surprise her," I said. Surprising a Kodiak was not something you wanted to do, particularly a mamma with cubs. We had been talking loudly as we walked the trail; guide-recommended advice.

"That's why they sell those bear bells in town. Sounding like Christmas must sub for loud talk," Dean explained with a grin.

"I doubt it," I answered, watching the sow and cubs. "Maybe an air-horn would produce enough decibels to warn them; at twenty yards those bells sound like leaves blowing in trees. But what do I know? Kodiaks have bad eyesight but good hearing and an exceptional sense of smell." She knew we were here, it didn't seem to upset her at this distance. The cubs were playing in the lake. I felt the center pocket of my backpack for the unmistakable feel of the big revolver.

"Got it?" Dean asked.

"Yup."

"Can I see it?" I unzipped the pack and handed him the stainless-steel Ruger Alaskan chambered in .454-Casull. A powerful handgun.

"Be careful, it's loaded!" I warned. "Beats Dirty Harry's .44 magnum."

"It must kick like hell," Dean figured.

"Took me a box of fifty cartridges to consistently hit one-gallon water jugs at twenty-five feet. It's loaded with 300-grain solid-core bullets. 'Solids', as Hemingway called them." I had grown up around guns—my dad was a policeman in Milwaukee for thirty years. He taught me the two Gun Rules: Rule Number One, don't shoot anyone. Rule Number Two, disregard Rule Number One if you're being attacked. The Ruger .454 was life insurance in Alaska.

"Ted told me a guy got mauled up here two years ago—lost his leg. He hit a charging Kodiak four times with a .44 magnum and it didn't stop the bear!" Dean remembered.

"They have tough hide and thick gristle; gotta hit the right spots. The .454 has one up on the .44 magnum!" I pointed out. We both looked across the lake at the bears, they hadn't moved much. "Let's try a few casts from here and keep an eye on them," I suggested.

"You're the man with the gun!" Dean said.

"Yup, indeed I am. Now let's get some of those dolly varden trout before the bears change their minds and start chasing us!" The dollies were abundant; they hit anything we threw at them, as did small kings. We caught a total of ten fish in thirty minutes and released them all. The sow must have smelled the fish; she had her nose in the air. The cubs were running ahead of their mother along the shore, in our direction. It was time to go.

"Good Short-Time Lake," Dean noted. "I'll mark it that way on the map."

Walking back to our spot at the mouth, a cow moose crossed in front of us. It stopped, gave us a stare, then moved on.

"They can be more dangerous than bears—bull moose for sure," Dean warned.

"The .454 Ruger doesn't know the difference," I replied.

Dean laughed, "That's true!"

There were no guts on shore when we got back but plenty of eagle dung around the cooler. We had two hours before Todd arrived. We sat on a log and ate ham sandwiches loaded with lettuce and spicy mustard—one of Lynn's special creations—and drank a cold can of Coors. The nutritious beer-jerky lunch needed some assistance.

Dean was casting the same white trout fly while I snapped on an eight-inch bucktail spinner used for muskies in Wisconsin. It had a heavy wire with two spinner blades that could slide and spin in front of a tuft of deer hair which hid the hook. It was three times the size of the Panther Martin I had used before. We were back in the mouth of the river, knee deep in cool water—ocean ahead to the left.

"Big lure for river salmon," Dean commented.

"Maybe not! I'm motivated—gotta beat your seventy-six-pounder. Big fish eat big baits." The fish we had caught in the morning were nice for eating, eight to fourteen pounds, but Todd told us there were monster kings in the river's mouth. We hadn't seen any big fish in the lake the short time we were there.

"Come on, bucktail!" I commanded, reeling fast so the lure's twin blades buzzed just below the surface. "No Alaskan salmon has ever seen one of these!"

We were casting toward the ocean; right where Todd would be landing soon. The water was as gray as yesterday but with less wind. A light chop moved the water toward us, disguising the lure, making it look less artificial and more like an acceptable meal. I had no idea what a bucktail spinner looked like to a fish; a wounded sardine, a big leech, a huge bug? I didn't know. But it sure caught muskies and northern pike in Wisconsin—big ones.

Dean couldn't out-cast me with his light-weight fly. My bucktail sailed ten yards past his fly on a cast. I held the rod high when reeling in, getting the lure to skip on the surface, in and out of the chop.

The king salmon hit with ferocity, slamming the lure's spinning blades. "Look at this guy!" I shouted. The fish was high-jumping about forty yards out.

"It's a big king!" Dean shouted back. He was downstream of me and could see the fish better. The fish kept running and taking drag. I held the rod up at a high angle over my head. The twenty-pound test-monofilament line buzzed off the reel. The fish, well over thirty pounds, tested the limits of the spinning equipment, which was much lighter than the trolling rods and reels used yesterday. The big salmon's powerful muscles were propelling it at full speed. Big ones don't jump often; they swim hard against the resistance and take line, like Dean's had done yesterday. But this fish had read a different rule book: this was one pink-bellied, blue torpedo that jumped frequently.

"Can't believe he hit that musky lure," Dean exclaimed. He had reeled in his line and was standing next to me now.

"He's spinning on the surface—look at that large, curved snout," I was excited. The fish was in the middle of the river's mouth, out as far as the mouth was wide—fifty yards. It was running away and taking line. I tightened the drag slightly and walked into deeper water to change the angle of the line. The angle change got him to turn ninety degrees to my right. Then he was swimming sideways, swerving with half-jumps. I had to get the fish turned toward me before it got into the rocks on the opposite shore. I kept medium pressure on the fish, walking left to change the angle again. I was waist-deep and the bottom was mucky.

"You got him turned!" Dean was as excited as I was. "He's sidewinding toward us."

"I don't want to over-pressure him, this is a big fish." I reeled faster to keep the line tight as he swam toward us.

"I'll grab him when he gets close," Dean was ready. We had no net along, just our bare hands. With those old rodeo hands, Dean was an excellent fish-grabber.

"Be careful of the hook!" I warned him.

"Let me get in front of you!" Dean instructed as he walked out chest deep. On the second try, he grabbed the fish inside a gill plate, skillfully avoiding the hook. Then, quickly, he put his right arm under the belly keeping his left hand inside the gill plate, pinching nerves to calm the fish while I removed the hook with a small pliers tied to a chain around my neck.

The big Chinook was forty-five inches long with a twenty-eight-inch girth. By formula, forty-eight pounds! We both took a good look at the big salmon—my camera was in the backpack on shore. "Forget it," I said when Dean asked about it, "We need to release this fish now!" I could tell it was exhausted. Dean put the fish in the river, holding its tail while pushing it forward, then back gently, then forward again with more force. He repeated this sequence several times. Then let go of it. The fish stayed between us for a minute or so, then with a powerful tail splash, bolted upriver. "Good release," I blurted, totally wet now. Dean gave me a thumbs-up.

We teased each other about fish caught trolling versus casting. I, of course, tried to convince him that a forty-eight-pound king caught casting from shore with twenty-pound line was equal to a seventy-six-pounder caught trolling from a boat with sixty-pound line. I was very pleased; this was my largest Chinook salmon and it had put up a great fight. It was bigger than the ones mounted in the lodge, but not on equal ground with Dean's fish—casting versus trolling notwithstanding!

There were two cans of Coors left under the fish in the cooler, which we finished while continuing the debate. Todd arrived right on time.

Flying across the island, I noticed the moss-green mountains of morning had become whisky-brown in the dusk, and the blue rivers and lakes now looked steel-gray. A line of stratus clouds in shades of purple hung low above the western horizon. My mind would hold onto that picture.

We landed on the lake behind the lodge, slowly approaching the outer dock. When we got out, I held the plane steady while Dean unloaded the cooler and fishing gear.

"Thanks for the business! Watch out for bear!" Todd shouted as he turned and revved the engine. We watched him take off; he was in the air before we were off the dock. We carried the cooler together and the other gear in our backpacks on the seventy-five-yard walk to the lodge.

"Hello gentlemen!" Lynn said, greeting us as we entered the lodge's back door. "How was your day?"

"Another great day fishing in Alaska," I replied. Dean did a quick recap of it.

"And another big fish! Congratulations!" she said. "Did you bring any fish back?"

"Four nice eaters," Dean answered.

"Where are they?" she asked.

"In our cooler on the porch," I replied. She poked her head out the door and looked for the cooler.

"You don't want to leave that cooler there! Better take it downstairs now and put the fish in the freezer." There was an urgency in her voice. Dean and I carried the cooler downstairs. "Did she think we wouldn't do this?" Dean asked me.

I shook my head. "It seemed like she wanted us to be quick about it! That's my reading." Lynn was still by the door looking out when we came back up the stairs.

"Let's go inside and get comfortable," she said. "Sorry I was so abrupt. We had some excitement at the lodge today." Dean and I followed her into the great room and sat down in the large comfortable chairs. Lynn remained standing.

"A male Kodiak bear—a huge old boar, figured out how to open our garbage dumpster today. He made a big mess."

"When was that?" Dean asked.

"About four hours ago."

"Did the bear leave after making the mess?" I was thinking about our walk from the dock to the porch. I felt the pocket on my knapsack again to be sure the gun was still there. An old habit I'd inherited from a policeman—my dad.

"No! I had to get the .450 Marlin rifle and chase him away. We've seen that one before: Fifteen-hundred pounds, coffee-brown, white ears, paws larger than a dinner plate. I put a shot in the ground next to him and he high-tailed it."

"Do guns frighten these bears?" Dean asked her.

"They do if it's a local one, but you can't count on it. I shot at it from the back door with two guests behind me, ready to rush inside if necessary. That damn rifle kicks like a bloody bull."

"Dinner will be ready in one hour. Ted should be back from his meetings in town soon. Go get cleaned up," Lynn ordered with a wink. "We're having fresh king crab; all you can eat!"

After dinner, we relaxed in Ted's room drinking herbal tea with fresh wild-berry muffins Lynn had baked for dessert. She joined us, knowing we had something to discuss. Ted recapped last night's sightings. Lynn did not interrupt him, but nodded with understanding.

"Is it possible all three of us were hallucinating?" Dean asked. "I'm a retired jet airplane mechanic; the speeds we observed were difficult for me to imagine." Lynn kept still, looking at me now.

"I had never seen a UFO before, then three at once! The objects we saw were like stars and very high, satellite-high. In fact, they looked like satellites but moved sixty times faster. That's a million miles per hour! They made sharp turns and full stops at that speed, all while in geometric formations."

Lynn cleared her throat, with the look a teacher has when trying to answer a student's difficult question. "None of you were hallucinating!" She said. "I've seen them too."

"Recently?" Ted asked.

"Last week, on the dock around 2:00 a.m."

"How often have you seen them?" I was really into this now.

"Many times, starting five years ago."

"Do they appear in different parts of the sky?" Dean asked.

"Yes, but mostly to the north." Lynn was dead serious and knew the implications.

"Do they move in different formations, like the ones we saw?" Ted interjected.

"Yes, but always in straight lines; no curves or circles," She answered. We paused to drink some tea and take a couple bites of our muffins.

"What do you think they are?" Lynn asked, looking at me.

"I don't know. I do know the astronauts on the International Space Station have seen bright, fast-moving objects on many occasions. Internally, NASA calls them 'Fast Walkers' and cuts live transmissions when they show up. I haven't paid much attention until now; measuring their speed was mind-blowing."

"I don't discuss this with guests—you boys are an exception. I don't want guests to think I have nuts and bolts loose in my head. It would be bad for business."

"Nuts and bolts work best with lock washers!" Dean said. We all laughed. Still in disbelief, he was trying to lighten up the conservation.

"What about locals; do they see them?" Ted questioned.

"Many Indigenous Natives see the moving lights, like the coastal Haida and the Tlingit. But they don't make a connection with UFOs. Most simply regard such lights as part of the night sky. One Haida Indian man that used to come around called them star-spirits. As far as the non-indigenous locals—they don't say. And tourists just want to see the Northern Lights," Lynn explained.

"Do you see them when the auroras are strong?" I was curious. "There were no auroras last night and tonight is overcast."

"Good question! Don't recall I have," Lynn answered. "The aurora's shimmering brightness overwhelms everything else."

"If you've seen them for over five years, they're not here to attack us," Dean said, analyzing the situation.

"Maybe they're here to monitor our development." Ted proposed.

"Or, to alert us to an incoming asteroid or comet," Dean remarked.

"Maybe they're really here to protect us from ourselves!" I suggested.

"Well," Ted concluded, "last night gave new meaning to Alaska as The Last Frontier! There is a lot more than big fish and big bears up here. . ."

Postscript:

I have personally repeated the UFO sightings of the type described in this story. Most notably four years ago in Key West, Florida: Late at night above Mallory Square while lying in a lounge chair.

Male lion's kill, the "Fatally Distracted" impala

4

Fatal Distraction

A Lion Seizes Opportunity

A large, black-maned lion lies hidden in long grass near the river at the edge of the savannah. The animal faces into a gentle breeze coming from the river basin. It blows over him and out to the flat plains where elephants march along the horizon. Governed by primal patience, he scans for opportunity.

Masai Mara, Kenya, 1998

We drive onto the savannah from the dirt road that parallels the river. The steep escarpment beyond the boundary of the reserve is behind us. Four giraffes are feeding on thorn trees nearby. Benson stops the Land Rover and shuts the engine off, allowing us to take photographs without vibration. We already have photos of Masai giraffes, but new angles on animals this close are worth a stop. Standing up in the vehicle, through the open top, I aim my camera at the head of the nearest giraffe. He looks straight at me and cocks his head. What is he thinking? I wonder. I thank him mentally for the pose.

"Perfect," I say quietly. "Everybody still." I take two shots; *Zip Zip*.

The giraffe hears me and steps back. It keeps looking directly at us; its head filling the camera's viewfinder. I turn the camera vertically, hold it steady, and take two more shots. Four photographs at 1/250 of a second; in total, a sixtieth of a second in the giraffe's life. Hopefully, they capture the high perspective, extreme caution, and wary curiosity that defines a giraffe.

In silence, we watch the four giraffes. They lope around several fever trees, scenting the cool river air while looking out at the savannah. Staying close together, no longer distracted by us, they resume feeding. They've seen Land Rovers before; a common sight, like fever trees and elephant grass. The giraffes grew up with them as did the other animals on the Mara except the oldest elephants. Only they might remember a time without Land Rovers.

Suddenly, the silence is broken by the sound of two dueling impalas. They are about forty yards in front of us. Benson starts the Land Rover and drives toward them, off the dirt road and into the grass, thorn bushes scraping the rover as we get closer.

The two male impalas ram their ebony horns into one another. Heads down, eyes canted, they try to get a head-on view of each other. They engage and disengage. Their facial expressions are strangely innocent, the same expressions they have when grazing or mating. They have no way of changing them. Internally, however, hormones are flowing and something like hate is raging.

Horns lock, then burst apart. It's a distinctive sound—hollow horns ramming hollow horns—like bamboo chairs slamming together. They stomp and mash the grass beneath their feet. We can smell the fresh-crushed grass. I pick up a second camera loaded with slide film and begin shooting. I want to get some quick shots before they break apart and run off. I set the camera to automatic program mode, aim, and shoot. I take four fast shots, holding as steady as I can, camera pressed tight against my face. The shots are okay, not great. The light is wrong, but I capture the essence of the fight.

"Benson, drive around them!" I shout. "Get the sun behind us."

"Yes," Benson replies. He drives around behind the impalas who have no awareness of us. They are transfixed with no intention of quitting. They ram and reposition constantly. Benson tells us one is a vibrant young male. He points to it. The other an older territorial male. Both rams have two formidable cobra-shaped horns, widespread and sharp-pointed, each close to a meter in length. Serious weapons! Bachelor herds of young males abound throughout East Africa. I've seen them practice dueling on previous trips. But a real fight for territory—which includes exclusive access to a harem of females—is not commonly seen. A ruling male can service harems as large as forty or more; he cannot allow another male to enter his domain without a fight. We see the female impalas in the distance.

When we arrive on the other side of the animals, sun behind us, my son Jeff begins shooting black and white film with his camera. He aims at the impalas and waits for unique shots. I'm aiming too. Father and son—amateur photographers immersed in an African adventure. My sister, Kitty, alert and excited, watches from the back seat.

The light is much better now. Jeff and I try not to disturb each other when taking shots. It's difficult and some get wasted, but that's why we brought sixty rolls of film. Perfect, flawless shots are the goal: where the light is right, obstructions avoided, reflections and shadows considered, and the animals uniquely positioned.

"Thanks Benson. We're right on top of them!" I shout, over the bamboo-clanking. My voice has no effect on the Impalas.

"Welcome," Benson answers. He's a Kakuru man of few words, tall, dark-skinned, and lean with ten years guiding experience.

I sit down on the seat so I can shoot straight at them with no down angle. They're not distracted by anything. They don't know we're watching them; only the fight consumes their attention. Strangely, the fight itself is the distraction that limits their awareness. I zoom out halfway, getting their connected heads to fill the viewfinder.

Zip. Zip. I take two more shots. I love the essence of still photography because it immortalizes moments. Jeff keeps up with me shot-for-shot. There's no question some will be perfect.

The impalas are brilliant in the sunlight, their upper bodies a gleaming golden-tan that enhances their gypsum-white bellies.

Their horns lock together for a dozen seconds then jerk apart. Then slam back together with force, sliding and sawing, making rasping sounds. They are intent on killing each other, but no blood is visible. It's amazing. All it takes is for one to miss the advance of the other, not engage properly, and a jugular gets pierced. The two rams fight without blood. Moments of engagement lengthen; they waltz with each other when their horns tangle. Even Benson is impressed with their tenacity.

Jerking up suddenly, the older ram disengages and steps back. The younger ram comes at him full force and re-engages. Both stomp and bang into each other again with fierce intensity, wide-eyed but not seeing each other straight on when engaged. Brown dust flies up, hitting their faces. They spin in a circle, then more circles in reverse, becoming entangled. I take two more shots. I retract the zoom to get background scenery in the viewfinder and find the elephants who have been on the move, they are closer now. They pay no attention to what is happening.

I look at the giraffes behind us. The two bulls are twenty feet tall; the cows are shorter. They stay together and appear to be looking out beyond the impalas, stretching their necks, instinctively curious. What are they looking at? The elephants?

The older impala disengages and runs off rapidly, out toward the flat savannah and the elephants. He pauses for a moment and looks back. The young ram is victorious—he has won. He can walk away and claim the territory and the harem of females. This place on the Mara is his!

But no! In seconds, he's off after the old ram with remarkable speed, catching him about sixty yards out. They engage and begin fighting again. I pick up the camera and check the number of frames left—twenty. "Good," I say out loud. I can sense it's not over and new perspective at this distance is desirable.

"Benson, stay here, don't move."

"Okay," Benson replies, practicing word conservation.

Jeff loads a thirty-six-shot roll of 400 ASA color slide-film into his camera. He can sense something too. More Fuji moments.

I lean forward and switch the camera to multi-frame mode, take four shots quickly getting the impalas in the foreground with elephants behind them. I switch to shutter priority and set 1/500 second. I scan with the lens fully extended, out beyond the impalas, then rest the camera on a small beanbag on top of the door. I aim close to where the giraffes had been looking and something that wasn't there before—a blur in the grass.

Moving now, the blur comes out of the long grass. It's a large animal.

"Lion!" my sister shouts.

"Yes," Benson confirms. He has binoculars on it.

"Big male!" I shout. Jeff is looking at it through his camera lens.

"Yes, very big," Benson says. The blur speeds up. My sister is holding her mouth and screaming.

"He's coming. He's coming on!" Benson shouts.

The lion moves toward the impalas at a controlled pace, its black mane flaring and radiating, fully charged with static electricity.

"*Jeff, get this—don't miss this!*" I shout.

Jeff aims his camera and starts shooting. The lion is running now.

I do the same, keeping my camera on the beanbag. I take multiple shots by just holding my finger down. The lion runs—steadily and deliberately—toward the impalas. More deliberate than fast. He can be precise because both impalas are totally distracted by the fight. Merely trotting works well for the lion. He closes the distance, chooses the old ram, and tears into him with fully extended, four-inch claws. He mauls the animal and bites solidly into its upper back—missing the neck. The young ram disengages and stays to watch. He still wants to fight the older ram and does not grasp what's happening. I can't believe this. Jeff can't believe it. My sister Kitty is screaming again and holding onto me. The lion eyes the younger ram and switches its hold on the older ram to one paw, then lunges at the younger ram trying for a double kill. The younger ram jumps back, then returns to fight the older ram. He partially engages his horns with the older ram's without regard for the lion, but the lion digs its claws deeper into the older ram, securing it, then lunges at the younger ram, missing again. Finally, the younger ram becomes aware of the threat and bolts away, running out into the savannah toward the elephants; it stops once and looks back, part of him still wanting to fight! The older ram, in an unbelievable second effort, gets out from under the lion's paw and tries to escape by lunging forward. It doesn't work. The lion sinks its claws back into the impala, pulling it close and biting into its thigh, eating on it! The Impala kicks hard while being eaten alive, convincing the lion to launch another mauling thrust and vicious bite, this time into the neck!

"He's got it! He killed it!" Benson shouts. A full six words—he's excited! The safari guides in this part of Kenya speak English quite well but you need to nudge it out of them.

The male lion is huge, easily nine feet long. He's on top of the dead impala—all over it with an irrevocable grip on the neck. I take three photographs of this scene. My son is stunned. He doesn't say much in situations like this. His face is full of amazement that says it all. We're both pumped with adrenaline. It's that fire-in-the-gut feeling you get when immersed in a momentous experience. My sister is overwhelmed with it all and begins to cry, shedding tears for the dead impala. There is no perfectly clear and accurate way to describe such an event. It's where words fail.

The male lion drags the impala toward the river and heavy bush. We follow him closely. Halfway to the bush he stops, turns toward us, and displays his prize. He's five yards away.

The lion is impervious to our voices and the Rover. They have been around for his entire life. He treats us as a curiosity. But—take one step out of the Rover and you are dead meat! All the lodges and guides make this perfectly clear, and guests must sign a disclaimer. Some get out of vehicles anyway.

"Get this," Benson says. "Get this picture."

"Yes, Mr. Benson. A huge male lion pausing with its kill, fifteen feet away! Count on it," my son declares and starts shooting.

I aim directly at the lion's profile and zoom out to get seventy-five percent of the viewfinder filled with him and the impala. I take three shots. Then, zoom in to get only the two heads, predator and prey. I move left and right as I shoot from the open top of the vehicle trying to get annoying blades of grass out of the lion's face. Odds are that some shots will be unobstructed. Lesser evils have demoted African wildlife photographs.

"Rare to see this," Benson says. "Male lion alone, making kill. Females make kills, sometimes get help from males. But not often on the Mara."

"Yes," I acknowledge, happy he's talking more.

"Simba is the king," Kitty says. "The Lion King." I give her a hug as she wipes her tears. "At least he only got one of them," I tell her. She nods.

"It was very special to see this. You're a great guide Benson," Jeff says, patting him on the head.

"Welcome," Benson replies, smiling big.

The lion, monstrous with its huge hips and bulging shoulders, continues to drag the impala away from us into heavy bush, passing over where the impalas fought. But now there is blood. Lots of blood.

The giraffes had moved away, going down along the river toward the escarpment. The taller bull had stopped before disappearing, turning its head back for a departing look—a last trace of curiosity. The elephants are out of sight, somewhere beyond the horizon.

We continue to follow the lion, but with difficulty. We are in heavy bush. The lion dragging the dead impala is directly ahead of us. The cat's paws are the size of dinner plates, its claws sharper than fishhooks used for marlin. It's frightening to see this. He drops the impala at his feet and stands over it, turns and growls at us. His growl, a deep guttural resonance that all of Africa can hear, runs a chill down my spine. We have the windows up and doors locked, but the top is open. Vehicle conditioning since birth is one thing, but being hard to see in high grass is another.

I wondered what goes through a lion's mind at a time like this. *Might he think we would we try to steal his kill?*

"Be careful Benson, he can't see us clearly," I say loudly.

"We're okay," Benson says. The lion picks up the impala and drags it again. We follow him deeper into the bush; Benson shifts into four-wheel drive. Thorn bushes scrape the side of the Rover, like fingernails on a blackboard. "Waste-paper" flowers, like bits of scattered Kleenex, dot the grass. The lion moves straight ahead for another thirty yards, then turns and takes the impala behind an expanse of broadleaf plants. I feel we are pushing him too much, his growl is no joke. It's a stern warning!

"Benson, stop here," I repeat with authority.

"It's okay," he says back. "Masai Mara lions will not hurt us if we stay in the Rover." These are words that could become famous and last... I remembered a story from the past about a leopard that jumped into a minivan of French tourists in Samburu because they wouldn't stop aggravating it. Last week's guide had witnessed the attack from another vehicle. He told us three of the people were helicoptered to a hospital in Nairobi. No, we're not ready for an encounter with an angry lion and join the impala behind a bush. We need to pause and consider the danger.

"This is far enough Benson!" I was emphatic. "You said it was rare for a male lion to make a kill, but this one did, and we're in high grass with it and he can't see us!"

"Okay we go," Benson agreed.

It's such a rare event to see—he just wants to give us our money's worth," Jeff said.

"I understand, Son, and he did!" At eighteen Jeff was bulletproof—he thought we could follow the lion a bit farther. Kitty was a picture of relief that qualified for the Louvre.

Benson backed the Land Rover out of the heavy bush until he could circle around and go forward, out to the dirt road that followed the river that would take us back to camp. When I looked back—the lion and dead impala were out of sight.

We passed a troop of baboons on the way back. There were a dozen of them from teenagers to pregnant females plus one large male—The Dictator who had a bad case of hemorrhoids! These baboons could jump into a vehicle, particularly the teenagers. They were in the middle of the road so we had to stop.

Benson grabbed a big can of wasp spray from under his seat, one that shoots out twenty feet. He held the can high so they could see it and gave it a spritz. Instantly, the baboons recognized it and moved back. Getting squirted in the eye with wasp spray was worse than with Mace or pepper spray! Benson smiled at them. The Dictator looked at Benson, made some guttural babbling sounds, then gave him the finger! I'm not kidding. My sister was laughing hysterically. Jeff took a picture. Last year in Benson's Land Rover a group of Swedish tourists had an open bag of potato chips when they came upon these same baboons. Several of them jumped into the vehicle and went crazy fighting over the chips. Two of the Swedes got bitten before they could throw the chips out. Benson told us the big male had escaped from a private zoo in Arusha and had joined up with the troop. A zookeeper had taught him how to communicate with his finger.

Back at camp, it was already dark. The peanut butter and cheese crackers we'd had for lunch were ancient history and we were hungry. We went to our tent and cleaned up. It was a large army-style tent on a wooden platform with an operational bathroom. It had two double beds and a cot. Jeff got the cot. I called for a guard to walk us to dinner. According to house rules, a guard had to accompany guests to the dinner tent, and for good reason; we were close to the river and its plethora of wild animals. A tall Masai man in a red uniform showed up promptly, carrying a kerosene lamp. The dinner tent was about fifty yards away. When we got to it, there was quite a surprise waiting: A seven-thousand-pound male hippo was blocking the entrance! The Masai put his arms out, like a school crossing guard, and made us back up. There were other guests waiting behind their Masai guards too. The hippo was a giant male—a gray oval of flesh, wet from the river, with pink eyes and ears, and a monster mouth. At least that's what we could see of him under the kerosene lamps.

"They are very dangerous," a young German man told us while standing with his wife behind their Masai guard. "More locals die from hippo attacks than from any other animal."

"And they don't eat meat," his wife said, "but kill over three thousand locals a year. They can bite your head off!" Kitty felt sick after hearing this. Jeff made sure he had his Buck knife in his pocket. He told me he'd read that you could kill one by stabbing it in the ear. "Before or after he bites your head off?" I asked him.

"I heard they have a bad disposition," I added; an obvious understatement. My sister moved to the very back of the line of people waiting to eat. She had the most Masai guards in front of her! Jeff, still fearless, was just fascinated. We had seen hippos in the river but none this close. The animal grunted and shuffled its feet but didn't move from blocking the entrance.

"I know this one," a voice behind me said. It was Benson holding a large garden rake. "Big Hippo dangerous."

"So are big lions," I said, smiling. He gave me a serious look and disappeared. What was I joking about? This monstrous hunk of meat could take my head off! The Hippo held its ground.

"He's the dominant male in a pod of twenty, upriver from here," a cook in a tall white hat said, standing with us now. "He just comes to scare and aggravate us. Benson will get him to move." The other guests were whispering to each other. Four Masai guards formed a line and were holding spears, looking quite imposing in crimson-red uniforms. They stood together making sure we were all back far enough.

"They must be the backup to Benson," I said. The German man looked at me and frowned. "It is important not to move—a hippo can run thirty-two kilometers per hour!" He said. *Where was Benson?* I wondered. *What could he possibly do*?

The rake had fresh reeds and green sprouts twisted into a large ball on its end. Favorite hippo food from down by the river. Benson came carrying the rake, holding it straight out from his body. He was grunting like a hippo. The animal jerked and turned to look, but mostly could smell the sweet ball of vegetation. Slowly, it followed the smell and the grunts. Benson had come up from the river the back way by a steep trail. Now facing the hippo and sticking the ball of vegetation in its face, he backed down the trail. When the animal got closer, nose on the vegetation, mouth open, Benson threw the rake with the vegetation down the trail toward the river while ducking into the bush. It was too steep for the animal to turn around. It ignored Benson and followed the enticing aroma.

"How about that!" Jeff said, not thinking about his Buck knife anymore. "I was ready to back up the Masai!"

We were all amazed and relieved. The cook in the white hat shouted, "Follow me!" We gladly followed him into the dinner tent.

The aromas in the dinner tent were scrumptious, unless, of course, you were a huge oval animal that could mouth a basketball and loved to eat river weeds. The waiters and cooks were moving fast after the hippo delay. The three of us were seated next to Heino and Anna, the German couple we met in line. We were at a large circular table with a yellow table cloth that had four large candles in the center. Candlelight was by necessity—the generator had been misbehaving. Light reflecting off the table made everyone look yellow.

"Where's Benson?" I asked Daniel, our waiter.

"He's eating with the other guides," Daniel answered.

"Go tell him we insist he eat with us." I looked at Heino and Anna and they nodded yes in agreement. "Tell him he has no choice!"

Daniel had to drag Benson in. Normally, it was verboten for guides to eat in the guest tent. Everybody clapped when they saw him sit down, I had been pointing to an empty chair at our table. Nobody in camp, including management, dared to disagree.

"We need a drink," Kitty realized.

"That's for sure," I said. Jeff and the German couple ordered beer—Kenya Tuskers. Kitty and I opted for gin and tonic. Benson stayed with water. It was busy, everybody was drinking something. We had time to talk about Africa.

"To a great day in Africa!" I declared, holding up my G & T. Every guest in the tent took a drink, including Benson, enjoying his Evian Water.

"And to Benson, a great guide!" I added. "Scaring us with the lion forgiven."

"To 'The Hippo Imitator,'" Jeff announced, holding up his beer. We all drank again. Benson was happy. This may have been the first time a safari guest ever toasted him!

"Benson, I have a question for you: How did you learn to grunt like a hippo?" I asked.

"I listen to them," he said. "And practice grunting like female hippo in heat."

"So, it took both food and sex to get it to go down the hill," Anna declared.

"And the rake!" Benson added. We all laughed.

Food was finally on the way. Daniel brought out a house special for starters, Kenyan mushroom soup containing tiny shrimp. It smelled terrific. "They're from Mombasa," Daniel claimed.

"The shrimp or the mushrooms?" Kitty asked. "Both," Daniel affirmed, smiling. Jeff was horsing it down; I forgot how hungry he was. Daniel quickly brought him a second bowl.

"Jeff and Kitty explained the details of our day to Daniel. Then, Heino and Anna told about their day. They had seen three cheetahs hunting Thompson gazelles; 'tommys'—half-size versions of impalas.

"The mother cheetah was teaching her offspring the rules of the hunt. Rule Number One: lie patiently hidden in the grass for a long time. Rule Number Two: jump up when food is close, and run like hell after it," Anna explained. "The mom caught one, and we watched them have lunch."

"Poor little tommy," Kitty lamented. "Fully nourished cheetahs," Heino said. "Africa," Anna added.

"Did the cheetahs hit eighty mph?" I asked Heino. "They may have—I didn't have a radar gun," he replied with German seriousness. "Then you need to get one!" I told him. Heino frowned at me. I maintained a stern look. Anna laughed immediately and whispered something to Heino. Then he laughed too. "He's still sorting out the hyperbole in American humor," she said.

"Very exciting to see such amazing animals on the hunt," Daniel remarked. He was native Kakuru and spoke the Queen's English perfectly. "This was a special day for all five of you! And now for your main course!"

An assistant waiter brought in six steaming plates: "Impala medallions in wine sauce with red beets, plantains, and sweet potatoes." Impala medallions were the filet mignon of Africa, they were magnificent and tender with no game taste, cut from the narrow end of the tenderloin.

For dessert: Kenyan coffee and crème caramel with coconut sauce, a perfect finale.

The next morning Benson took us back on the river road to the high grass where we last saw the lion—he had moved. There was a gentle breeze blowing out from the river into the barren grass.

We did see hippos and crocodiles in the river and elephants eating trees, but no lion. Out in the shorter grass of the savannah we were treated to large herds of animals: zebra and wildebeest; steenbok and eland; and a cackle of hyenas that were chasing impalas. The impalas were running away from the hyenas at full speed, long jumping—several body lengths with all four legs in the air—one jump after another, touching down for an instant, then back up, flying. They were not easy to catch—for that, they needed to be distracted!

Returning for breakfast after the morning game drive, we heard another party talking about their morning. They had seen three cheetahs and one lion, all sleeping with full stomachs. The lion was a large, black-maned male lying upriver from where we had been. A gentle breeze blew over him, rustling his mane. They tried to rouse him by shouting and banging on their Land Rover. But he slept through it snoring loudly, paws covering his face to keep the flies off. It was boring to see a big lion sleeping like this.

Postscript:

Africa is an amazing wonder; a diversity of life was everywhere in the 1990s. I was fortunate to have travelled to East Africa and South Africa five times during that period. But since 1998 when this story took place there have been changes. The population of Kenya has grown from 38 million people in 1998 to 44 million in 2015 and is expected to reach 53 million by 2020. This has put tremendous pressure on the animals and many species are now endangered. Cheetahs are critically endangered in 2017 with leopards and giraffes not far behind. If you have never been to Africa to see its animals, and you have a burning desire to do so, now is the time. Don't wait. And if you want to help Africa's wildlife survive, there are many credible associations that need donations.

Fez Gate (Blue Gate)

5

Danger in Morocco

Discovering the Unexpected and Bizarre

Tangier, May 1968

East of Tangier in the foothills of the Rif Mountains the turquoise Mediterranean sparkled in front of us. A guesthouse in Chefchaouen was our destination. I was driving a Renault rental; Dave Trebatsky (Treb) my fraternity brother, sat beside me in front, instinctively trying to brake whenever I did. Professor Norman Catell was bouncing around in back. The road was rough, a Moroccan hybrid of pavement alternating with gravel. Well disguised potholes—axle-breakers—were a bonus feature to watch for. This was the scenic route along the coast—a long way from Stevens Point, Wisconsin!

Treb had gotten sick after dinner the night before, probably from the couscous we ate at the hotel restaurant. He'd hugged the toilet in our room most of the night and was dehydrated and looking green in the morning. I'd pulled into an Arabic grocery store before leaving Tangier and bought six cartons of yogurt, and insisted he eat three of them immediately.

"I don't eat yogurt," he told me.

"Eat it, or you're going to feel like crap all day." He choked them down as we bounced along. "Yogurt contains beneficial acidophilus bacteria; they'll kill the germs that are making you sick! I know what I'm talking about!" I instructed him.

Treb was tall, medium build, with blonde hair and blue eyes. At twenty-one, two years younger than yours truly, he was learning how to become a world traveler.

Couscous is a Moroccan delicacy—a dish of Berber origin that is prepared for special events. Norm Catell, in organizing our trip, made sure our arrival would be considered a special event. So, the hotel made couscous for all the guests. It's a complex casserole that starts with a layer of hard-rolled semolina grain steamed until plump and fluffy, then piled high with meats, veggies, nuts, and dried fruit. It's quite a creation. The final touch is a spice mix of thirty ingredients sprinkled on top called *Ras El Hanout*: ground leaves and roots with emphasis on turmeric, cardamom, nutmeg, ginger and cinnamon.

You eat couscous with your hand—your *right* hand in a Muslim country! Left hands were deployed for less sanitary activities. Everybody at the table digs into the same dish, which is the size of a large pizza. Norm and I made sure to sample the undisturbed side of the dish. Treb was digging in with three strangers on the opposite side, eating like a horse. *E. coli,* or some germ may have been in attack mode. Thinking back, I recall Norm sprinkled our side liberally with the spice mixture, and we felt fine. Maybe because certain spices kill germs. Otherwise, the strangers were to blame for contaminating the couscous.

A truck passed us throwing chips of pavement into our windshield right when we hit a serious pothole. "They didn't tell us in Tangier the road would be this bad, just not to drive at night," I remarked.

"My nuts are in my throat," Treb declared. "Ditto," Norm agreed. We were in second gear and going seventy kilometers per hour. I slowed down to sixty. The scenery was stunning with buff-red hills, green forests, and the blue Mediterranean Sea domed by streaks of white cirrus clouds. The road followed the sea east for four hundred kilometers before making a sharp turn south and following the Algerian border. We would turn well before that and head south to Chefchaouen.

May is hot in Morocco. We had the windows half open—a compromise between dust control and cooling. The rental car had no air conditioning.

"Feeling any better Trebby?" I asked him. This was only his second trip out of Wisconsin; he had been to Kansas once!

"I feel like dog shit," he said.

"Drink more water," Norm told him. "You're dehydrated."

"You were barfing all night," I reminded him.

"I know it—I had the dry heaves," He took a long drink of water. "What I really need is a quart of Point Special!"

"Beer's not a good idea." Norm shook his head.

"Why not? It's good rehydration," Treb responded.

"Think about drinking water," Norm repeated.

"You're just an old leaker, Norm." Treb managed a smile. "Someone who can't hold their liquor."

"Trebby, Morocco is a Muslim country. We're on a back-road, we won't be zipping by dozens of taverns like in Wiscon-sin!" I reminded him. The road was sandy now and we were still going slow. The mountains changed colors as clouds redirected the sunlight. Cedar and oak forests with exposed rocky spots were interrupted by fields of spring-green vegetation. When the road went through a small village and became overrun with goats and chickens, hooded beings appeared.

"How can those Arabs stand the heat in hooded sweat-shirts?" Treb asked Norm.

"They're called *djellabas,* and they're Berbers not Arabs," Norm instructed. Both Treb and I had taken his "Introduction to Geology" course the previous year; he was a smart guy who had the classic look of both a professor and someone named Norman. Known as "Normal Norman" at the university, he was in his mid-forties, about five-nine, thin, and wore glasses. He and Treb had sparred for the last two weeks as we traveled through Europe—Morocco was our last lap.

Darker green fields in the distance resembled corn fields in Iowa, and the hills behind them were terraced. I had the car in second gear on steep inclines; fifty kilometers per hour was hard to maintain—we needed more power. The Renault's small twenty-horsepower engine was overheating. We finished a long uphill climb—shifting into first gear frequently with a hot clutch pedal—and came to a summit where we could see down into the Rif Valley for several kilometers. We drove down into it and, rather abruptly, revised our perspective.

The countryside was deep green with tall stalks of cannabis, this was the "corn" we had been seeing in the distance. Signs of "Hash for Sale" and an army of persistent salesmen—men and boys—suddenly surrounded our car. They had come out of nowhere from hiding, awakened by our vehicle approaching. Heads covered except for their eyes, they tried every pitch they knew to get us to stop. I had to slow to a crawl to keep from hitting them. One man sat on our trunk, glaring at Norm. A boy, maybe twelve years old, was holding onto the hood of the Renault, running backwards as we moved slowly ahead, staring at me and smiling. He had sprigs of cannabis stuck in a headband and was pointing to it. "Premio-qualitee!" he shouted. "Forty-dollar kilo!"

"Now we're talking my language!" Treb was excited.

"Settle down Treb, it's strictly illegal!" Norm said. "Big fine if the police catch you."

"Yes, and it's often a setup. The police share the fine with the guys who set you up," I added, having read it in a tourist guide. Treb's face morphed from a smile to a frown. Up ahead, mules were in the road, loaded up with the long, leafy stalks, carrying them for processing into hashish or kif. We had to move on. I handed the boy who was running alongside us a five-dollar bill for his efforts.

"*Allah Esahel,*" Norm yelled out to him. The boy smiled and backed away.

"What's that mean?" Treb asked.

"It's Arabic: May God make it easy on you," Norm translated.

On Treb's side two men were still running, one holding onto the car's mirror, the other on the backdoor handle. They were shouting "*La, La, La,*" holding up bags of dry marijuana. La meant no.

"*La Shukran*!" Norm shouted. "No thanks!" We accelerated slowly.

We drove on at eighty-five kilometers per hour. The road turned south toward Chefchaouen as the Renault threw hot dust into the hot day. Cannabis fields were now higher up in terraced foothills. An old car was stalled with its hood up in the middle of the road. Two men with blue tee shirts wrapped around their heads were waving for us to stop.

"I'm not stopping," I said. The car rental agency had warned us about this.

"Go around to the left," Treb urged. "There's a dead tree on the right."

"I see it," I swerved left as they ran toward us. "Close the windows; lock the doors!" I shouted. I never saw Norm move so fast. There was a tree on the left too, hidden in the grass. I swerved right, just missing it, and almost hit the front of the stalled car when we got back on the road. I floored the gas pedal.

"The blue-heads just got into their car!" Treb shouted. Norm was quiet, holding onto the back of my seat.

"It was a setup! We were lucky as hell to miss those trees," I realized.

"A robbery setup!" Norm exclaimed. We were about fifty meters in front of them, but they were gaining.

"How far is Chefchaouen?" I asked Norm—he had the map.

"Maybe thirty kilometers." I had the Renault topped off at ninety kilometers per hour.

"You're making them eat our dust," Treb said as chips of road flew back at them hitting their car. "They're getting close—twenty meters now."

"The guesthouse is on this side of town; its road will be up ahead on the right in about ten Kilometers." Norm read his notes on the map. "Their road comes in perpendicular to this road, so you'll have to make a sharp turn."

"I hope they have security!" I was scared. We had no weapons!

"They're trying to pass and cut us off!" Treb yelled. I'd been swerving to prevent this; the road was coarse gravel now and bigger stones were flying back at them. With no mud flaps, the Renault really threw dust and gravel—it was good for something.

"Flat tire and we're dead meat!" I shouted, creating as much dust and flying stones as possible. Fortunately, their old car was not much faster than ours.

Whump, Whump! We partly dipped into a large pothole with the back tires while making a tight swerve! I was astounded the

Renault could still function; I steered back into the center of the road. "They smacked the same pothole straight on—almost going ass-over-appetite!" Treb yelled out. Norm nodded, he was whiter than a ghost in fresh snow. The pothole appeared to have slowed the blue-heads down somewhat!

In the distance, on the far hills, we could see the blue-washed buildings that defined Chefchaouen. Norm pointed at the road to the guesthouse coming up on the right.

"I'm going to take it at full speed," I shouted. "Hold on!"

I made the turn sharply. "Stay behind me Norm—hold onto the back of my seat!" We tipped about thirty degrees, two tires up, then back to flat. The blue-heads kept going straight, missing the turn. "The dust saved us; those scumbags didn't see us turn." Norm shouted.

"Scumbags—good word, Norm!" Treb shouted.

"We have to be sure they don't turn back." There was nothing in sight but the new dirt road. "Good news—nobody's behind us!" I shouted.

When the road made a wide turn, we could see where it became asphalt—my pulse finally slowed down. On the right was a sign with an arrow: "Weber's Guesthouse, One Km."

When we could see the guesthouse, we stopped before getting any closer and checked behind us, again confirming nobody was there! We got out and shook off the dust. Treb's blonde hair was brick red. Norm's glasses were opaque. I had to rinse mud out of my mouth with the last of our bottled water.

"Thanks a lot for suggesting the scenic route, Norm." Treb was on the road to recovery from his couscous event.

A jeep, with two men in beige uniforms and red skullcaps drove out from a garage next to the guesthouse. One man held a shotgun. We didn't move. When they got to us, they identified themselves as security for the Weber Guesthouse. The driver looked us over without getting out. "Follow us," he said, easily recognizing three authentic Americans looking as if they'd come straight out of a western movie.

The spring sun was bright and warm and green grass bordered the circle drive to the entrance. I finally shut off the smoldering Renault. Treb opened its trunk and hauled out our luggage. Very dusty luggage. Before we could decide what to do—not wanting to take it inside—a young man came out with a broom. "Welcome to the Weber Guesthouse!" he said as he swept the dust off our luggage.

The guesthouse was a remodeled *riad*: a large, single-story, square building made of pink sandstone. Everything was spotless and organized. A sizable, open garden was in the center of the building—guest rooms surrounded it. We had entered a different world.

Two lovely Berber ladies in bright patterned dresses and jeweled hairpieces greeted us inside. "Welcome to our *riad,*" they said.

"*Shukran!*" Norm thanked them. "I can't tell you how happy we are to be here." Then he apologized for our appearances.

"This is Morocco, dust is part of the experience!" Izza said, then introduced her sister Kella. We don't have many Americans visit. We're pleased to honor you with our hospitality."

Both looked to be in their early thirties with daffodil blonde hair and light complexions accented with lilac eye shadow and a touch of rose lipstick. They were truly a sight for sore eyes. We introduced ourselves and briefly explained our eventful road trip from Tangier and the couscous episode the previous night.

"You went the dangerous way!" Izza confirmed. "Those outlaws never come on our road, they're allergic to shotguns!"

"We know that now," I said. "It's always best to live and learn—with emphasis on 'live.'"

"Mr. Treb, how are you feeling?" Kella asked.

"Better, after eating three cartons of yogurt and watching out for Norm."

"There's still three left!" I reminded him. "Your dessert tonight."

"Yummy," Izza said. "Lots of beneficial microbes." I was astonished she knew this. "Follow us and we'll check you in, we can talk over mint tea in the garden at 15:00."

"That translates to 3:00 p.m. for Mr. Treb." It was Norm's turn to take a get-even shot. "A talk in the garden sounds wonderful." The ladies' perfect English and exceptional beauty captivated Norm. I swore to keep an eye on the professor.

They showed us to our rooms. The walls in the room Treb and I shared were pure white, curving around two comfortable beds with blue sheets and pillow cases that matched the blue-tiled bathroom. A large ceiling fan turned slowly, gently moving the air as I looked out the window at the garden, alive in the sunlight. We had time to clean up and recalibrate before tea.

After refreshing showers, we walked together into the garden at 3:00 p.m. It was fully enclosed; no openings to the outside except at the top. A clear, crescent swimming pool in the center had two fountains at each end—marble lions with water pouring from their mouths. Colorful flowerpots hung from the walls, each with flowers that matched the pot's color. Various African cactus plants thrived in large pots and decorated the floor.

Guests were sitting at a large round table in an alcove where Izza and Kella were managing a tea-preparation cart. We joined them.

"Pour it high," An Englishman said to Kella. She held the metal teapot high above his head and poured the tea into his glass, almost a meter below, without spilling a drop.

"It's about the bubbles," he declared. "It drinks best with bubbles."

"I think it's about watching Kella!" Norm teased; Kella blushed. There were six other guests besides the three of us, Kella and Izza poured the tea high for everybody; it was a Moroccan custom.

"Welcome to Chefchaouen," they both said while adding a bundle of mint leaves to each glass. The mint was added after pouring so as not to disturb the bubble- formation. The clear glasses were tall and wide without handles. Around their center was a band of leather so ladies could hold the hot tea; men were expected to hold their glass above or below the leather band. Like in Russia! The tea was fresh-brewed green tea with a touch of raw honey. The finished creation looked nothing like a cup of tea but more like a miniature hydroponic garden. The mint taste developed quickly.

"Absolutely delightful!" The Englishman's wife declared. Izza introduced them as Mr. and Mrs. Patrick Taylor. "Call us Pat and Diana," Pat said, as we all took sips of our tea garden before Izza and Kella introduced the rest of us.

Enjoy your "Berber Whiskey," Kella declared.

"That's what we call it," Izza added. Sometimes Berber men add a splash of Judeo, a local anise-flavored vodka brewed from figs!" She winked as us. "It's one of the adjustments some have made to Muslim law."

"Berber folk dancing at festivals is very special. We call the women dancers Marrachias." Kella smiled. "They wear long red or violet dresses with black belts and bells—hair loose swinging with the music!"

"I'll drink to that," Treb said. We all smiled and took sips of tea. The conversations continued for about an hour before the guests were ready to head out for the afternoon.

"Anybody going into town needs to take a Grand Taxi—a Mercedes van with a licensed driver! I will call it for you. It costs five-dollars per person and will drop you at the town center, the medina. You can walk anywhere from there." Kella explained. Four of the guests decided to take the Grand Taxi.

"Be sure to see the Kasbah! And make sure you take the same taxi back!" Izza added.

"They call regular taxis 'flying coffins,'" Pat said. He was a tall, distinguished Englishman, smartly dressed like he was ready to umpire a cricket match. He spoke the Queen's English, of course. "You lads have your own vehicle?"

"Yup, a beautiful Renault subcompact," I responded proudly. "Twenty horsepower!"

"Brave lads," Pat smiled. "Don't drive at night."

"After our day, I would edit your advice to 'don't drive period.'"

"Bang on, Chap!" Pat agreed.

The garden cleared and we had a chance to talk more with Izza and Kella before going into town. The five of us sat back down.

"Norm started off by explaining that Treb and I were his students from the previous year at the University of Wisconsin at Stevens Point. He was a professor of geology and specialized in fossils. He liked to travel and frequently made trips with students.

"There are many fossils in Morocco," Kella said. "But not here so much—more down south around Quarzazate and the Draa Valley."

"Yes, I was there two years ago; found some beautiful red ammonites and large black trilobites. I'm back to see north Morocco now; we only have a few days. There is a fossil shop in Fez we're going to visit."

"Tell us more about your road trip," Izza asked. I gave my summary, then Norm and Treb added what I'd missed.

"Do you know the history of marijuana in Morocco?" Izza asked us.

"Does it have to do with the Spanish Conquest?" Norm responded.

"Yes, it was back in 1860 after the first Spanish-Moroccan war. To calm the population down and make it easy to take over the country, particularly the Barbary Coast cities, the Spaniards promoted the use of marijuana, or kif, to get people relaxed and less willing to keep fighting," Izza explained.

"How about that!" Norm said. "It's a war story."

"It is, but there's more to it. We're Berbers, indigenous people; many of us have light skin and hair and blue eyes. Kella and I have a German father and a Berber mother, a rare combination. Berbers have been in Morocco for thousands of years. The Muslims took over in 700 A.D. Many Berbers integrated into Islamic society but many did not. Those who did became Sunni Muslims." Izza explained in more detail.

"Is there a name for those who did not integrate?" Norm asked.

"The government called them 'cultural militants' for a time. Now they're just Berbers," Izza answered.

Then Kella took over. "You might say that many Berbers semi-integrated. Like the Mughals in India who also made adjustments in Islamic law. For example—like Izza said—many show skin and hair, dance, and listen to music. Some also drink alcohol, smoke kif, and eat during Ramadan. These are options for the individual to decide. Some Berbers accept them, others don't. There are no religious police in Morocco, like in most Islamic countries."

"Doesn't this create problems with the Arab Muslims who rule?" I asked.

"Yes, it does, but there are nine million Berbers in Morocco. King Hassan doesn't want to fight them; he looks the other way most of the time. It is said he dances and drinks vodka in private." Izza giggled. I was thinking it would be hard for her to visualize the king dancing.

"That's the guy with a red sock on his head you see on postage stamps," Treb said. Both Izza and Kella laughed. "You'd look good in one, Treb!" Kella remarked. She had her eye on him.

I disregarded that observation. "This tells me there are options to being entirely wrapped in the shroud of Islam. More power to the moderates!"

"It's truly a discussion for the ages," Norm said. We all agreed.

We had planned to go into town but were too beat up from the intensity of the day. The pool looked inviting—we had it to ourselves. After a swim, we went outside and walked the countryside around the guesthouse. "Don't go too far!" the boy who'd swept our luggage yelled from a window. Hearing him, the two security guards came out of their quarters, looked at us, saluted, then sat down and watched us take our walk. One had binoculars.

"We know firsthand there are dangers in Morocco!" Norm reaffirmed. We appreciated the security.

"I'd like to meet George Weber sometime," I admitted. Norm agreed. I couldn't help but wonder what Kella and Izza's father was like. *A moderately stern German man? Certainly not unconditionally stern!*

While finger-combing his hair, and watching two very green birds in a tree, Treb interjected, "You'll have to go to Berlin to find out. Kella told me he lived there."

The next morning, it was 9:00 a.m. when we hit the dusty trail. Chefchaouen was close. Nestled high in the Rif Mountains it was indeed, "The Blue City," a collection of blue-plastered buildings and riads in all shades of blue—from robin's egg to cobalt. Norm had given us different explanations for all the blue: "It was a cool color for long summers; dry, blue paint was cheap and mixed well in water; blue kept mosquitos away; it was not Muslim green; blue signified sky and heaven." Norm had done his homework on this.

We drove close to the medina and parked next to an abandoned building; hopefully nobody would risk stealing a Renault subcompact. The medina comprised the old city. It was completely walled-in and off-limits to cars.

We entered it through the *Bab el Souk*—the market gate. Two Arab men immediately approached us.

"I'm Ahmad; this is Mohammad."

"Want to smoke kif, excellent quality?" Mahammad asked in an assuming voice. Kif was a mixture of marijuana and tobacco.

"La, La," I said.

"Say *no,* we understand English. Where you going? We can guide. Take you to leather tannery? The Kasbah?"

"No thanks, we just arrived," Norm told them. We started walking in the direction of the Kasbah and they followed. We walked faster, they followed faster.

"We'll guide you, keep you safe. For small money." Ahmed raised his voice. "Don't worry."

"These *touts* are right out of the tour guide's warnings section," Norm said to me. Ahmed ran ahead of us then turned around, walking backwards, and tried again in an even stronger voice. "You should try our special kif. Free samples! Relaxing experience!"

"Best *Kif of the Rif,* Best *Kif of the Rif,* yes, yes, *naam, naam*!" Mohammad repeated over and over in a nauseating voice behind us. I told Norm and Treb to be quiet, stop walking, and get an angry look on their face. The three of us stopped and stood shoulder-to-shoulder, like we had rehearsed this, and glared directly at the two Arabs. There was a moment of silence. Then I yelled: "*In The Name of Allah, No Thanks!*" as loud as I could.

Norm and Treb remained silent; Treb had the best angry face. The Arabs walked away without another word.

"They didn't even try to be friendly." Norm looked disgusted. "What would you do if you were alone? It wasn't this bad down in Quarzazate two years ago."

"You were with a group of rock hounds with hammers!" Treb pointed out.

"And probably short on tourists," I added. The best advice was to stay in a group. There was an inherent desperation in these people, I could feel it. The bright sun helped calm us down. It was warm but dry; we were comfortable walking around in long pants and short-sleeved shirts, following the guide book's advice on dressing.

The Kasbah was not far ahead as we walked the old, narrow, blue maze of streets. An old man was blue-washing a fence in front of a small *riad*. Not whitewashing, but blue-washing. He mixed blue paint powder in a bucket of water, then brushed it on. Made me think of Mark Twain and *The Adventures of Tom Sawyer*. It was "work if he was obliged to do it—play if not obliged." The old man smiled when he saw us! There was a crowd up ahead in an open *souk* and we could smell food.

"Have a look at these," I said, pointing to some ungodly-looking sausages with bulges and a weird odor. Norm winced. Treb simulated puking.

"They're camel spleens stuffed with camel meat," a tourist lady told us. "Very gamey."

"I bet they are! That settles it, we know what's for lunch," I said to her. She laughed.

"You might want to share one of these too," she teased, pointing to a large simmering pot.

"Sheep heads, with bulging eyes!" Norm exclaimed. "At least they smell better."

"They're loaded with red pepper and cumin," she remarked. "Good way to eat old mutton."

"We'll have them as a second course. With plenty of beer!" I kidded.

"This sure isn't Kansas," Treb said. "It's bizarre!" She laughed again and waved as she walked on.

Strangely, no shopkeeper was around trying to sell us something. We walked on, investigating more. The amazing lack of symmetry created a special charm. Most of the *riad* dwellings were well-kept. Dark blue clay pots housing small palm trees were abundant. Most buildings and *riads* were largely cubical and nestled together. Because the city was built on a mountain-side, steps were everywhere—wide or narrow, long or steep—there were lots of steps. Subtract the issue of scary *touts* and old mutton, and it was quite lovely.

We bought tickets and went into the Kasbah, an old fortress with a garden and museums inside. That was where cobalt blue was prominent—the darkest of blues. Men stood around in hooded, striped *djellabas.* Hot clothes for a hot day. None of them were moving fast! Climbing the Kasbah's tower produced stunning views of the medina and several ounces of sweat—the views were worth the effort!

Leaving the Kasbah, we walked into the plaza and found activity: bars, cafes, shops, and people. Here were the tourists, including the lady who had explained the camel spleens and spicy sheep heads. I tapped her on the shoulder from behind.

"There you chaps are; you found the plaza," It was time to introduce ourselves. Her name was Beverly Limerick, a retired school teacher from South Africa. Norm invited her to join us for lunch provided she could recommend a good café.

"The place I like is a bar—over there." She pointed to a square, blue building with a small *Flag Special* sign hanging over the door.

"It's my treat," Norm insisted. The four of us went inside. Mostly European tourists were sitting at small tables, drinking beer and eating fried fish and flatbread. Ceiling fans kept the air moving and dispersed the alluring aromas. It was warm but not uncomfortable. Colorful woven rugs with exotic designs hung on the walls—one wall held local paintings that were for sale.

There was no typical bar to sit at, just tables. Two perfectly white cats walked between the tables diligently searching for scraps. The place had no name—Beverly called it the Flag for the Moroccan beer it served. It was well organized and clean; busy but not noisy.

"Their Mediterranean flounder is lightly fried in coconut oil, fresh from Tetouan. It's a gift from God," Beverly asserted.

"It smells great in here, I'm as hungry as a Barbary Ape…" I said, but before I could finish my analogy, a blue-eyed Berber boy greeted us. His light complexion was highlighted by rosy cheeks and a blue, pink flowered shirt. "*Marhabaan*," he said to us in Arabic.

"*Manzakine*," Beverly replied in Berber. The boy smiled in surprise, "*Manzakine*," he repeated.

"*Matghette si sem*?" Beverly asked him his name in Berber.

"Amenzu," he answered, grinning, holding up an index finger.

"His name means first one, the oldest. But he's only five," a tall Berber lady behind him said. "He's happy you answered in Berber, tourists never speak it. I'm his mother, this is our family's bar."

"Looks more like a restaurant than a bar," Treb observed. He was accustomed to sitting on the floor at Little Joe's bar in Stevens Point on a crowded Thursday night watching coeds in mini-skirts dance to the Rolling Stones.

"Thank you. It was called 'The Bar' when my father bought it, so we kept it a bar." She recognized Beverly. "Your name is Bev! I remember you from last year!"

"And you are Ohana. I remember you, too. Please meet my new-found friends: Norm, Stan, and Treb!" We exchanged greetings and listened to Ohana explain the menu, making a strong recommendation for the fried flounder and flatbread that came with steamed vegetables from local gardens.

"Sounds spot-on," Norm said, trying a touch of South African slang. "How about we start with four cold Flags."

Treb and I nodded in agreement. Norm was enjoying the conversation with Beverly.

"I better go with mint tea," Beverly said to Ohana. "These chaps are much younger than me!"

"Except Norman; he's an old guy," Treb amended Bev. "They call him Normal Norman at the university."

"Good thing you're not my student anymore!" Norm said, grinning. Norm could easily withstand Treb's attempts at humor after yesterday's car chase!

Ohana brought three steins of Flag Special and Amenzu pushed the apparatus cart for making Bev's tea. It had been awhile since we'd had any liquids—we each took a long drink of Flag while Bev's tea was being prepared. "Pour it high!" Treb insisted. "Make lots of bubbles!"

"Let me propose a toast." I lifted my glass. "To meeting Beverly!" The three of us each drank several ounces of Flag; a smooth pale lager. Bev took a sip of her tea.

"Tea doesn't count for rehydration," Treb proclaimed. He wasn't green anymore; the six cups of yogurt had sped his recovery. Of course, he would give the beer credit for his return to normal skin color—fast-acting beer.

"I beg your pardon young man, it surely does! It's called Berber Whiskey, you know." She took another sip, almost a drink. "There is no alcohol in tea unless you intentionally added some."

"Don't mind him, he's only a sophomore—needs a couple more years of seasoning," Professor Norm explained. "Water does rehydrate better than beer, providing it has the right balance of minerals. Beer provides some nutrition; it's considered a food in Germany."

"That's right, Norm!" Treb was at full attention now. "I don't drink beer—I eat it."

"It's been around since the beginning of time. I'll give it that." Beverly tried to intercede with a neutral comment.

Ohana was enjoying the conversation as she poured more tea into Bev's glass. "I know what Bev and I are having," Norm asserted, pointing to the fish and bread on the table next to us. "How about you guys? I mean chaps."

"Same for me," Treb said. "Ditto," I made it unanimous. Ohana nodded and headed to the kitchen with Amenzu.

"How did you get here, to Chefchaouan?" Norm asked Bev.

"On a bus from Tangier; a good one!"

"There are bad ones?"

"Many."

"Sounds like you've had some compromising experiences." Norm looked concerned.

"That's an understatement!" She clarified: "Two years ago, my friends and I got robbed on a minibus east of Marrakesh. We were stopped by the police—they wanted to see our passports and airplane tickets. They took them from us and made a radio call, then came back and told us we had to pay a fine of two-thousand dirhams each for touring in an illegal vehicle. We had no choice; had to pay. Later, our driver told us there was no such law.

"Robbed by the police," Norm lamented.

"Yup," Beverly said sadly.

"There's more. Three years ago, I was in a minivan with mixed company; four men and five women—strangers—going from here to Fez by way of Ketama. About ten kilometers before Ketama we came to a road block—an old log truck was parked sideways in the middle of the road just before a small bridge. When we stopped, two Arab men came toward us wielding machetes. The driver tried to turn around, but they were up to the van in seconds. They ordered us out and forced us to stand in a group, frisking and taking jewelry, watches, purses, wallets—everything. Everyone was scared to death..." Beverly paused and took a breath.

"Don't leave us hanging. What happened next?" Norm asked, looking at Treb and me, shaking his head. "We've been to the same rodeo," I whispered to him.

Beverly continued: "Everyone was scared but one man—a tall American wearing a cowboy hat who stayed near the back of the group while others were being frisked. He crouched down and slowly backed out. The Arabs saw him when he was about ten meters away. They were screaming in Arabic while raising their machetes and running toward him. He stood still, looking straight at them, not moving. His right hand was behind his back. The two Arabs stopped running and slowly approached him. They were obviously confused and must have wondered who this was. Quickly the 'cowboy' swung his arm out holding a huge revolver. I never saw a gun that big!

"He aimed it at them and yelled, *'Anna Khebir Shaytan!'* Then shot twice. The explosions were deafening. Clouds of dust flew up!" She paused again.

"Did he kill them?" Treb asked. Norm was silent, hypnotized.

"No!" She said. "He put the two shots in the ground, right in front of them—at their feet. Then he cocked the gun and held it out again, straight at them. I can still hear the clicking sound of that gun cocking."

Norm, Treb, and I were transfixed. Until this moment we had not realized that two other tables—eight more people—had been listening to her intently. One woman at the closest table wanted to know what he'd said in Arabic.

Beverly translated: "It means "*I am big devil.*"

"What happened then?" Treb asked.

"You never saw two Arab men turn and run so fast in your life, screaming in Arabic. Our hero was a Texas oilman who travelled to Morocco often, he had a local Berber friend keep the Smith and Wesson .44 Magnum for him. He carried it in a shoulder bag when touring.

"Never bring a machete to a gun fight!" Treb declared.

"John Wayne would have been proud!" I added. We were ravenous by the time Ohana brought the food. The fish and veggies looked great. Beverly excepted, we ate big, as if the three of us had been raised on a Texas ranch.

Bev's stories were worrisome and confirmed our experience. She was a special lady; very smart and worldly.

"Which way are you driving to Fez tomorrow?" Bev asked me.

"Through Ketama," I said.

"Be very aware, it can be a dangerous place—it's serious kif country. A least there are three of you! Kif is that mixture of marijuana and tobacco.

"We know it," I said.

"Norm, thank you for lunch. Post me a note when you get home; here's my address in Durban." She handed each of us a postcard picture of a South African lion pride with her info on the back. "It was lovely meeting the three of you. Be sure to call if you come to South Africa." She was meeting friends at the Kasbah and had to leave.

"You're very welcome, Beverly." The professor was sad she had to leave. "We'll be careful," I assured her. We each hugged her, said goodbye, and had another Flag.

After lunch, we checked the Renault, making sure it was still there, then played tourist for the rest of the afternoon. Fortunately, we did not encounter Ahmed and Mohammad when we re-entered the medina, but there were other *touts.* A loud "*No thanks*" from the three of us usually turned them away. It was busier now—more tourists, more opportunities for the touts. We saw the missing shopkeeper, alive and well, tending his stuffed camel spleens and sheep heads. Then we further explored the medina, observing carefully when arriving at dead ends or *derbs.* Indeed, we had seen "The Blue City." I was deeply moved by my brief exposure to Morocco at this point; how its beauty contrasted with the bizarre and the perilous. *What would the grand medina in Fez be like?* I thought. It was a hundred times larger than this one!

Morning came fast the next day. We had bisara for breakfast; sweet Moroccan bean soup with tea and biscuits, then said our goodbyes with hugs and promises to tell our friends about the Weber Guesthouse. Kella and Izza were truly remarkable young ladies; proof that strangeness and danger can be minimized when cultures mix.

"*Be Slema, Shukran,*" Norm said in Berber as we got into the car. "Goodbye and thank you," they replied, smiling and waving.

I drove again as we headed southwest out of Chefchaouan, deciding to take different roads to Fez and avoid Ketama. We'd had additional stern warnings yesterday afternoon. A German man had told us that hooded men in Ketama pressured him to buy kif in brown bars—like candy bars. You could smoke it or chew it. He had to buy several so they would leave him alone, then discarded them later. It cost him sixty U.S. dollars to leave Ketama. A woman from Ireland told of old men, *Rifi-Berbers,* smoking water pipes in town. "Ketama is a lawless place," she told us. "The main street is only one-hundred-fifty meters long but it's opaque with kif smog. Only men standing around; no women."

"I'm happy we made the decision to take a different route to Fez," Norm affirmed.

"It's shorter—only two-hundred kilometers," I said; "three hours if the roads stay good." It would have been foolish to ignore the warnings.

"The guide book avoided mentioning Ketama," Norm remarked.

"I was hoping to see the epicenter of Morocco's '*Hash Capital,*' and inhale some of that special smog," Treb said in dismay.

"You've been Berberized brother. You'll survive the disappointment," I notified him. "Okay, okay," he eloquently replied.

"Norm, where are those apes you saw two years ago?" Treb sensed it was time to change subjects.

"Down south of Fez, in the Atlas Mountains. They're called 'Barbary Apes' and they live in the cedar forests—they're big monkeys; Macaques."

"Did you get close to them?"

"Not too close; there were about twenty in their troop. Some stared at us, others swung in the trees, disregarding us. The locals say there are three types: Those that like olives, those that like tourists, and those that don't like olives or tourists."

"That's funny," I said. "After all, Morocco is in Africa!"

We drove on. There were potholes now and chips of pavement hitting us whenever a truck passed. The guidebook said to look out for "road chips"—here they were again. So much for the good road.

We arrived in Fez at midday. Norm had selected another quality guesthouse. We were greeted by a bald, heavyset Arab man named Omar—unfortunately, not two attractive Berber ladies. Omar was polite but had a landlord's personality, very authoritative. Any Muslim woman in sight was covered head-to-toe.

"Come here. You must eat lunch," Omar commanded. He took us to a small dining room where *Bestila* was being served.

"Don't let it frighten you, it's safe," a familiar voice said. Pat and Diana Taylor were at a table waving us over.

"I'll be a monkey's uncle! What a nice coincidence!" Norm said.

"Sit down and eat with us," Diana insisted. Omar moved more chairs over. "You lads must use the same guide book we use!"

"Frommer's Morocco," Norm replied. "That's it!" Diana nodded.

"What are you eating?" Treb was studying the elaborate pie on the table, its crust bulging high. "It smells great."

"It's called *Bestila,*" Pat answered. "It's the Bee's Knees!"

"Speak American, darling. It's delicious." Diana looked at Treb. Using a spatula, she put a sample on a napkin and handed it to him. "We don't like to eat with our hands," she said. "Me, either!" Treb assured her, and carefully took a bite. We sat down and Omar brought another pie.

Diana explained what we were eating: "It's pigeon cooked in spices with eggs, roasted almonds, sugar, and cinnamon; then baked into a savory pie with *Warka* dough. It's called *Pastilla* in other countries but originated in Morocco." It was quite good, once I got my mind off eating pigeons.

Stork beer, another pale lager, helped me dismiss any concerns—like the recollection of fat pigeons eating worms in the grass outside Westminster Abby. I ordered five Storks for us; we all drank beer. We had an interesting discussion about London, our first stop on this trip and their home.

Pat advised us to hire a professional guide for the medina here in Fez, saying it was overwhelming without one. Omar was happy to organize it.

We parked the Renault outside one of the main gates leading into the medina—the largest medina in the Muslim world. The gate was a formidable construction with a Moorish arch in the center and a smaller arch on each side.

Dark blue swirling patterns covered the front of the gate—nondescript until I looked closely, then I could see they looked like tiny, interlocked monkeys. I'm sure the swirls were meant to be something else. There were many challenges to the imagination in Morocco.

As everywhere in Morocco, no cars were allowed in the medina. The gate was being refurbished, and workers were everywhere on ladders. Immediately I realized that hiring a licensed guide was a good idea. Ben was waiting for us; he called out to Norm as we walked through the gate.

"Mister Norman," he said, pointing at Norm. "Are you the professor?"

"Yes, I am. It's a pleasure to meet you, Ben." Norm shook Ben's hand.

"And hello, Mr. Stanley and Mr. Treeb."

"It's Treb, not Treeb," Treb corrected him.

"Sorry, sorry, Mr. T-R-E-B." Ben smiled, Treb nodded his approval.

"Easy mistake," I told Ben. "I call him that when we deer hunt together in Wisconsin—from '*treeb*' stands." Treb, not paying attention to me, was looking around at the scores of tourists mixed with locals who were coming and going through the gate. He unfolded a map of the medina and looked at it.

"We are right here." Ben pointed on Treb's map to a small dime-size area on the three-foot map.

"Big place." Treb raised his eyebrows.

"Yes. You can get lost. It's over 170 square kilometers!" Ben then explained the three-arched gate we just walked through, The *Bab Bou Jeloud,* "The Blue Gate." There were many gates leading into the Fez Medina; this was a popular one.

Ahead were two beige towers, the larger one was green at the top. Between us and these towers was a plethora of humanity, sorting themselves out within a labyrinth of alleys, narrow streets, *riads,* corridors, *souks,* and horseshoe arches. A cacophony of human voices could be heard: haggling, bartering, discounting, explaining, laughing, arguing; all blending together in a strange discordance. An unusual music; out of tune, but curiously inviting.

The Fez Medina was not only much larger than Chefchaouen's but older and more complex, ancient, built in 812 AD. The three of us had countless impressions after the first day. Most obvious for me was the panorama of differences in the medina—distinct dichotomies. There were clean and unclean places, repaired and unrepaired, even and uneven, light and dark, safe and unsafe, painted and unpainted, old and new. And they were not separated from each other! Opposites often alternated, adjacent. After spending the day with Ben, we certainly gained perspective that reached beyond Tangier and Chefchaouen.

Our countless impressions required a dictionary of words to describe, challenging the ability to be concise, accurate and meaningful. Pretend you have just one hour to run through the Fez Medina, the oldest and largest in the Islamic world. The faster you run, the more you see. Here—recognizing the limitations of words—is what your senses might record: Square buildings on hills, dilapidated riads, well-kept riads, uneven streets, crowded walkways, narrow passages, dark corridors, bright sunlit walkways, donkey carts, mountains of spices, cloves and cinnamon bark, bloody camel legs for sale, old masonry, haunting calls to prayer, colorful umbrellas, goat heads on hooks, unrelenting salesmen, fresh paint, leather curing, medieval weapons, fakes, swords and shields, white-robed beings, black robed women showing eyes only, kif smoke, canary yellow roofs, Muslims on prayer rugs, camel heads dripping, hides drying, beggars begging, women pounding goat excrement for Argan oil, pungent odors, urine, overloaded donkeys, pigeons in cages, woven baskets, Fez hats, snake skins, bronze statues, unrelenting salesmen, shoes of every color, woven tablecloths, artists, painted vases, piles of olives, snail soup, fried pigeon, camel jerky, donkey heads hanging, flatbread baking, enticing scents, flowers, clean souks, jewelry, large necklaces, and tourists—lots of tourists…

Treb had the best summary of the medina: "You'da had'a been there."

We walked out of the medina at one of the back gates where Ben had parked his vehicle. He would drive us back to our car outside The Blue Gate—several kilometers away. But first we had to reinstall ourselves on planet earth.

Outside the medina, on the back side, the extent of the wall that encircled its entire 170 square kilometers was most obvious—immense physically and mentally. In a way, it was frightening; it was either the end or the beginning of freedom, depending on your perspective.

The medina contained a unique civilization! Outside of it, there was no containment. The Moroccan government left the medina's exclusive culture to itself—an orphaned world. I couldn't determine in my mind whether this was good or bad.

Once I was out of it, I recognized that Morocco's attempts at emulating aspects of the modern world had a different discordance and music. Beyond the walls of the medina, in the distance, were the Atlas Mountains separated by green fields and forests. Human developments were sparse. And beyond the mountains, in the far distance, there was endless desert.

A few more days in Morocco were ahead. We still had to find the fossil shop for Norm. I had already learned many lessons in a short time. Maybe they would provide wisdom and intuition for future travels…

Postscript

We found the fossil shop on the last day. Norm was pleased and so was I—we both bought large trilobite specimens from the basement of time—600 million years ago. Treb bought a water pipe.

Morocco was the launching pad for my future travels, more so than central Europe.

I did eventually see the lady I designated as Beverly—in Durban, South Africa years later. She was 96 years young and remembered me well, and happy to hear Norman had found the fossil shop!

Augusto holding a Caiman in the Amazon

6

Soul Voice in the Amazon

Augusto's Special Universe

Prologue:

The two rivers came together at Manaus. The cola-colored Rio Negro joined the silt-laden Amazon which then ran a thousand miles to the Atlantic Ocean with an average width of twenty-five miles. The waters didn't mix at first; they formed a distinct boundary for several miles until the densities equalized. Neon tetras and other tropical fish stayed in the silty water for safety, darting in-and-out of the clearer water to feed. Locals in small boats pulled nets along the boundary to catch them.

At the docks in Manaus glass jugs of water bubbling with air contained hundreds of tropical fish. The neons were unmistakable with their fluorescent blue stripe. Rows of huge pirarucu—long, pike-looking fish with bronze and red scales—laid flat, ready to be fileted. Caimans in aquariums, squawking parrots, squirrel monkeys and three-toed sloths in cages, large spiders in jars, and snakes—anacondas and boas in wooden crates, were ready to be shipped around the world. Welcome to Manaus, the capital of the jungle.

Manaus, Brazil 1989

A low fog hung over the calm backwater. Not far away, great quantities of water rushed east in the Amazon—more water than from eight of the world's next-largest rivers combined. Various islands and bays created calm backwaters in the great river; of its two thousand species of fish, the pirarucu was the largest.

The two pirarucu I caught the first day—in heavy rain—were nice four-footers; big for most fish, small for pirarucu. We were after the giants...

Augusto's boat was small, he spent most of the time bailing and repositioning it in the wind. The rain obliterated anything beyond twenty feet, making the immense rainforest look small. Augusto paddled his flat-bottomed boat, the *Fativa Marie,* quietly and effectively. He kept a long wooden pole handy to push us off the bottom in shallow areas. Young and tan, he had curly black hair and penetrating brown eyes. His black mustache looked good under an authentic Portuguese nose. He was half Indian and half Portuguese. They told me in Manaus he was one of the best fishing guides on the river.

He didn't have to paddle far and excitement didn't have to wait long to happen! There were two giant fish near shore where the water was only four feet deep. I was casting a silver Rapala that landed in front of the larger of the two, which was over seven feet long. I jerked the lure twice, reeled fast for a few seconds, then stopped reeling. The fish hit immediately. I set the hooks and it sky-rocketed, clearing the water. When the fish fell back in the water, its weight pulled down hard forcing me to one knee on the bow's plywood platform—the monofilament line hummed at maximum tension! Fortunately, the rod and my body had absorbed most of the force. I backed off on the reel's drag just in time as the rod bent a full forty-five degrees.

I checked my position on the plywood board on the bow. It was only two feet square, just large enough to stand on and maintain balance. Augusto adjusted the boat's position to keep the fish in front of me. All I could do was hold the rod tight—it felt like the line was snagged on a crippled moose. The rod would vibrate a few inches due to line stretching. The fish didn't move, it was matching all the force I could apply.

After a minute of a tugging standoff—a long time in sport fishing—it began swimming in powerful S-shaped half circles, taking out line while shaking its head back and forth. After eight minutes of swirling and bulldogging, gulping air frequently and staying within a ten-yard circle, the fish surfaced and started coming toward the boat. I reeled fast to keep up with it.

"This fish breathes air," Augusto said. He paddled the boat to a sandy beach spot on shore while I held the rod out and pulled the fish along the short distance, not far from where I had cast. It was an Amazon monster!

"Get out here!" Augusto shouted. "Fight fish from shore." Holding the rod tight, fish splashing and head shaking, I jumped in the water as the bow touched sand. Now I could get line on the reel. The fish was huge—more than a foot longer than me, and I'm six feet tall! Augusto pulled the boat onto shore and jumped out, running in the water trying to grab its tail. The fish reacted and jumped straight up, halfway out of the water, pulling me to my knees again only this time in the water. I bowed the rod to it. Augusto grabbed at it again; it responded with more jumps, half-jumps, and swirls. It was gulping air and making coughing sounds continuously. Augusto kept reaching for the monster until it tired enough so the two of us could catch and hang onto it. Its head flopped over my right arm and its tail touched the water while hanging over Augusto's left arm. We were standing side-by-side holding it by the belly. It had been fifteen minutes since I made the cast, just one cast.

The *pirarucu* was seven and a half feet long, and fat. Over two hundred pounds, Augusto calculated. The front half had glistening bronze scales; the rear scales were red, like someone had splashed red paint on them, missing spots. I tried to imagine a northern pike the same size in Minnesota; a fifty- inch, forty-five-pounder was the state record.

"Want to keep it?" Augusto asked.

"No, release her. She's fat with roe – she'll make lots of baby *pirarucu*."

"Okay, Mr. Stan," Augusto agreed. He would have kept it for eating. "We can keep a small one, okay?" He asked me. "Sure, let's see if I can get a three-footer for you and ten-footer for me before we go to that island place for lunch."

I didn't know the *pirarucu,* also called *arapaima,* breathed air exclusively; it could only stay underwater for ten to twenty minutes. A fish that couldn't remain underwater!

We caught two more, the largest was a five-footer; we kept the three-footer for Augusto. There really were ten-footers in the Amazon, I'd seen one on the dock in Manaus. *Pirarucu* were easy to catch. Too easy. At some point—the sooner the better—conservation measures had to be established. Its brilliant scales were used to make expensive fish-leather boots. The meat was pink like salmon and eaten by locals—its tongue a delicacy! And, it was becoming a world-class game fish. All serious factors contributing to its vulnerability.

It was 2:00 p.m. and I was hungry, Augusto had been snacking on peanuts. "Let's go to that lunch place," I suggested.

We paddled around a long island to a small, five-building village on its west end. A wooden building on stilts extended out over the water. "Good fish to eat here," Augusto said while tying up the boat. The water was low so we had to climb a wooden ladder to get up to the restaurant. A teenage boy wearing a Miami Dolphins tee shirt held the ladder steady.

"What on earth is *that*?" I asked, looking at the four-foot tall, gray animal with a foot-long snout standing in a corner of the deck. One leg was tied to a floor board with a rope. When it saw us, it raised its head in slow motion.

"Giant anteater," The boy answered. I couldn't stop staring at it. "His name's Andy. He eats bugs; likes ants the best." The animal moved in slow motion, its black-marble eyes looked right through me.

"Incredible," I said.

"My name is Marco," The boy smiled, putting his hand out to shake mine.

"Call me Stan," I replied, shaking his hand. "Tell me more about this creature." I was curious. It had brown hair with black streaks on its back and a huge tail. It turned its head very slowly, looking at Augusto now.

"Andy has a two-foot tongue and six-inch claws. He can kill a Jaguar with those claws," Marco said proudly. I was astonished.

"Let's go eat," Augusto was hungry, he had seen Andy hundreds of times. Marco led the way and we went inside.

At the bar—an eight-foot wood plank—a man and woman sat drinking beer. There was a cooler on the floor filled with block-ice and Brazilian beer. The bar tender was an old Portuguese man who knew Augusto.

"Ola, Augusto," the old man hollered. "Ola, Tiago," Augusto replied. Augusto told me to grab a bottle of Xingu beer, I reached down in the cooler and grabbed one, handing it to him, ready to reach for another but he shook his head no. "I don't drink beer when guiding," he said dejectedly, giving it back to me. "It's the guide agency's rule," Tiago said, making a mark on a scrap of paper to record mine. The beer was a German-style lager brewed in the state of Mato Grosso in Brazil. It was ice cold.

Tiago and Augusto spoke in Portuguese to each other while I introduced myself to the man and woman. They were from Copenhagen and on their first trip to Brazil. Their guide had dropped them off for lunch. I had worked for a Danish company at the start of my career, so it was easy to talk about Denmark. The woman was explaining how much they loved Tivoli Gardens when we were interrupted by another mystery animal.

"*Oh! Neg. Ga Vaek*! (Oh! No. Go away!)" The woman screeched in Danish. Her husband pulled her stool closer to his.

Marco had carried in a three-toed sloth and put it on the floor next to us. The creature was all arms and legs—over three feet tall with long brown hair, two black eyes, and a flat white nose. Its three, six-inch long, curved claws on each hand and foot, presumably made it Andy's equal. This animal redefined toes! Like the anteater, it moved in slow motion and made no sounds—the sloth could hold onto anything.

"His name is Aldo," Marco said. The animal was standing up holding onto one of the legs of my stool, slowly moving its other arm to reach for a second stool. Its face was round and friendly with an up-curved mouth that produced a perpetual smile. The Danish woman had quickly pulled her legs up and was sitting cross-legged on top of her stool. Tiago and Augusto were still talking, paying no attention to Aldo that was now suspended between two stools.

"He sleeps a lot," Marco said. "He can sleep in the rain since it runs off his long hair. Nothing bothers him. He turns green in the wet months from algae growing on him." I laughed out loud. A sloth that changes colors; now, indeed, I'd seen everything!

"You speak great English, Marco. Where did you go to school?" I asked.

"I live with my father in Miami. I come here to help my uncle run his bar in summer." Another boat was being tied up on the dock; the guide was picking up the Danish couple. Marco excused himself to help them. Augusto had ordered lunch for us: a plate of fried cichlids, much like the ones I once raised in an aquarium. They were small and curled up but tasted good, like perch. I drank another beer.

After lunch, we went out on the deck. Marco wanted to show us his spider collection: quart jars with one spider in each—big ones. When he put two together, they fought nonstop until one was dead. Then the winner ate the dead one. Marco had a comprehensive guide book on spiders but several of his specimens were not in the book. That told me Amazonia was still undiscovered and wild! When he put the spiders away I went over to Andy, who was watching a large grasshopper on the deck. Slowly, he repositioned himself, looking right at it, then shot out his two-foot tongue. Bingo, a full meal in one slurp.

We climbed down the ladder to the dock: myself, Augusto and Marco. We talked some more and I mentioned I had relatives in Miami, and that we should connect again.

"I would like that very much," he said, and gave me his father's business card with their home phone number.

"There's a lot we don't know about nature." I remarked as Augusto untied the boat and Marco pushed us off. "I know," Marco said. "Like how to catch a twelve-foot picarucu!" That comment produced a big nod and smile from Augusto!

"Go Dolphins!" I replied loudly as we paddled away…

After lunch, we went looking for an even bigger pirarucu, the twelve-footer Marco told me to catch. But the afternoon fishing did not produce a world record pirarucu. I had to settle for two four-footers that I caught on a gold colored Rapala. They were caught in deeper water on one of Augusto's secret rock piles; both put up a good fight. The one that almost jumped in the boat was completely red. I released them unharmed. We got back to Augusto's houseboat around 5:00 p.m. for an early dinner.

After dinner, Augusto told me he had a special adventure planned for the evening. He wouldn't give me any details except to bug-proof myself. He gave me a jar containing a thick, oily liquid formulated by a local shaman. It smelled like a mixture of peppermint, lavender, and rosemary oils. Augusto only knew that several essential oils had been mixed into coconut oil. I knew anything was better than Deet, so I applied the shaman's potion liberally to all exposed skin and to my fishing hat. It smelled good.

The cool evening was filled with sounds of frogs, insects and unknowns, a relief from the oppressive heat and humidity of the day. The air was thick with a variety of river odors from the diversity of life surrounding us. Clouds broke just enough to let in a last glimmer of light from the west. Behind us, the sky was overcast and black. Amazonia had a voice and a collective consciousness, I could feel it. If we made a loud noise, like blowing a horn, the insects and frogs would go silent for a minute, then start back up in unison. It was like the totality of the life in Amazonia had its own soul.

Sitting in the front of the boat, flashlight ready, I looked east into the blackness wondering what to expect. Augusto turned the boat left toward shore and entered an expanse of giant water lilies that were six feet in diameter. As the wood bow touched the lilies it made a slapping sound until Augusto stopped paddling. I switched my flashlight on and noticed hundreds of lime-green butterflies resting on lily pads. Green frogs were eating them. There was a lot of green life in Amazonia. A mosquito buzzed around and I killed it. I had taken doxycycline this morning—the one anti-malarial drug I could take.

"Watch me!" Augusto commanded. He stopped paddling and turned his flashlight on. Looking in the water he spotted something and slowly moved the boat closer to it. Then, without warning, he grabbed the thing and held it high out of the water, showing it to me. With a slight smile on his face he threw it back into the water making a substantial splash. Then asked if I could do it.

I was a little unsettled but also amazed. "I think so," I said nervously. Then, with all concerns aside, curiosity in charge, I said, "*Yes!*"

Augusto paddled deeper into the lily pads. "Watch for orange eyes," he said quietly." We both had our flashlights on searching the water. "There's one," Augusto whispered, pointing to the end of his flashlight beam.

I scanned with my light until I saw its orange eyes reflecting. "I see him," I said quietly.

"You catch this one," Augusto whispered.

"Yes." I mouthed the word. "Get around behind him." I made a circle with my thumb and index finger, signaling okay. Part of me couldn't believe I was about to do this. It was black-dark when both flashlights were off. And we were alone on a cloudy night in the middle of the Amazon.

I had watched Augusto catch the first one, then it was my turn. Educational advice was demonstrated only once, then it was up to the student. Augusto put the end of the flashlight in his mouth so he could paddle and move the boat over to the motionless eyes.

"Grab fast behind head. Squeeze like I did," He whispered, then demonstrated with his hands. I nodded, staring into his nodding flashlight.

I kept my flashlight beam on the creature's eyes as we got closer. I could see half its body above water. The reptile looked right at me but was blinded by the light. I held the flashlight high with my left hand, keeping it on the eyes. I knelt on the front seat as Augusto moved the boat closer. The seat, an old warped board, creaked loudly. The eyes moved backwards and sank – disappearing below a giant lily pad.

"Gone!" I said. Augusto nodded his head. His flashlight beam, shooting from his mouth, nodded along. He jerked his head to the right saying nothing, just pointing with the beam. I scanned my light to the right, still kneeling on the creaking seat, and saw a bigger pair of eyes twenty-five feet away.

"More quiet," Augusto whispered, as he paddled slowly. I nodded in agreement and grabbed a flannel shirt out of my duffel bag, rolled it into a cylinder and knelt on it. The board was quiet. He brought the boat up alongside the eyes.

"Now," he whispered.

Holding the flashlight high again, pointed directly on the eyes, making no sound, I grabbed fast with my right hand. Not knowing exactly how big it would be or how to avoid getting bit if I missed the neck, I squeezed hard and lifted the reptile out of the water. It was heavy. All four legs and the tail were in motion. I was exhilarated! It was black with yellow stripes and had large golden eyes bulging from its head. These cousins of the alligator can get to be sixteen feet long! The ones bought as pets usually measured about a foot or so, like the ones for sale on the dock in Manaus.

Its neck was easy to grab and hold onto, the leathery skin had rutted scales that made gripping easy. No slime. The skin was clean feeling. The *caiman* let out a loud hiss when it opened its mouth. He was not happy to see me. Pointing the flashlight at his head, I saw the characteristic curved-up snout and bony-ridged eyes. Standing up, holding it out and away, putting my flashlight down, I grabbed its swinging tail. I was holding the caiman now with two hands. Success!

"You got him," Augusto said. "A big one!"

"He's a three-footer plus," I replied. "Big for hand-catching."

"You caught him good, like I do."

"Thanks – I watched you! You're the man, Augusto! Let's get a picture." I could feel the life in the reptile, subdued by my grip but very alive. It was like I had won a prize at the state fair and some gal was handing it to me. A living prize.

"Yes, I take picture." Augusto grabbed my waterproof camera.

"Take two, like I showed you." I held the caiman high and Augusto snapped two flash pictures.

"It must weigh thirty pounds." I was impressed. "A perfect black caiman."

"In Brazil, we say *jacares,*" Augusto clarified. "A perfect *jacares.*"

"He's beautiful, whatever we call him. Not a single blemish." With all my strength, I launched the *jacares* back into the water, making sure it cleared the boat. Its splash was what a full-grown Labrador would make jumping off a boat. Unharmed, the reptile disappeared with one tail kick. I imagined what it must be like to swim beneath six-foot lily pads in warm water in total blackness, searching for something to eat. The commotion woke the butterflies up and got them flying around our light beams, reminding me of the insect sounds around us. I had stopped listening in the excitement. None were bothering me; the shaman's potion was working.

"German tourists call *jacares* alligators," Augusto remarked.

"Alligators are only found in the southern United States." I remembered from zoology. "Do you speak German?"

"No, I speak English to Germans. Sometimes Portuguese."

"You speak English well."

"Not so well. I speak guide-English."

"Whatever you call it, it's good for me."

"You're a good man. We catch more *jacares*?" Augusto asked.

"Yes, absolutely." My take was that many clients had not been nice to him.

"We keep next one for eating?" Augusto said. "Good eating! Take this hammer—hit it on head." He came up with a rusty old hammer and handed it to me.

"No, we must let them go!" It was illegal to keep or eat caimans in the Brazilian Amazon but locals did it anyway. Rarely was the law enforced; it was on the books to please the environmentalists.

"Okay," Augusto shrugged, losing his enthusiasm, as if a switch shut off inside him, or he'd had a sudden spell of guide-strain. He wanted caiman meat.

"Tomorrow afternoon, when you drop me in Manaus, I'll give you a tip in U.S. dollars. You can buy meat with it."

"No, have plenty of meat. Fish meat and chicken meat," he said. "*Jacares* meat special. Can't buy." I let it go at that, dropping the subject. There was something else bothering him…

We went on and caught three more, another three-footer and two smaller. I caught and released them. One had a wounded front leg, probably caused by another caiman—that might have been one to keep for Augusto to eat? There were no two alike; their yellow stripes were like fingerprints. It was strange how rewarding it was to catch a wild reptile by hand in its native environment, take it completely by surprise, examine it closely, then release it unharmed knowing there was some skill involved. Grabbing a six-footer would not be smart! Obviously, you had to gauge the size before grabbing; one of the intuitive aspects a first-time student had to learn. There was an unexpected aliveness and mystery to catching these caimans by hand. Something I hadn't planned on doing but, in the aftermath, was very *pleased to have* done it. For me, immediately after such an experience, an internal voice, my soul voice, declares loudly: Yes!

Back at Augusto's houseboat, we relaxed on his back porch with a whiskey. It was past 10:00 p.m. and late for him; his family was asleep. There were no electric lights, he went inside and brought out a kerosene lamp.

"Here's to good American whiskey," I said, lifting my glass containing an inch of Wild Turkey bourbon. Holding it out, I pointed it at the great river, then at Augusto. Hoping that whatever was bothering him would be resolved by the bourbon.

"Salute," Augusto said, holding out his glass; we touched glasses and both drank our inch. Augusto closed his eyes, maybe trying to sort out his thoughts as he swallowed the whiskey. He was not on guide duty at 10:00 p.m.

We sat quietly for several minutes, looking out at the river. The insect hiss was ever present, crickets contributed to it now along with loud chirping frogs. Occasionally, a monkey would scream. The water was calm except when piranhas splashed, there was never just one of them.

"You live in a special place Augusto; this river, this land."

"All my life here—this place," he replied with a serious look, "this one place."

I poured another inch of the golden liquid into our glasses.

"To my home," Augusto toasted. We each drank the second inch.

"Easy whiskey to drink," he said.

"We say smooth." Its golden color, intensified by the kerosene lamp, looked like caiman eyes in a flashlight beam. I'm not a big whiskey drinker but I needed some assistance getting a good night's sleep. I would be sleeping in that hammock again with mosquito netting tickling me. Augusto's houseboat was largely open; the living room where I slept had two large windows that were permanently open. I poured us a third inch.

"To catching big *jacares* by hand," I proclaimed, holding my glass up. Augusto did the same. The Wild Turkey bourbon was starting to take effect.

"And to letting them go," I said, finishing the few drops left in my glass. "Do Germans like catching *jacares*? I saw a group of them at the hotel in Manaus a few days ago."

"They mostly watch me."

"Only watch?"

"Only watch," Augusto answered. "Only watch and worry about snakes. Always they worry about snakes."

"Spectators," I remarked.

"But they're not happy to watch. Not happy to be on river," Augusto lamented. "Shamans say their souls are not happy."

"So, what happens if your soul is unhappy?" I asked him, curious now.

"It can leave," Augusto replied in a somber voice.

"Leave for where?" I asked, sparked with sobering attention.

"For the spirit world," Augusto said.

"You believe your soul can leave while you're alive?"

"Yes," Augusto answered. "Shamans know this well."

"And what happens to you if your soul leaves?"

"You live empty, no soul to remember the rest of your life."

"So, when you die, that part of you that lived without a soul dies forever?" I asked him.

"Yes," Augusto said with a sigh and the same somber expression. I poured the last of the whiskey into our glasses.

Again, we both sat silent, maybe fifteen minutes, looking out at the blackness of the river. Insects, frogs, monkeys, piranhas—still there. Finally, Augusto broke the silence.

"My soul left me two years ago," he said.

"*What?* You can't be serious! No!" I was confused and disturbed.

"I was sick, malaria sick, bad fever. Could not eat. My soul left because it thought I was suffering, dying!"

"But souls don't die, they go on. They don't feel anything when you die. They just leave," I said, wondering how I knew what I just said.

"The Shamans said my soul did not want to feel me suffer. So, it left. Your soul has you—you don't have it!" Augusto was very serious and speaking clearly despite the whiskey.

"How did you know your soul left you?"

"Because its voice was gone," Augusto said. "That voice inside you. The one that gives advice." I felt a cold shiver go down my spine. My internal voice talks to me often.

"My Soul Voice is gone!" Augusto repeated. "Nothing I do now is important. When I die, I'll be completely gone since the malaria."

"Are you sure of this?" I asked him.

"Yes! Shamans have examined me. Augusto tired now, whiskey tired."

I slept well in the hammock, thanks to the bourbon, until I had to urinate at 4:00 a.m. It was a challenge to negotiate the hammock and netting in the dark. It might have been amusing without a headache. After three misses, I managed to get into it and fall back to sleep.

When I awoke, the day was bright and warm; a flock of red parrots flew overhead just as a very green arowhana fish jumped and caught a beetle in the river. Augusto's wife brought me a plate filled with slices of mango and the best papaya there is, red Brazilian papaya.

"Good Morning," she said perfectly, not knowing many English words.

"Good Morning. Beautiful day," I responded.

"Yes, very beautiful." Her three children, one a crawling baby, hugged her feet. She looked down at them with pride, they were her life's priority.

I rolled out of the hammock, sat up, and squeezed some lime juice on the papaya. It was splendid.

I was already dressed for the day: shorts, tee shirt and flip-flops. Here, you could begin the day in the same clothes you slept in. Nothing was complicated. Most everything worked because there was little that could break. This old, wooden houseboat was their home in the universe.

"Delicious!" I said, after finishing the papaya, now sitting in their kitchen. I offered the children some mango, checking for the woman's approval. She nodded, and I gave each of them a slice. I held the baby's while he sucked on it.

"Come here." Augusto was motioning with his hand at their bedroom door. I got up and followed him into the bedroom. He looked tired but had forced a smile.

"Meet Toco." Augusto was giving the bird a slice of mango. Sitting on the windowsill was a fabulous toucan.

"He's our pet," Augusto's wife said, standing behind me. The bird was spectacular. Its bill was the length of its body, black with a streak of yellow along the top, blue feathers surrounded its eyes. Its breast was brilliant yellow complimented by crimson-red in the tail. The rest of the bird was jet-black. It nabbed the mango with the tip of its bill, threw its head back and swallowed. It watched me, the stranger in the room, carefully. Augusto gave it more mango, which it quickly nabbed, then, looking at me again, opened its wings, fluffed its feathers, and flew away.

"He comes every morning." Augusto looked happy. I was glad to see he still could experience joyful moments.

"Magnificent bird!" I commented. Augusto's wife nodded.

"Do we cast lures for *pirarucu* today?" Augusto asked.

"Not today Augusto. It's a short day—you need to get me to the dock in Manaus by 3:00 p.m. Let's go downriver where the waters meet and look around, photograph birds, look at trees, butterflies, Amazonia! Toco has me inspired."

"Okay, we do this." He said, still looking tired to me.

Too much whiskey. My fault. My inner voice lectured me.

"We take bigger boat today," Augusto said. I looked out the window and saw a long, wooden boat with a canvas canopy and a forty-horsepower motor.

"Where did that boat come from?" I asked him.

"I bring from Manaus this morning. Belongs to guide agency."

"When did you sleep?"

"Only sleep short time. Let's go find birds."

I could see his enthusiasm was being challenged. The whiskey had opened Augusto's Life Book to its Life-Changing chapter.

We went out to where the Rio Negro joined the Amazon. Two huge rivers became one—then it was only the Amazon after that. It carried one fifth of the world's fresh water! All of it, the land, the river, the jungle, was Amazonia. There were twenty-five hundred species of trees and over two thousand species of birds out there. When the rainforest got thick, trees grew into each other, so from the boat I couldn't tell where one stopped and another started, except the big, majestic mahogany trees; they stood out as did tall groves of slender acai palms. Those palms were quite imposing at eighty feet tall with their white bark and palm leaves at the very top. Some crossed and fell into each other and looked like a giant pile of *Pickup Sticks*—the sweet fruit was used to make exotic drinks, desserts, and acai wine.

It was a good day to photograph birds, and we found many exotic species including two of Toco's relatives. Seeing blue and gold macaws, the largest of parrots—four feet long—flying in flocks and squawking, put an exclamation mark on the trip. But, it was a tough day to enjoy because Augusto had been preoccupied…

We returned to Manaus where we had started three days ago. After Augusto tied the boat to the dock, I hugged him and patted him on the back. "Thank you, Augusto, you are a great guide," I handed him two one-hundred-dollar bills, more than the recommended tip. Then grabbed my rod and reel and duffle bag.

"Thank you, Mr. Stan. This will buy much food for my family," Augusto said, bowing his head. I put my rod and reel down and put my hand on his shoulder.

"Augusto, help your family with their souls! Help grow their souls by giving them great experiences and lots of love. Then, if your soul has truly left you, you will not live empty because part of you will live on in them. And tell the shamans that departed souls can come back! If they can leave, they can come back! It's only logical. Call your Soul Voice, tell it to come back, it's missing great experiences and the love you share with your family. Your suffering from malaria is history!" I stepped up on the dock.

Augusto stood at the back of the boat, absorbing my words. His tall frame looked holy in the glitter of light reflecting off the river. His face, less sober, had a hint of a smile. "Go home safe my friend," he said to me as he started the motor.

"Let all those *jacares* go," I said. He nodded.

"Don't drink whiskey with Germans," I added, jokingly. "Only Americans."

He nodded, with an emerging smile. I was trying to think of one more thing to say to him. He untied the boat and backed it away from the dock.

"Okay, Okay!" He shouted, forming a circle with his thumb and index finger like I taught him, holding it high for me to see. "I will help my family and tell my soul voice to come back," he had a sparkling smile on his face now. "*Thank You Very Much!*"

I held my right thumb up high while walking to the end of the dock where he could see me better. Augusto had the outboard at full throttle and was waving. I could still see the sparkle in his smile…

When leaving the dock, I saw a large wooden AMAZONAS sign overhead. The smell of river water blended with boat exhaust and myriad live animal aromas. Strangely, it was not objectionable but more of a signature—humans interacting with the wild. A young boy wearing an eight-foot snake around his shoulders followed me off the dock. He wanted to sell me the snake for ten dollars. It was a healthy, young boa-constrictor. I told him no thanks but gave him five dollars for showing it to me. He walked away quite happy.

I threw the duffel over my shoulder and headed up the hill to where the taxies waited. I glanced back at the Amazon, it looked more like an ocean than a river from here. My soul voice was singing…

Lion patrolling at night

7

South African Mystery

Don't Read This One Alone!

Northern Transvaal, South Africa 2001

It was a cool morning and Graham was already up having tea with the others. Several guests had collected outside the camp office and were holding their tea cups and talking, looking at baboons out by the water hole. Three giraffes had watched me shower; my bungalow had an outdoor shower enclosure that a giraffe could see over. I dried off, dressed in nylon safari clothes, and reviewed the camp rules posted on the door:

1) No walking outside camp.
2) Ask a guide to walk you to and from your bungalow.
3) Don't feed any animals.

I walked over to the office where tea was being served, realizing I had just violated Rule Number Two. Maybe they only meant at night? Other guests were milling around without guides.

"I saved you a cranberry muffin," Graham said in his Irish brogue as I sat down next to him outside the office. "It'll have to keep yeh going for three hours."

"I'll bring a couple Snickers bars for us—appetite buffers!" I said. "How did you sleep?"

"Well, for a short night," he said. Graham O'Brien was my business partner in South Africa, born there of Irish parents; medium build, clean shaven, red hair and blue eyes under bushy eyebrows. We were in the business of using beneficial microbes to boost soil fertility and had worked together for five years. We were now relaxing in the Sabi Game Reserve in South Africa's Northern Transvaal. On the map, Mozambique was directly east and Zimbabwe to the north.

"I heard some interesting news while you were in the shower," Graham reported.

"Sorry, I was watching giraffes watching me. What's the news?"

"Lions in camp last night! Two females. The ladies in bungalow number six saw them drinking out of the pool at 12:30 a.m."

"That was just before we got here," I said. "Close call!" When it comes to lions, we needed to be in a vehicle or inside a building to be safe!

"Right, we were lucky lads," Graham responded. "A German man told me only elephants and lions come into camp, mostly late at night." There were no fences around Sabi, no lights for miles. We were in the middle of the South African bush. I felt in my pocket for my Gerber knife, serrated blade model—*like it could have saved me from two lions?* We had time for another cup of tea.

"You boys will be in Rob's Land Rover with Hans and Hilda Zimmer," the guest services manager said when he came over. "Pleased to meet you both, my name is Neville Adams. Missed you last night."

"Got in late," I said. "KLM from Amsterdam was delayed—a bad habit they have. We went right to our bungalows, so thanks for having everything ready, light on, key in the door, whiskey in the minibar… "

"No problem, pleasure to be of service. Better get ready to go. I see Hans and Hilda are all set. Rob will be here in fifteen minutes; see you both for breakfast." Neville had to rustle up other guests."

The German couple was sitting on a bench under an acacia tree by the driveway. Graham was ready, I had to run back to the bungalow to get my backpack. I wondered whether Neville heard there were lions at the pool last night...

Rob showed up at 6:30 a.m. sharp and introduced us to Elliot, who would be our spotter. He sat on a swivel seat on the front left fender. A Winchester .458 rifle was mounted under the dashboard within easy reach. Three rounds of "solids" were loaded in the magazine; the chamber was empty. The Land Rovers used by Sabi were open with theatre seating behind the two front seats and room for nine guests, six comfortably. The four of us had plenty of room. I introduced myself to Hans and Hilda. Hans was the German man who had told Graham about the lions. He was retired from his job as head brewer at Lowenbrau in Munich. Both Hans and Hilda were dressed in brown shirts and pants, their white hair sticking out from under small cowboy hats—cute. I had a light rain jacket on over my safari shirt, Graham wore a sweater jacket.

Before starting, Rob gave us the rules: "No standing. No arms or legs outside the vehicle. Hold onto your handle bar tight if we move fast. And, most important, do not aggravate any animals with loud noise or fast moves. It's not a zoo out there. The animals—even some birds—are wild and dangerous." Rob was in his mid-twenties; tall and lean with sandy hair, and he arrived wearing a clean ranger's uniform. This was his fourth year as a safari guide. Elliot was native Zulu; shorter and stockier than Rob with big brown eyes and a pleasant smile. He was wearing tan camouflage.

Hilda, feeling the cool morning air, took two brown jackets out of her day-bag, giving Hans his before putting hers on. They were matching Lowenbrau jackets from last year's Octoberfest. "Now we're ready to go into the bush," she said to Hans in German.

The drive started at the gate. A dirt road took us out of camp down into a ravine that smelled of elephant dung. The cool morning dampness enhanced the odor. We drove over large circular footprints, wet in the muck. Then the road went up a gradual hill with green thorn brush scraping the Land Rover on both sides. Its tires crushed brush that released a rosemary scent, neutralizing the dung odor. I'd experienced this welcome chemistry on other game drives. Cheers for rosemary!

"Do you know elephant dung is medicine?" Hans said, turning and looking back at us. "They make tea from it for bronchitis and diarrhea."

"And the fresher the dung, the better," Graham added. Having lived in Johannesburg all his life, he had become quite knowledgeable of such details. I was still learning.

"I heard a bottle of Lowenbrau beer works even better!" I quipped. Everyone laughed, including Rob and Elliot.

It was getting brighter now and we could see better—enough to make out animals grazing in the distance. As we drove on, the road firmed up into clay-like brown dirt, quite comfortable compared to roads I'd been on in other African reserves. "Is this high veldt or low veldt?" I asked Graham.

"It's wild veldt," Graham answered. "Wide open with thorn trees everywhere, spaced apart in high grass with more thorn trees." The grass on high ground was brown, green in low areas. Out to our right, in the distance, zebras and impalas were grazing. Elliott was glassing them with binoculars. We drove on at a good pace, the air was fresh and warming up.

I took my bush hat off and sprayed it liberally with forty-percent Deet—African black flies were on the attack. I passed the can to Graham. Hilda was spraying on a mixture of essential oils in alcohol: Lemon, clove, and rosemary. It smelled great and she insisted it worked better than Deet. Using Deet was noxious, it only produced a trifling improvement over being eaten alive by an assortment of African bugs. Graham and I switched to Hilda's formula.

"Last year we had record floods," Rob said. "The spring rains of the new century were the worst in a hundred years. The Sabi River was up over twenty-feet, uprooted trees were everywhere along the river. Huge stumps and broken branches are still suspended. Trees in trees. You'll see when we get to the river—be ready to duck if I shout! The animals knew the flood was coming. Hippos moved up river to higher ground and the crocs followed. They got wet but didn't get washed downstream in the deluge. It wasn't all bad; the rains gave the bush a good washing."

"I'm glad we didn't come last spring," Hilda said.

"Hello, Hilda! I was hoping it wasn't just Hans who spoke English." I was happy and pleased. Other than hello, I hadn't heard her speak it.

"No, I taught Hans how to speak English when he was in training at the brewery—he was a stubborn student!"

"She used to teach English in Frankfurt when we first got married," Hans added. I could tell Hans felt lucky to have Hilda; she had a joyful caring spirit. They obviously had been married a long time. Without her taking care of life's details he might be back scrubbing beer barrels at the brewery.

"All four of you men need to keep me informed about Africa. My husband knows only a little about it." *Teachers never stop learning,* I thought to myself. She could have passed for a Hummel figurine in her youth; there was a humble wisdom hiding in Frau Zimmer.

"Rob, did you ever shoot that .458 rifle?" I asked him.

"Yes, at a target range. It kicks like a drunken giraffe."

"Ever at an animal?"

"No, and hope I never have to."

"You may have to someday if those man-eating lions in Kruger Park get down this far," Hans was not a man to mince words.

The road was bumpy, with yellow thatching grass and thorn bushes scraping the Land Rover like fingernails on a blackboard. We had dipped into a low, wet area and the Rover's big tires were throwing mud. Rob kept driving and ignored Hans. Elliot had heard Hans but didn't say anything either. It was the first I'd heard of these lions! Old Hans was adding some serious spice to our conversation!

"The last incident was up in the Punda Maria area of Kruger Park, considerably north of here," Graham said in a low voice to Hans, holding onto his shoulder. "We can talk later, I'll show you where it is on the map." I was also curious to see where Punda Maria was—I hadn't looked at the map in the office yet.

We moved closer to the zebras. There were eight of them, two of the mares had foals and a stray wildebeest was hanging out with the one stallion. "The wildebeest don't herd up down here like in Kenya and Tanzania," These were Elliot's first words. He looked back at us, swiveling on his fender seat.

"How do zebras protect their young from lions?" Hilda asked Elliott.

"They kick very hard at the lion and run around the foal to protect it." Elliot said. "They keep kicking – nonstop."

"When there's more than one lion attacking it's difficult to protect a foal. The herd tries to stay together, but many foals are lost. They're a favorite food for lions." Rob added.

It was warming up so I took my jacket off, rolled it up, and stuffed it in my backpack. Hilda folded both of their jackets neatly and put them away. Graham kept his sweater jacket on—it was still a bit cool for him.

We were on smooth dirt, throwing dust with the zebras behind us. Rob's VHS radio beeped loudly. He answered it and didn't say anything for about two minutes, then spoke in Afrikaans to the caller. "Rhinos," he said to us. "Four of them in the bush." He made a U-turn and headed back the way we had come. He stepped on the gas, and we moved fast.

"First of the Big Five coming up," Graham announced. Rhinos, elephants, Cape buffalo, lions, and leopards comprised the Big Five. The universal bucket list for African safari's.

"We never saw rhinos up close in Kenya," Hilda said. She was excited, as were the rest of us. Hans told us this was their second trip to Africa. It was my fourth.

When we got to a spot on the side of the road that looked no different than any other spot on the side of the road—just high grass—Rob braked and turned right, driving directly into the grass. Going off-road was allowed in Sabi but not in Kruger Park to the east. It made a big difference in our ability to get close to animals like rhinos. Ahead of us was an outcropping of several different trees—some were sausage trees with large zucchini-shaped seed pods. Rob kept driving toward the trees and a clearing of shorter, greener grass. And then, right where the grass turned green, they appeared in front of us; four rhinoceroses. I grabbed the camera. We were alone with the huge animals.

"These are white rhinos," Rob said. "The big bull weighs at least two and a half tons." It snorted and started spraying urine back toward us right when Rob began talking. Then the rhino kicked backwards, wiping its feet, a huge bulk of an animal. "That's to let us know he's not happy with us being here," Rob put the Rover in reverse and held his foot on the brake. "The small one is a yearling calf; it weighs close to a ton. The other two are females, cows. These rhinos eat twelve hours a day—they like the Guinea grass. This is a good sighting. We are right next to them, but can't stay long. That bull can run forty kilometers an hour for short distances. We don't want to aggravate him too much. He could tip this vehicle over!"

I was impressed with Rob's concern for Africa's intrinsic dangers and his extra concern for our safety. It was different in East Africa. The guides in the Serengeti in Tanzania, for example, were more flexible with the rules. I recall safari vehicles pulled over near lion prides that allowed their guests to walk around! "Get back fast if lion comes" they would say. Something to keep in mind when planning an African safari!

We watched quietly as the rhinos grazed, their heavy heads hung low. Except for the bull and the calf, the two cows paid no attention to us. The bull did not raise his head but looked at us with one eye, slightly tilting his head, keeping his square lips just above the ground. Perfect grazing lips. The calf was more curious, he stood up straight and looked right at us. I took pictures at several angles, as did Hans. The bull was dirt-brown with two huge horns, gray underneath the dirt. One of the females was dark gray, and half wet; the other was a lighter brown, coated with different dirt. The yearling was gray with zero dirt; Graham had declared him "clean as a whistle." None of the four were black or white!

Elliot told us there was no color difference between black and white rhinos and that all rhinos were gray. Any other color was due to mud (dirt). Black and white were just names from colonial times used to describe the two species. The difference was the shape of their lips! White rhinos had big flat lips for grazing on grass; black rhinos had narrow pointed lips for picking fruits and leaves. There was a pervasive odor of urine mixed with dung. "The smell is the same for both species," Elliot added.

"Look at those oxpecker birds on the females," Hilda observed.

"They're the cleanup crew—bug eaters," Hans said. One bird was on the back of each female rhino, pecking bugs. They looked at us for a moment, then went back to pecking.

"These are red-billed oxpeckers that fancy ticks and horsefly larvae," Rob explained. "They fly away noisily when they see a predator, warning the rhinos. Lions will kill a rhino calf when desperate, so warnings are vital."

The big bull snorted and sprayed again, his rear end facing us. He backed up several steps when he heard Hilda's voice. He could turn and face us, aiming his two horns in seconds. Rob asked if we had taken enough photos, Hans and I said we had. He backed slowly out of the clearing, made a circle in the high grass, and headed to the road. In all my trips to Africa, this was the best rhino sighting by far. It was exciting to get so close!

Back on the main road we headed back to where we had been before the rhino detour. A herd of impalas, running at full speed, ran across the road thirty meters in front of us. Behind them was a pack of wild dogs chasing and yelping. Rob stopped and we watched the seven dogs. They were black and white; skinny and long legged with large black ears. They all looked like they needed a meal. The impalas were winning the race, running fast and jumping with all four legs off the ground. Rob turned off the road and followed the dogs following the impalas.

"Let's see if the dogs can catch one of the small ones," Rob said, driving right behind the dogs. There were two small impalas at the rear of the herd, but they were holding their own, swerving and turning. We stayed behind the dogs until they slowed down and gave up. "A larger pack would have gotten one!" Rob said. "I've seen packs of forty dogs chasing Impalas. They divide and come at them from each flank so they can't turn."

"Those dogs look hungry," Hans said.

"That's their normal look," Elliot replied. "Never saw a fat one, they're better scavengers than hunters."

Rob was turning the Rover around and heading back to the road when another call came in on the radio. He didn't talk long. "*Luiperd!*" he said excitedly.

"What?" Hilda asked, winking at Rob when he turned around.

"Sorry, I meant leopard—sometimes I switch to Afrikaans without knowing it. The guide on the radio has a nice one up a tree near the Kruger border. If we move fast, it will still be there. Hang onto those handle bars."

We travelled fast over lumpy savannah heading east on a diagonal from the main road. Here the grass was shorter and wide open. The ride had occasional bumps and jerks. It was like riding an old horse at half speed. Hans and Hilda were hanging on tight and bouncing along, their cowboy hats pulled snug on their heads.

Now there was more game; big eland and hartebeest and the smaller steenbok. I was looking for kudu but didn't see any. Kudu were among the most stunning of the grazing animals.

"They like the savannah," Elliot said, referring to all the grazing animals. We raced toward the leopard and became airborne twice with all four wheels off the ground. "Termite mounds! Hold on!" Rob shouted. "These clay mounds range from six inches to six feet high and come straight up out of the ground! Termites build them."

In the distance, straight ahead, we could see a group of large trees with wide trunks and heavy branches. Rob aimed the Rover at them.

"Those are Sycamore figs; the *luiperds* like them," Rob said, smiling. He slowed down as we got closer and stopped about fifty meters away, grabbing binoculars. The other Sabi Land Rover had already left and a Mala Rover from a different reserve had arrived with a full load of young men. "There is a big male in the middle fig tree with its kill." Rob pointed out, putting the Land Rover in gear and slowly moving toward the leopard, shutting the motor off ten meters from the tree. The Mala Rover was closer, it was from a game reserve southeast of here on the Sabi River. Beyond the Mala reserve was the south end of Kruger Park. There were no fences, so animals were free to move between Kruger, Mala, and Sabi.

The leopard was lying on a long, horizontal branch parallel to the ground, about fifteen feet up. Brown spots, many with yellow patches inside them, covered the animal's white body in a brilliant pattern. Around his head and shoulders and on the legs and tail the spots were solid brown. There were many subtle designs that branded each leopard a separate individual like fingerprints. The cat's tail was longer than his body and provided stability when climbing trees. This leopard was a perfect specimen. Stomach full of impala, he kept one paw on the half that was left. Hans and I got great shots. Didn't need fast film, 100 ASA was fine.

The Mala group started making noise—all were young men wearing sports jerseys and short pants. Each one was trying to whistle by putting fingers in his teeth; that loud wolf whistle sound you get when you know how to do it. About half were successful. The leopard growled at the disturbance. Rob and Elliot were angry; Rob's face was red.

"It's crazy what they're doing," Rob said. Just then the leopard stood up and looked around, seeing both vehicles clearly. He growled again, grabbed the impala carcass in his mouth, and bolted up the tree to a higher branch. He didn't lie down, he kept standing and looking at both vehicles. The Mala boys were waving small flags now and either whistling or shouting. I could sense that Hilda wanted to run over and scold them face-to-face, the stern-teacher part of her, but instead she stood up and put her left index finger over her lips while shaking her head no. She kept repeating this.

"They're a soccer team from Argentina," Elliott informed us. Rob didn't say anything.

"This is scaring the mickey out of me," Graham said in a shaky voice.

Rob started the rover and put it in reverse keeping his foot on the brake. "Can he attack us?" Hans asked. Hilda was nervous but kept shaking her head, less scared than mad.

"Do they ever jump in a vehicle?" She asked. The Land Rovers were completely open above the seats.

"I have never seen it happen in South Africa, but it has in Kenya." Rob was being cautious. "We're going to move. Take any last pictures now."

As Rob backed out slowly, the leopard started down the tree with three paws holding wood when possible. This was one heavy cat—going down a tree was harder than going up. It was amazing to see but scary in an open vehicle this close. The Argentine boys had quit whistling and shouting—all nine of them. I called it the "Hilda Effect!"

Rob had our Rover back from the tree now by twenty meters or more. The leopard stayed on the ground near the tree, impala meat safely above him, as he switched his gaze from one vehicle to the other.

"Why don't they move?" I wondered out loud as we kept backing up.

"This will be reported." Rob had a serious look on his face. "That guide will lose his job. He's putting those crazy kids in danger!" There was only one guide with them who was also the driver, no spotter.

The leopard held his ground, still standing by his tree. The Mala vehicle started up and drove off. We did the same, only in reverse. Rob did not want to take his eyes off the cat. It's amazing how fast a Land Rover can go in reverse. When we were fifty meters away Rob stopped, and we all looked back. We could see the leopard was back on the high branch with the impala. It was a great sighting except for the annoying soccer team. I felt both excitement and relief. "You may have saved everyone, Hilda!" I gave her a thumb's up smiling. She smiled back, her eyes wet with tears. She wasn't accustomed to compliments.

"That's number two of the Big Five," Hans squeezed Hilda's hand.

It was 8:30 a.m. and time to start back for breakfast. Going back, Rob took an alternate route along the Sabi River. There were hippos in the river but we didn't stop. "We'll get to them after lunch, and elephants too," Rob said. The next game drive was at 4:00 p.m. I noticed I had at least two mosquito bites. I needed to remember to take 100 mg of doxycycline after breakfast. Malaria here was the non-repeating type that could be treated. Graham had it previously. It was less devastating than the type in East Africa, but nevertheless preventative medicine was a requirement. Doxycycline was an alternative to mefloquine, which I couldn't take. We moved on in the direction of breakfast.

After two delightful veggie omelets and two glasses of mango juice, I wasn't in the mood for any of the wild-tasting steenbok sausage. I was ready for a nap.

While walking back to my bungalow, leopard memories still fresh in my mind, I noticed Graham talking to Hans and Hilda. I changed directions and went over to them. I was right about Camp Rule Number Two being broken—everyone was walking around without guides during the day.

"We were discussing the man-eating-lion dangers in the north." Graham's dramatic eyebrows were working overtime. "That was the spice Hans tried to add to our conversation in the Rover."

"Hans and I would like to hear what Graham knows about it." Hilda had a sobering expression on her face. "Can you join us?"

"Sure. Can we do it after I take a short nap?" I was very interested, and surprised I hadn't read about it somewhere. We had the middle of the day to relax so there was plenty of time to talk; I just needed to go horizontal for a while—without bumps.

"Yeah, I need a bit of a lie-down myself," Graham admitted.

Hans checked his watch. "It's only 10:00, lunch is at 1:00, and another game drive at 4:00—plenty of time."

"How about 11:30 by the pool?" I suggested.

"That's good; nobody has used it since we've been here. You know, most older Europeans don't swim," Hilda reminded us. "Only lions use that pool."

I slept for an hour; the travel and jet lag from yesterday had made me tired. Then I laid awake thinking about the morning game drive before getting up. I took a second shower outside—there was jungle grit in my ears and elsewhere that required removal. The cement enclosure covered me from the neck down. This time there were no giraffes to admire me and make my wife jealous! I dried off and was energized again, ready for the meeting.

It was a beautiful day by the pool, with authentic South African sunshine and a fresh, mild breeze. We sat at a table and opened the umbrella above us. Graham went into the office bar and brought back four Castle Lager beers. Looking out to the water hole, seventy-five meters away, three muddy warthogs were rutting around grunting and snorting. "*Hakuna matata,*" I yelled in their direction.

"Hopefully no worries," Hilda interpreted.

"There may be a *few* worries, no matter what the warthogs do." Hans added.

Hans started the meeting that he had requested. "First, before Graham speaks, let me tell you what is believed in Germany about the man-eating lions of Kruger Park: Everyday there are illegal immigrants—or refugees depending on your politics—who cross the Mozambique border into Kruger Park and attempt to make their way into South Africa to find work. During the daytime, South African air and ground patrols watch the border. During the night is when the refugees cross. They can't use lights of any kind, so they follow the power and telephone lines using starlight on clear nights. Some cross over on totally black, cloudy nights. The lions, hunting at night, find them. A large unknown number, hundreds per year, are eaten alive. Most of this occurs up in the north section of the park, 360 kilometers from here." Hans paused.

"Graham, it's your turn," Hilda said.

"Yeah, the whole thing is tying me in a knot. I'm a native South African. I believe in laws. We have immigration laws. But I also know the refugees are desperate people. This has been a problem my entire life and before that. Whenever a human body part is found in the bush such as a head or arm, like they have recently, it makes front page news in Jo-Burg. The government gets constant heat from the U.N. to do more. Whenever rangers kill an entire pride of lions suspected of being man eaters—as they have several times—a new pride moves in. And the taste for human flesh grows. Kruger Park is a big place, twenty-thousand square kilometers! It's estimated there are two thousand lions in the park and no fences between here and there." Graham paused.

"What measures are being taken by Mozambique? Isn't it part of the problem?" I asked.

"Hans started to answer, but Hilda interrupted. "Let me tell you what I know about Mozambique. It has a long, dirty history that I won't bore you with. Just to say it started in the Stone Age and wound up being a dysfunctional democracy. The good news is that German and other western money is being invested there in natural gas and clean coal production. Infrastructure failings are being corrected. But there is no opportunity for the unskilled. They are the refugees. The current government of Mozambique must initiate training programs to prevent foreign workers from competing with the indigenous people."

"Brilliant, Hilda," Graham declared. When Hilda knew something for sure she wasn't bashful about telling it! *She was one smart woman in a small package,* I thought.

"I agree. It will require some rethinking by the U.N. to do that. They typically blame the country where refugees arrive, not the country they leave. The problem has two faces."

"Night patrols using night-vision equipment might slow things down," Hans said. "Turn more refugees back."

"We do need something that can help now—maybe flashing warning signs with a lion eating a refugee." Hilda said firmly. "Something seriously scary!"

"I know some legislators in Pretoria, I'll schedule a talk with them," Graham said. "We need a plan for now and a plan for the future. I can't imagine how it feels to be eaten alive by a lion."

"I think we need another Castle Lager," Hans insisted. "Too bad they don't serve Lowenbrau." Nobody disagreed.

That discussion brought us to lunch—we didn't have to move an inch. While eating, we talked about family and friends; the lion worries were put on hold.

Neville walked over after lunch to visit with Graham and me. We were sitting outside Graham's bungalow.

"Good afternoon, gentlemen." Neville looked a little nervous compared to this morning. This told me that managing a safari camp was not without stress.

"Good afternoon, Neville," Graham and I replied in unison.

"I have to change the time for your afternoon drive to leave at 3:00 instead of 4:00. I hope that can work for you," Neville said apologetically.

"Yeah, why not?" Graham said looking at me.

"It's fine with me," I agreed. "May I ask why?"

"Rob has a special assignment to check on some game that involves a longer drive," Neville informed me. "He needs the extra hour."

"What about the Zimmers?" Graham asked.

"I've already talked with them. They agreed; no problem."

"We'll be ready at 3:00," I said. Graham nodded. Neville thanked us.

We were down at the bench ready to go at 3:00 p.m. sharp. Rob, right on time, pulled up with two older rangers in the Land Rover and no Elliot. "Good afternoon," he said without making any introductions. The four of us got into the seats we'd had in the morning: two bench seats in back. Both older rangers sat on the bench seat behind Rob and were armed with .44 magnum Smith and Wesson revolvers.

We headed out the gate down into the elephant dung ravine and up the hill with the scraping thorn bushes, then out on the road we'd taken this morning. The cool dampness from the morning was gone and we were comfortable in shirt sleeves. Rob was looking straight ahead while the two older rangers talked to each other in Afrikaans.

We stayed on the morning road for about forty-five minutes before turning onto another dirt road that climbed abruptly. Rob shifted the Land Rover into second gear. We drove faster after reaching the top of the hill and passed a flock of guinea hens walking single file, bobbing and pecking along. They were about two feet tall and looked like small blue turkeys with white heads and red caps. Rob kept going without stopping. It was odd for him not to stop and explain the birds.

"Something is strange," Graham said to me in a low voice. Hans and Hilda were also whispering to each other. "Did you see those handguns?"

"They're Smith and Wesson .44 magnums," I said. "Very powerful; they would make Clint Eastwood proud." The Winchester .458 rifle was still under the dashboard.

We were on flat, high ground heading northeast and had run out of road. There was brown grass and a variety of trees, including acacias. I noticed they didn't umbrella out as much as those in the Serengeti. Since we couldn't consult with Rob right now, I paged through a field guide to see if I could identify them. Some were green thorn trees that looked like they had been half-eaten.

"Elephants eat those thorn trees." Hilda said, glancing back at my book. Obviously, she had done some studying also.

"Are you sure you weren't a biology teacher too?" I asked her smiling.

Just then a radio beeped, and one of the older rangers answered it speaking in Afrikaans. He listened for several minutes, turned around and looked at us, then resumed talking on the radio. I could see that Rob had heard some of it and said something in Afrikaans to the ranger. The ranger nodded.

"What do you think that was about?" I asked Graham, who understood the language.

"It was hard to hear them—something about our nationalities," Graham said.

"We're still going forward. Looks like we passed the test," I quipped. *This is all very strange,* I thought.

"I think I know where we might be going." Graham whispered to me.

We continued travelling through savannah-like terrain and could see elephants in the distance. Ten of them. "Are they eating green thorn trees?" I asked Hilda. She laughed. "You know I can't see that far."

"Elephants!" Hans said loudly, pointing at them. Rob kept on course as if he hadn't seen the ten elephants. It was our number three of the Big Five.

"Later," Rob replied. He kept on a northeast course and was heading in the direction of the Kruger Park border.

"We'll be out of the Sabi reserve and into Krueger Park soon. This is scaring the mickey out of me again." Graham was startled.

Hans had bought a map of Kruger Park at the office after lunch. "We're somewhere south of the Talamati Bush camp,"

Hans said, showing Graham on the map. The older ranger with the radio had made a call and was talking as Rob drove on.

After an hour of driving off-road, a large rock outcropping, called a kopje, could be seen ahead. Huge rocks were surrounded by a mixed stand of trees. It stood out from the terrain we were in, a boulder pile in the middle of flat savannah. We kept on a course toward it. The two older rangers were talking to Rob—giving him instructions? Graham could not hear what they were saying.

As we came up to the rocks and trees we were stunned. A pride of lions had taken them over. Two large females were sitting on the top rock; we could see them in profile. Two other females played with their cubs farther down while two junior males, their manes just developing, were sniffing each other's genitals. A large, black-maned male was stretched out under a bush at the bottom of the rocks, stomach bloated, alert to our presence. I had my binoculars on him. Rob had the vehicle close, fifteen meters away. I could count the flies on the big male's head. The two older rangers, still in the vehicle, were looking at everything but the lions, glassing up and down with their binoculars; beyond the rocks, between the rocks, in the trees, on the ground.

"What are they looking for, Rob?" Hilda asked. She looked as though she was already thinking worrisome thoughts while squeezing Hans' hand.

"What the lions have been eating," Rob answered. The two rangers immediately looked at him. Rob was irritated and told them something in Afrikaans. One ranger just shook his head. I was starting to figure things out.

"We're too far south in Kruger for such a worry." Graham was moving his finger on the map.

"Probably not, or we wouldn't be having this ordeal," Hilda said in a shaky voice, turning back toward Graham. Hans was glassing the lions and not talking. They were sharing a zebra kill. The four cubs were crawling on each other and fighting over a piece of meat that had separated from the carcass. In the sun, the females sitting on the top rock—probably mother and daughter – were just looking out with their sparking golden eyes.

Hans and I took photos, but neither of us felt completely comfortable. I had that sick feeling you get in your stomach when you know something isn't right. We were sitting with a pride of eleven lions in a totally open vehicle and they were eating red meat. *What was the worry*? I thought ironically. I took the Gerber knife out of my pocket, opened and closed it—double checking it. It was the only weapon we were allowed. I had read an article in Tanzania last year that a man killed an attacking lion by stabbing it in the neck and slicing open its carotid artery. *But these lions here are not from north Kruger. Their taste was for zebra,* I kept thinking.

Nevertheless, Graham looked jittery. He didn't have a camera, so he was unable to take photos as a diversion. Hilda had put down her binoculars; she had been worried from the start. Rob looked at the two rangers; they nodded to him and he started the Land Rover.

We started backing out a short distance when the older ranger with the radio yelled "Stop!" He pointed to a large Volkswagen-size rock we couldn't see before. We all looked with binoculars. It was a frightening sight. Sitting on top of the rock, standing straight up, alone, was a white tennis shoe. The four of us were shocked. Rob was stone faced. We were absolutely in the middle of nowhere; no roads, no villages! Where did a tennis shoe come from? The implications were frightening! The older ranger with the radio made a call. The other ranger looked back at us. "Time to go," he said in English. We moved away from the rocks, the lions, and the tennis shoe.

By 6:00 p.m. it was overcast and dark. We had a long drive to get back to camp and, adjusting for the darkness, it would be slower. By 7:00 p.m. it was ink-black. *Is this how the refugees felt?* I wondered. Rob was following our tracks back over the brown grass; he slowed down so the younger ranger could move up to the spotting seat. We had been moving fast considering the darkness, the Rover's lights only illuminated the grass directly in front of us.

The younger ranger, using the Rover's spotlight, moved the beam around and found zebras grazing off to the right. We couldn't see their black stripes, only their "white stripes." It was scary; anything crossing in front of us would be dead meat. The

Land Rover was a big truck with a cattle-guard, but still, I could imagine what a five-hundred-pound Eland would do to us flying over the windshield! We trusted Rob because he had been operating under orders without a choice. We drove without incident until we got to the first road where we had to watch for low tree branches. Rob slowed down while the ranger flashed the light on the trees. We turned off the grass and onto the road.

At the intersection with the main road, just a 'T' in the dirt, we were feeling better. Just beyond the intersection we had to stop. A giraffe was blocking the road while grazing on a green thorn tree. Rob blew the horn and it moved.

"I thought only elephants ate green thorn trees," I said to Hilda. She laughed.

"Thanks for lightening things up," she replied. "It will be good to get back to camp and relax without rhinos, leopards, lions, and bumps. Today has certainly been something more than a day at the Berlin zoo."

Hans then reminded us: "We did see four of the Big Five, two in the a.m. and the two in the p.m."

"Hans! Whatever happened to 'morning' and 'afternoon,'" I quipped. "Nobody uses a.m. and p.m. where you come from! I was toying with him.

"He was trying to 'Americanize' for you," Hilda explained, faking a stern look.

"Thank you, Hans! Your humor was appreciated," I replied.

"I wasn't trying to be funny," Hans said. "Was just trying out the American version of English." We all laughed even though it wasn't that funny.

We continued talking for the sake of talking—we needed the levity. The last serious thing said was Graham confirming we couldn't count the elephants in the Big Five because they were too far away.

We arrived back to camp late, after 8:45 p.m. Rob walked us to our bungalows after dropping the Zimmers off first. "Freshen up and get ready to go eat at 9:00," he told them. On the way, he stopped by the restaurant and told the head waiter we might be late for dinner. As I was climbing out of the Rover, Rob had asked Graham if the three of us could have a talk before dinner. Graham, seeing me nod, said "Yes."

Rob started the discussion in Graham's bungalow: "I know you were confused by our drive this afternoon. You have probably figured some things out. It's a very serious, compromising situation. Park Headquarters called Sabi last night and told Neville to cancel the drive with the four of you this afternoon, and take two rangers to southeast Kruger where we saw the lions. Neville told them no, that we had paid. The rangers could go along but no cancellations. Due to the urgency of the investigation, they agreed and you know the rest." Rob paused.

"It was a brilliant lion sighting, but scary as hell knowing the implications, particularly seeing that shoe at the end," Graham looked a bit disheveled.

"I know. This was the first time in four years I had to make such a drive," Rob admitted.

"What facts can you share with us?" I asked.

"There was an incident with tourists last week near the Tamboti bush camp in southeast Kruger. A teenage girl from France had gone out of a safari vehicle to relieve herself. It wasn't one of our Rovers! She disappeared behind some thick bush well behind the vehicle. She disappeared without a sound; nobody saw or heard anything, but they did find one of her tennis shoes. This was not a refugee event, it's too far south for that. The two rangers today were visiting nearby prides, looking for clues. They had been in a Mala Lodge vehicle yesterday."

"Well, we certainly found a clue today," You could see Graham was perplexed by it. He was a strong promoter of Kruger Park. I suspected that only one or two lions were involved, like in the *Ghost and the Darkness* movie. I couldn't imagine an entire pride migrating that far—hundreds of kilometers.

"Will they kill this pride?" I asked Rob.

"I hope not, I really hope not," Rob said. "Several prides visit those rocks. This pride killed a zebra and, hopefully, it doesn't have a taste for human flesh."

"This ties me in a knot." Graham remarked. "There's a lot at stake here, from both sides. The government has killed complete prides in the north after finding the remains of refugees, and it has not stopped the problem. A new pride moves in and tragedy continues."

"That's right." Rob said. "The problem with tourists can be solved with rigid rule enforcement. The problem with refugees is another story. I will talk to Hans and Hilda after dinner. You guys better go eat. They are keeping it warm for you. Be sure you don't walk to your bungalows after dinner without me!

"Oh, one more thing," Rob added. "That Argentine soccer team was ordered to leave the Mala reserve and the guide—a part time guide—was fired."

"Besides Evelyn and Barbara in bungalow six, did anyone else see lions drinking out of the pool last night?" Hilda asked the group that was gathered in the office, waiting for dinner. Nobody else had. Hans was quiet, holding his hands behind his back and pacing, master-brewer style, as if a tank of beer had gone sour. Some of the other guests had read last week's newspapers about the disappearance of the French girl, but no details had been given. So, the subject at the pre-dinner gathering, to the dismay of Sabi management, was: "What do we know about the man-eating lions of Kruger Park?"

The other guests knew that special rangers had been with the four of us today. "What did they find?" was everyone's question. The four of us had discussed what to say if this came up: "We had a long drive to the Kruger border and saw a pride of lions eating a zebra. The rangers had been with a Mala vehicle yesterday." We let Graham explain. He did not mention the tennis shoe!

The dinner tables, setup outside in a large semicircle with a blazing fire in the center, were covered with white tablecloths. Each table had a kerosene lamp that gave off a warm, orange glow. Electricity was limited to fans and air conditioning in the rooms and a few lights in the office and bar. There were no other electric lights. Out in the distance was the water hole, but in the black night you couldn't see it.

"Can you see any invisible animals?" I asked Hilda, smiling. The four of us were sitting together and she had been looking in the direction of the water hole.

She just smiled back shaking her head as dinner was served. The appetizer: salmon caviar followed by chilled tomato bisque soup. The main course: either roast lamb or grilled sole with red potatoes and local vegetables. French style caramel custard and Kenyan coffee created a superb finish. The dinner was a comforting conclusion to what had been a dramatic first day.

Rob walked us back to our bungalows, about forty meters. The clouds had cleared and the Southern Cross was high and bright off to our left, thousands of light years away. Frogs and crickets were making sounds that frogs and crickets make in Africa. Lions might be down at the water hole.

Rob was ready with Elliot at 6:30 a.m. for day two. Hans and Hilda wore matching camo outfits and the same small cowboy hats. Graham and I were dressed in yesterday's clothes and ready, in Graham's words, "to have a go." Rob and Elliot were smiling.

"Today we will spend time down by the river. There will be a lot to see." Rob said. Elliot put his right thumb up. Hans and Hilda did the same. Graham provided a wide Irish smile. It was a bright clear day, and I could tell everybody was trying to forget half of yesterday. The South African government had a conundrum to solve.

We're weren't a mile out of camp when a large kudu bull jumped out in front of us. This was one special antelope animal I hadn't seen up close in Kenya or Tanzania. Its magnificent large black horns swirled out of its head like two coiled cobras, perfectly complementing its tan, white-striped, black-maned body. The kudu made a full stop in the middle of the road and stared directly at us. This was the prize, the trophy of trophies that Hemingway dreamed about and slept in hunting blinds overnight to surprise.

Once the kudu crossed the road after stopping in front of us, it ran perpendicular to the Land Rover for ten meters. Then stopped again, turned its head, looked at us once more, and bolted away. Its hooves threw brown dirt and small stones as it ran. I could feel the animal's weight vibrating the ground. He was the star of the show for me!

"Grand kudu," Graham said. "There are more down here than up in East Africa. This bull is stunning!"

"We see this kudu often," Rob remarked. "He lives around here with four smaller bulls. He recognized our Rover." Rob drove past the intersection where we saw the giraffe last night but stayed on the main road.

"Did you get good pictures, Hans?" Hilda inquired.

"Yes, mommy, I did." Hilda smiled when Hans said this and pinched his ear.

Graham and I laughed—so did Rob. Elliot on the fender seat didn't hear it. Then we wondered why it was funny? "Hilda, please explain. If I said that to my wife she'd get angry and not talk to me for an hour."

Hilda explained: "It's an ironic expression Hans uses to kid me; he learned it from his father. Hans' mother was ten years older than his father. With us it's just the opposite. Hans is ten years older than me! I love the irony if he doesn't overdo it."

After driving close to an hour with a minimum of bumps we got into elephant and Cape-buffalo territory as we headed toward the river. "We have to be careful in here; these are the two animals we fear most. They are unpredictable and can charge," Rob said. "The buffalos are the worst—they don't adjust to our presence like most of the elephants do."

"Watch for low tree branches in case we have to move fast," Elliot said, swiveling back toward us on his fender seat. "And hold on!" We slowed down as we got closer to the Cape buffalo herd. There must have been two hundred of them, all wearing sharp curled horns—powerful weapons! They were facing toward us, lying in rows in the course grass.

Rob told us a chilling story about them: "Last year a group of hunters that were permitted to hunt Cape buffalo encountered a major problem. As they approached the herd, getting ready to shoot their selected animals, the whole herd charged. Their Land Rover was right in the middle of it. The hunters ran under the Rover, down on the floor inside it, some on top of each other.

Two got badly gored and had to be helicoptered to Johannesburg."

"They look so tame lying there." Hilda's glass was always half-full, not half-empty and we appreciated her perspective. The herd was forty meters away, lying in a line parallel to us. They were being annoyed by large black bugs, some beetle with big mandibles. It would be a hellish experience if they all charged at once—the river was not far behind us and the Land Rover didn't swim. They reminded me of two hundred army tanks, lined up ready to charge at a moment's notice, hopefully able to recognize us as tourists, not hunters.

"We'll get a bit closer to the buffs then call it number five of the Big Five," Rob declared. "And then we'll go find those elephants we saw in the distance yesterday. Today you'll see them up close."

The elephants were pulling trees apart when we got to them. There were crashing sounds of trees falling into each other that only elephants could produce. "They strip bark away from large branches and eat it with its sweet cambium layers," Rob explained.

"Just like a six-ton beaver would do in Canada," I joked. Hilda laughed.

"A typical adult elephant in South Africa eats six hundred pounds a day. It takes a lot of trees to feed a herd of elephants," Rob added.

There were seven in this group. One big male and six others; two adult females, two teenagers, and two little guys. The bull was huge, with two great tusks that almost touched the ground. As we drove closer he began trying to locate us with his trunk, lifting it vertically while coiling and uncoiling it. He didn't trust his eyes like he did his sense of smell. He had smelled Land Rovers with people before. He honored us with a thudding bowel movement that slapped and dented the ground.

"He's making medicine!" Hilda announced, remembering our discussion from the day before.

"Look at him, what a huge tusker!" Graham declared.

"His name is Big Al," Elliot said. "He knows us."

"Did he ever charge?" Hans asked.

"Once," Rob answered.

"Well, what happened?" Hans was curious and so was I.

"I never knew how fast a Land Rover could go in reverse until then," Rob admitted.

Everyone laughed, especially Hilda—she had told us she couldn't drive a truck with a clutch in forward much less in reverse with an elephant charging.

"We men have to be good at something!" Graham instructed her, smiling. "Running the world keeps women so busy they can't find time for insignificant matters!"

"Big Al must have a deep understanding of people; you can see it in how he looks at us," Hilda remarked, ignoring Graham's comment. Al was swishing around a large tree branch with his trunk. His tusks helped keep it off the ground while he stripped the bark—still able to watch us during the process. The little guys stayed clear of him.

"One thing's for sure, he has the biggest brain of all the animals in Africa, including us," I added.

"Big Five complete. Let's do it again!" Hans said.

We finished the morning drive down by the Sabi River watching hippos and crocs, along with a plethora of birds. It was almost 9:00 a.m. and time to head back for breakfast. "Afterwards you all can relax, take a swim, read a book, or go on a guided game walk around the camp perimeter—but be ready for the afternoon game drive at 4:00 p.m. And don't scare any giraffes in the shower!" Rob pointed at me.

The game drive started right on time. We went out and made a left turn after the gate and then another into the bush, avoiding the ravine and eventually coming out behind the water hole. Rob stopped the Land Rover and we started glassing the area. Camp was a hundred yards in front of us—the shower-curious giraffes were behind us eating leaves off high trees. I recognized them, all three had long necks.

"An adult giraffe eats sixty to seventy pounds of leaves a day, one-tenth of what an elephant eats. Watch them... See how the tallest one mouths a high branch, both wood and leaves, and then pulls its head back, mouth closed, and gets only the leaves. It takes a tough mouth and tongue to do that!" Rob explained.

"And a long neck!" Hans said. We all laughed. The shortest of the three was eating on an acacia tree—a favorite—violently shaking its head to weaken the leaf stems on a branch.

"When a giraffe drinks, it splays its front legs out so it can get its head down. It takes time to get back to vertical. That's when a lion can attack it." Rob continued our education. It made me recall how brief another guide was on my first African safari. We were in Nairobi National Park and had come up on two giraffes eating trees, the guide pointed and said: "Two giraffes eating trees." By comparison, Rob and Elliot were real pros.

"I read that a giraffe can kill a lion by kicking it," Hilda said.

"I've seen it! Elliot said. "A giraffe kicked a lion in the head and broke its neck." *I never thought about this when they were watching me shower! Good thing the containment was concrete.*

Hilda turned to me and asked, "What do *you* know about giraffes?"

"I believe Rob and Elliot covered everything I already knew." I was joking of course. "Let me think...Okay here's something Rob and Elliot don't know: When I was a kid, Groucho Marx sang a song describing a giraffe's neck: 'Half, half, half of the neck of one giraffe is just twice as long as it should be.'"

Hilda clapped. "Can you sing it?" I tried, but it wasn't an award performance; in fact it caused the giraffes to move!

The warthogs we saw yesterday were still at the water hole, mud-drenched and snorting around—not paying attention to us. They didn't have any worries. Rob started up and drove out of the open swampy area, away from the water hole.

"Monkeys," Hans said, looking through his binoculars. They were in trees to the west, not visible from camp. Rob drove over to them through another swampy, shallow area—he had to put the Land Rover in four-wheel drive.

"Vervet monkeys," Elliot said. There were lots of them; gray and white with black faces, orange eyes and extra-long tails.

Some had brown hair patches on their heads, like a Moroccan skullcap. Several were swinging around in the trees—going from one tree to another—making full use of their tails. Some were eating and watching us.

"What are they eating?" Hilda asked.

"Bugs," Elliot answered.

"Grubs are their favorite high-protein snack," Rob added. "Lots of grubs here in the swamp. You all should try a few! They taste like almonds. Mix them with sugar and you'll have a high protein almond custard."

"Yum, yum!" Hilda interrupted. "Go on Rob, sorry."

"These monkeys are smart; they alert each other with specific alarm calls when predators are spotted. High pitch 'chutters' for a python; low pitch grunts for a martial eagle; and short, tonal inhales and exhales for a leopard; their three greatest worries."

Rob got us out of the swamp. Hilda waved goodbye to the monkeys and told me later that one had waved back to her—seriously! They were her favorite sighting.

We got back to the main road and headed to part of the river basin we hadn't seen. Soon there were plenty of hippos and crocs to watch, and a Peterson Field Guide's collection of birds. It was like this for most of the afternoon. A smorgasbord of African wildlife: More rhinos—black ones this time; another leopard—alone without soccer players; a family of baboons with babies clinging to their mother's belly; spotted hyenas eating a leopard's leftovers; and myriad miniature creatures, some new to Rob.

Just before dark, on the road up from the ravine by camp, we came upon a large male lion lying across the road, sleeping. As far as we could tell he was alone.

"Wow," Hilda said. She grabbed Hans' hand and squeezed—first out of excitement then out of fear. The huge lion was right in front of us.

"Don't make any noise," Rob whispered. He had the Land Rover running in idle with the headlights off. "If he doesn't wake up and move, we'll have to go around him. Don't want to do that if we don't have to." It was rocky and thorny off the road on either side. Turning around would mean a two-hour detour in the dark to get to camp the back way. It would take a mixture of guts and stupidly to try and force the lion to move just to save us from taking a two hour detour. Beyond the lion, camp was only a quarter mile away.

"It would be slow going up in those rocks and thorns. Could get stuck," Elliot said to Rob. *"Ja nee,"* Rob agreed.

It was now that time—just before complete darkness—which was very concerning. If the lion woke up startled by us the surprise would aggravate him. Smelling humans without seeing a vehicle was not something he was accustomed to.

Rob had a small flashlight with a red beam. It did not disturb the darkness. He held it between his teeth, so it moved with his head. It was enough light for him to see and unhook the Winchester .458. Elliot watched carefully. He knew what was happening. Rob pulled the bolt back on the rifle and chambered one of the cartridges, leaving two in the magazine. He put the safety on and pointed the light at it, then showed Elliot, who nodded. Rob reached into his shirt pocket and pulled out another cartridge, opened the magazine, and carefully inserted it for a total of four including the one in the chamber. Four shots of .458 caliber lead bullets, "solids," the most powerful rifle bullets available. Then, with the safety on, he handed the gun to Elliot. At the same time, Elliot handed the Land Rover's spotlight to Rob. Elliot had the gun, Rob had the spotlight. It was black-dark except for the small red light.

The lion was breathing heavily; the idling sound of the Rover did not wake him. Straight ahead of the Rover was total blackness, the lion was not visible. *What next,* I thought. We were all scared to death.

Rob hoped they would not have to shoot—this was the last thing he wanted to do. But in this situation, where a lion could charge and maul everyone, he might have no choice. It was a necessary preparation they had rehearsed in training. They had to be ready.

Rob leaned forward and whispered something to Elliot who felt for the gun's safety, turning it off then back on to recall exactly where it was. He nodded at Rob who put the Rover in reverse, holding the wheel with one hand, the spotlight with the other. The spotlight was *not* turned on. Rob slowly backed up the Rover as Elliott held the gun pointed at where he could hear the lion snoring. The large mud tires crushed the bush as Rob did his best to weave and stay on the road; when he heard scraping sounds on one side he turned until he heard them on the opposite side—the average direction was straight back. The lion was about ten meters away. Moving in reverse changed the pitch of the motor. That combined with the bush-crushing sounds, woke the lion, but in the first instant we didn't know it. Graham and I were in the back seat with the Zimmers directly in front of us, an empty bench seat was in front of them. The vehicle was completely open at the top. Elliot was still on the left front fender seat when the lion roared.

The roar was ear-shattering. A sound that could be heard five kilometers away exploded directly front of us. Rob turned the spotlight on as he backed away. He was weaving slowly, making S-passes. The lion roared again, much louder now that he was fully awake. It was a deep, guttural, gulping sound with staccato interruptions—then huge air gulps, powerful and penetrating. I had my Gerber hunting knife out and open, gripping it tightly. *How do you stab a charging lion in the carotid artery in the dark and stay alive?* I wondered, while more than a little shaky.

"Is he moving toward us?" Graham shivered as he asked. It was hard to tell in the glare of the spotlight.

"It looks like he's where he was when he woke up." Hans said. Rob and Elliot were not talking; we were about fifteen meters from the lion, very vulnerable to a head-on charge. This is when we needed those rangers with their .44 magnum revolvers. They could be shot and reshot quickly at short distances. And each gun had six shots! Trying to swing that rifle around for more than one shot would be very difficult. The odds were with the lion. It roared again, louder than the first two times. The sound was deafening. Everything in the Rover vibrated in the thunderous vocal bolts. The spotlight seemed to blind the lion and hold him in place. He stood in full profile with his head turned, staring into the spotlight. He desperately wanted to see us—instinct was holding him back until he could be sure of what we were.

"His roar gets louder the more he wakes up," Hans said nervously. Hilda was shaking and covering her mouth with a tissue. We were about twenty-five meters from the lion, still backing away slowly in S-turns. The spotlight was suddenly less intense for some reason! Rob rotated its connection to the cigarette lighter and it brightened.

"We need to make a U-turn and get out of here bloody fast!" Graham said loudly. Rob was already in the process of doing that. He handed the spotlight to Hans and told him to keep it on the lion. Elliot was holding onto the rifle with one hand and the circular swivel seat with the other. The lion wasn't coming; the spotlight was still confusing it, like a deer in a car's headlights. Hans was doing well aiming the light. After making the thorn-scraping U-turn, we could see the lion drop down—like big ones do—and reposition itself for sleep. Rob, going forward now, headlights on, could see the road ahead. He made a radio call to camp and explained our situation. The lion was where he had been when this all started. We had to take the detour!

Going off the main road onto an old bush trail, "the back way," was a serious detour in the dark. Tedious and slow. I cut my two Snicker bars in half, happy to use the Gerber knife for this, and shared the four pieces. We all drank the last of our water after eating the candy. It was 8:30 p.m. and we had over an hour to go on the detour. Without the lion, the Sabi camp was less than fifteen minutes from where we saw him! As we travelled the detour, deep within me a true realization was developing—how terrifying it must feel for a refugee to face a roaring lion in the dark on foot. What would a person's last thoughts be?

It was 9:45 when we got back. "I need a double Crown Royal on the rocks," I said, after getting out of the Rover. The Sabi camp never looked so good. Neville and two other guides were waiting for us.

"Glad to see everyone is safe." Neville appeared relieved.

"Rob and Elliot did a brilliant job," Graham gave credit where it was due. Neville nodded.

"And Hans too," Hilda said, gradually getting back to her normal self. "He held the spotlight in the lion's eyes!" Neville nodded again.

"Did that lion have a bulge in its tail, right in the middle?" Neville asked.

Rob and Elliot shrugged their shoulders. Graham and Hans didn't know nor did I.

"It certainly did," Hilda confirmed.

"Are you positive?" Neville asked her.

"Quite positive," Hilda insisted. "The bulge was the size of a grapefruit. I was so scared I couldn't talk or move, only look!"

The next day, morning game drives were cancelled. Heavily armed rangers went out to find the lion. This lion was not from any of the prides in the area. A large male lion with a lump in its tail was responsible for refugee killings up in the Punda Maria area of Kruger Park. It had to be killed.

It was a revelation to find a lion that would migrate hundreds of kilometers. This one was a rogue. Was it a rare exception or the beginning of a trend? If just one percent of the two-thousand lions in Kruger Park had this tendency, it meant twenty lions were potential man-eaters. Even experts couldn't predict the actual number. The tennis-shoe event was separate and solved to some extent. The shoe on the rock did not match the French girl's shoe found where she went missing. Did it belong to an unknown victim? That mystery has not been resolved.

Postscript:

The incidents and sightings occurred in private reserves and Kruger Park located in South Africa's Northern Transvaal. Getting true, unexaggerated information was one of the big challenges. Africa is a beautiful place. Nature at its wildest. Safaris are wonderful, but have intrinsic dangers. These events and others signal signal the need for expanded safety measures, better guest education, and improved border controls.

Author's son, Jeff (left), with his 60-pound Mahi Mahi

8

Rarotonga - a South Pacific Gem

Wild Times Somewhere West of Tahiti

Prologue:

My son and I flew to Rarotonga in the South Pacific, the largest of the fifteen islands that comprise the Cook Islands. We were seven hundred miles west of Tahiti and a thousand miles east of Tonga. Rarotonga is mountainous with a dense jungle. White sand beaches and a coral reef create a turquoise lagoon surrounding the island. The Cook Islands were named after Britain's Captain Cook who first visited them in 1773. But long before this, around 1000 BC, they were discovered and colonized by tribal people from Southeast Asia. Today, they are part of a vast 1,600 square mile area in the Pacific Ocean called Polynesia.

Rarotonga, Spring 2000

It was a short drive from our hotel to the trail head where the Cross-Island Track started. There was a small parking lot but no sign—we had been informed there would be a sign. At 8:30 a.m. a guide called Pa was scheduled to meet us; his real name was Papa Teuruaa, meaning "The Son of Polynesia." He was relatively young, had crazy blonde dreadlocks, and knew the jungle. That's what we were told; we hadn't met him yet. His logo showed him holding a machete in one hand and a rope in the other, running with his dreadlocks flying. We were excited to meet him. My son Jeff and I, dressed in shorts and tee shirts, assumed we were the first hikers to arrive. We walked around until 9:30, waiting. No Pa

"What do you think?" I asked Jeff.

"We're either in the wrong place, or Pa forgot about us."

Ahead was a path leading into the green vegetation. "Forget Pa, let's go," I decided. Jeff agreed—he'd wanted to go thirty minutes earlier.

We entered the narrow path. It had heavy vegetation on both sides. Large tropical ferns were thick with black spore clusters under their leaves. Hibiscus trees with twisted roots and white flowers engaged the ferns. We headed into the jungle away from the ocean and the lagoon. It really was a jungle, even without snakes and large animals; instead, big centipedes, spiders and ferocious red ants were chased by lizards and salamanders.

The narrow path didn't go far before becoming a muddy hill ten feet high. Rarotonga was having the wettest rainy season in years. The hill was wet with maroon-colored mud scattered with sparse vegetation—mostly it was a mudslide.

"Dad, do you think we're in the right place?"

"I hope so," I responded, a bit confused. "The guide book said the trail would go downhill and cross a small stream before climbing steeply."

"Well, we'll be climbing steeply without crossing any stream," Jeff noted.

"Let's give it a try," I suggested. "The book showed another path that also lead up a hill and then joined the main path. This could be why we didn't connect with Pa."

"Here's where we could use Pa's rope," Jeff quipped.

Both of us clawed our way up the muddy hill, grabbing tree branches and roots on one side or the other. What saved us were loops in the roots that we could put our feet into while pulling by hand on others. We had been warned about this.

"I'm on top of the hill, Dad."

"How did you get up that fast?" I was halfway up and wishing I had brought a walking stick; I could have used it for leverage. My white tee shirt was already turning maroon from the mud.

"Go more to the right—better roots to grab," Jeff instructed looking down at me. I could see the sprawling, twisted hibiscus branches on the right.

Once up, I caught my breath and we followed the path—if you could call it that. It kept rising steadily; at least it was not a sheer mud-cliff anymore. But the slippery didn't quit; last night's rain had been significant. Without good hiking shoes, we'd still be there! I had to stop and use the saw on my Swiss Army Knife to cut a walking stick from a fallen branch; three legs were better than two in mud. Jeff, at age twenty, was faster and more flexible than his dad. He kept moving ahead while I stopped briefly to smell the white hibiscus flowers above the twisted branches—aromatherapy in the jungle. To me, they smelled like Jasmine tea spiked with honey.

This cross-island trek was turning into more of a challenge than I expected.

"It's very steep again!" Jeff shouted back to me. I had to get down on my knees and pull forward, digging into the mud with the walking stick. The stick was vital. There were no tree branches to grab or root-loops for the feet now, just mud and slippery vegetation.

"This has got to be the tough part!" I exclaimed. The guide book said the first couple of hours would be difficult, and worse after a rain—it was a book I could now believe. An hour went by; bright sun was shining and starting to evaporate the wetness. We had to stop and drink from our water bottles. If necessary, we could drink rainwater that had pooled in large arrow-plant leaves. We continued slipping, sliding, and sloping upward. It was slow going, with Jeff staying ahead of me. It was harder than climbing the higher but drier rock trails in Utah's Canyon Lands National Park, another tough trekking adventure. There, it was rocks crumbling beneath your feet or under a handhold that enhanced the challenge.

I stopped to look around and stood straight up—an improvement from being on my hands and knees. I could no longer hear the surf pounding the reef; we had made some progress. Two small, yellow birds flew from tree to tree above us, something I would normally appreciate when not in a mud circus. Jeff was checking his arms and legs for scrapes and bites, applying tea tree oil to any he found. We took another drink of water then started uphill again; Jeff took the lead.

"It's steep again, but there are roots to hold onto," Jeff observed, doing a good job substituting for Pa. My knees were stressed from having to angle and dig through the mud. Ankles were something to pay attention to; my hiking shoes gave traction but didn't support the ankles much. While climbing in the mud and slippery leaves, I had to imagine that we were on an actual trail and not lost.

Another hour passed and I started to get a second wind, feeling stronger.

Maybe my body had been fighting jet lag. Or my cortisol levels had increased with the unexpected rough start. This is not uncommon; once the mind adjusts to reality, it moderates the stress hormones like cortisol and the false fatigue they create.

It took us a total of two and a half hours to get to high ground where there was a flat area with a large boulder. When we got to the boulder we could see "The Needle," a welcome sight. Called *Te Rua Manga* by the natives, the famous landmark was dramatic and imposing. At thirteen-hundred feet high, the sharp-faced, unobstructed rock pierced straight up through the jungle into the sky. It rose out of a deep valley surrounded by mountains and meant we were halfway through the Cross-Island Track. The most difficult half, we hoped. I felt a touch of accomplishment as I kicked mud off my shoes by the boulder.

At the boulder, we met a young couple from New Zealand who had started from the other end of the trail. I asked them how long it took to get here. They said they'd left the trail head at the waterfall two hours ago and that it was slippery. They didn't like what they heard from us. We were covered with mud so they had no doubts. The girl was looking down at her new trekking clothes and frowning.

We looked at The Needle once more, a quarter mile away and gleaming in the sunshine—a big rock for sure. Looking ahead, there was a signpost.

"Which way do we go Dad?" Jeff asked. He knew I had read the guide book. I would have memorized it had I known Pa wouldn't be with us!

"What does the sign say?" I asked him.

"It just says 'The Needle' and points to it."

"That's cute, like anyone could miss it. Does it point to the trail down?"

"No."

"Which way did the couple come from?"

"Don't know, they were at the boulder when I got there." Jeff had gotten to it before me.

For God's sake, why didn't we ask them directions? I thought.

"It looks like there are two different paths going down," Jeff said. We walked to a "Y" in the path coming from the boulder. One arm went down to the left and one off to the right into flat jungle. We could hear water rushing on the left where a PVC pipe headed down.

"Let's go left and follow that PVC pipe, it should take us to the stream that goes to the waterfall. At least we'll be going down," I suggested, and Jeff agreed. Now that we were in the middle of it, I couldn't believe how mountainous this island was.

We followed the PVC pipe. It started as a well-defined trail. But after about fifteen minutes the pipe turned left and went up a small hill. The rushing water was down and to our right now so we ignored the pipe and went right. It was a nine on the "slippery scale" so I sat down and slid, using the walking stick to guide my descent. It was like sliding on my butt down a Colorado ski hill after falling—a black-diamond hill with moguls. Jeff walked it holding onto various plants, but I got down to the water first!

It was a substantial stream with huge boulders and plenty of rushing water. There was no evidence of a trail. Mini-waterfalls were everywhere in the stream.

"Lost again, Dad!" Jeff declared.

"This stream has to wind up at the waterfall," I asserted.

"Makes sense," Jeff agreed, hopeful. I couldn't recall from the book if there was only one stream. It was about six feet wide and full of rocks. Winding up ankle-deep in the water after winning the race with my son on my rear end slide, it felt refreshingly cool.

"Now you know how hard it rained last night," I reminded Jeff.

"I must have slept through it," he said.

"It poured down in sheets of water, not in raindrops; billions of drops coalesced high in the sky and then fell together in sheets. I couldn't see the ocean from our room's deck. There was minimal lightning and thunder—just massive quantities of falling water." I had been up using the bathroom or I would have missed it, too. It was a powerful South Pacific drenching.

"Well, here's the rain I missed." Jeff smiled, pointing to the water rushing over a large boulder. We slowly followed the stream going downhill, side-stepping and over-stepping wet rocks. It was a winding stream and our forward progress was slow.

"Look here." I pointed at the water.

"Salamanders," Jeff said. Small, brown salamanders were eating red ants that had washed into the water in a calm eddy behind three boulders. The ants were swimming, trying to avoid the aggressive amphibians. Some had even climbed onto the backs of salamanders, likely biting them. These were the ferocious red ants of Rarotonga. The salamanders—snapping at the ants in the water—also tried to eat those that were on the backs of their comrades. Jeff picked one up; it wiggled like it was still swimming and, ignoring Jeff, snapped at an ant on its leg. I didn't need lions or tigers to be impressed by a jungle. I wondered if the New Zealand couple had seen this.

We continued downstream crossing back and forth across the stream whenever the rocks were level on one side. The deepest areas were only a couple of feet deep. Ahead of us, walking upstream, was an older couple coming our way. They were speaking Serbian to each other. Having Slavic ancestors, it was easy for me to recognize the language. I tried English on them.

"Hello!" I called loudly. Both, probably in their sixties, were not looking very happy. They were dressed in long pants and shirts and were wet from the waist down.

"Did you come from the waterfall?" I asked as they got closer. The man shook his head no and put a hand over his mouth, "English no good," he said.

"Waterfall?" Jeff asked, pointing downstream, holding his hands up and curving his fingers over and over. The man nodded his head yes, then pointed into the lush vegetation behind them where there was a trampled down area.

"The trail?" I asked. They both nodded. "How far to waterfall?" I pointed to my watch.

"The man looked at his watch, "*Zwei Stunden,*" he said in German, holding up two fingers.

"Two hours?" I confirmed, holding up two fingers. They both nodded yes. Then they walked in the direction we had come from. When I shouted, and pointed to my watch again, then pointed in their direction—the man shook his head. Apparently, he didn't want to know they had three hours to go.

Lost souls, I thought. *Like us?* Maybe. We knew we would get to the waterfall; just didn't know exactly how, yet.

We had washed most of the mud off each other while sitting on a rock near the salamanders, so we were completely soaked. We had even stripped down to our underpants and washed our clothes in the stream. It was a warm humid day and the cool water felt good. We must have looked scary to the Serbian couple.

We continued the trek—Invigorated by our bath in the stream—heading into the trampled-down ferns where the Serbian man had pointed. The ferns were wet, and as they got thicker, the trampled path disappeared. If the Serbians followed the sound of the stream to find it, we had to do the opposite, go away from the sound.

"Have your compass with you?" Jeff inquired.

"No," was my short answer. I was mad at myself.

"It helped us in Africa," he reminded me.

"My mistake—didn't think we'd need one on this trip, tropical island and all." We were surrounded by ferns waist-deep. It would be easy to walk in a circle and not know it. I took hold of my senses and carefully looked around. Jeff stopped and did the same.

"Here's where we could use Pa's machete!" Jeff deduced. Now we understood his logo: conquering Rarotonga's trails required both ropes and machetes. His dreadlocks were probably optional…

One thing was for sure: we had to head downhill. The ferns were in a flats area. Going back to the stream was not an option. Too many boulders blocked the way to the waterfall. I noticed some differences with the trees in the distance beyond the ferns; there were two stands of several trees that were separated from each other.

"Let's head for that gap between those two stands of trees," Jeff suggested. "At least it will give us something to aim at."

"You took the words out of my mouth, Son. I'll follow you." We pushed the ferns aside using a version of the breaststroke to somewhat clear the way. Water from their wet leaves flew everywhere! We were swimming through them, charging straight ahead toward the gap between the two stands of trees.

I was about twenty yards behind Jeff when he stopped swimming in the ferns and held his arms high, clapping his hands. I swam faster, pushing fern leaves and water away. When I got to him there it was: a defined trail! A sign was posted ten yards further down. Jeff ran to read it.

"What does it say?" I shouted.

"The Needle! And it points downhill." We both laughed out loud! We found the right trail; some comedian had turned the sign 180-degrees.

After another hour on the downward sloping trail—slippery, but controllable, able to walk it standing up—we stopped and took a break. We had refilled our water bottles earlier with rainwater collected in pools on leaves from arrow plants. Both of us took a long rehydrating drink, realizing we should have taken the other arm of the "Y" in the path by the boulder. Looking back, we could see that this trail kept going uphill from where we entered it after swimming out of the fern-ocean.

We continued downward and came to an open area with hundreds of plants showing off yellow-tipped leaves resembling snake plants but with thinner leaves. Large, golden dragonflies were feeding on mosquitoes above the plants. Just beyond, we could hear the waterfall.

We were ecstatic to finally see it! The water came from the mountains, winding its way through rocks and vegetation until it could fall free from twenty feet into a cool, clear pond. We jumped in and swam under the falls—a soul-cleansing swim in fresh rainwater collected in the mountains last night. We didn't want to leave; we had the place to ourselves. Both of us did the backstroke as we watched and listened to the falling water...

Jeff and I both had a strong feeling of accomplishment. Altogether, the adventure had taken five-and-a-half hours. It was more of a challenge than we had anticipated; but we conquered it and the spectacular ending framed it for posterity.

The main road that circled the island was a fifteen-minute walk from the waterfall. When we reached the road, we saw a private home about a quarter mile away. We walked to it hoping somebody would be home so we could call a taxi to take us to our car; we knew hitchhiking was a backup.

There was a man working in the garden. Jeff waved to him as we got closer. Starting with hello, we introduced ourselves to Wayne, whose name was on his shirt above a jumping blue marlin.

Wayne, a robust middle-aged New Zealander, quickly sorted out what had happened to us and was happy to give us a ride to our car on the other side of the island. We were not the first adventure seekers to get lost.

We talked about deep sea fishing on the drive—he was the captain of a charter boat. Wayne was an easy guy to like, courteous and hospitable, like many Kiwis I had worked with in New Zealand. He had moved to "The Cooks" ten years ago.

The next morning, we drove to Avarua, the largest town on Rarotonga and only four miles from our hotel. After passing Trader Jacks where we'd had dinner last night, we parked on the road behind two charter boats. Wayne was in his boat already preparing for the day. He did a convincing job of selling us a fishing charter yesterday. It didn't take much effort to sell me, ocean fishing was on our must-do list for the trip. He smiled when we arrived early and helped us board The Sarah Jane.

His boat was in a slip next to an old remolded tuna boat. He told us a man from California had bought it, cleaned it up, and was taking his family around the world in it.

Wayne's boat was a thirty-two-footer and well equipped with quality fishing tackle. The large Penn International fishing reels on heavy fiberglass rods pleased me. The boat's hull was bright yellow and had an upper deck above an enclosed cabin. A sun awning hung above the upper deck and the boat could be operated from above or below. Everything appeared to be in good repair and was clean and organized. It made me recall the opposite—a grimy old wooden trawler I once got stuck on in Acapulco; it took over a day to get a tow back to the harbor.

Wayne didn't believe in wasting time—we were on the boat and backing out of slip when he introduced us to Ian who had just walked out of the cabin. "He's the best mate on the island!" Wayne said, steering from the lower deck, following the harbor channel out to sea.

"There's only two mates on the island!" Ian replied with a grin.

We moved slowly out of the harbor, then fast until we were two miles north in ten thousand feet of water. Deep water. Ian had been busy getting six lines out. Within twenty minutes of leaving the harbor we were trolling for marlin, but we'd settle for anything big. All lines were rigged with freshly-thawed flying fish; four on outriggers and two on flat lines off the transom. All six baits were splashing on the surface—looking alive.

Jeff and I sat out on the lower deck watching Ian rig more flying fish. He was tying large hooks into the fish with dental floss to keep the hooks from pulling out while trolling. Wayne had switched to steering the boat from the upper deck. All six-flying fish splashed on the surface over the deep water for two hours. The sea was rolling with six to eight-foot swells as the fish flew out then back into the waves as if they were alive. Even when dead, their pectoral fins or "wings" were spread wide by one of Ian's secret techniques that made them look truly authentic. Living flying fish could jump out of the water and glide in the air over 150 feet when it was calm, and as far as thirteen-hundred feet when updrafts provided extra lift. The ones we used for bait were eighteen inches long with green-sparkling backs and white bellies.

"What were those two boats doing with spotlights out beyond the reef last night?" Jeff asked Ian. "We could see them from the dock at Trader Jacks."

"Catching flying fish like I'm rigging here. The lights you saw were on the men's helmets; they scare the fish out of the water. When the fish reenter the water, they get stunned for a few moments and are quickly netted with a long handle net. Those fishermen can bring in two hundred a night; the locals eat them," Ian explained.

"We fish with flying fish in Key West, but nobody eats any—too bony," I said.

"Aye, down here they soak 'em in vinegar to soften the bones. Then deep fry 'em in hot lard and eat the bones with the meat. We fish with flying fish most of the time, they're the best bait," Ian elaborated.

"And always on the surface?" Jeff asked.

"Always. A thousand-pound marlin will hit a one-pound flying fish on the surface! The marlin prefers to eat a stunned fish; it takes less energy. When a marlin follows a bait, Wayne often slows down to simulate a stunned fish, then speeds up and slows again. It depends on what the sea is doing. The sea has a soul, you know!" Ian had a wise expression on his face.

Wayne spoke on the intercom and told us he was going to turn toward shore and find the drop-off where five-thousand feet became five-hundred feet. "I don't see much on the sonar out here."

The sea was still ten-thousand feet deep under the boat, so as Wayne headed for shore the depth gradually rose to five-thousand feet. At this depth, he watched the sonar for a shelf that came up quickly to a depth of five-hundred feet. Then he turned and ran parallel to the island, trolling the baits over this sharp change in depth. Schools of bait fish often suspended around such drop offs, becoming easy targets for big predators—like marlin!

When shore was about a mile away we passed a large patch of floating weeds. Wayne steered the boat so the starboard side baits came close to the weed line.

"*Wham, Wham, Wham!*" A starboard outrigger rod bent and pounded, Ian got over to it in seconds, pulling it out of the rod holder, pushing the drag lever forward on the reel, and then pumping the rod to set the hook. With the hook set, he quickly reset the drag lever back to the fighting position. Jeff had been sitting in the fighting chair when Ian handed him the rod while placing its butt end into the swivel cup on the chair.

"Hold on tight—let the fish run," Ian told Jeff. Line raced off the reel. Wayne kept the boat steady in the swells, stern toward the fish, as Ian reeled in the other outrigger lines. I reeled in the two flat lines off the back—necessary to keep these lines from tangling with the fish. Fast action for all of us.

"Big mahi!" Ian yelled as the fish jumped. Its brilliant, turquoise iridescence was unmistakable! It was the same in all oceans: Blue-green on top, yellow on the belly and tail. It was called a dolphin fish in Florida and a dorado in Mexico. This was a big male.

No other fish looked like this. Jeff was alone with the mahi, pumping it up with the rod, then down to reel line in. He kept the line even on the reel with his left thumb. When the fish took line out fast, he didn't crank, when the line slowed down, he started pumping and cranking again.

"He knows what he's doing." Ian seemed impressed.

"This isn't his first fishing rodeo," I said, proud of my kid. Then suddenly, the fish turned toward the boat and swam at it. Jeff had to reel fast to get line in without giving the fish slack. This was a critical time when a fish could get off the hook. When it was about fifty yards out, it did a full 360-degree flip and came completely out of the water.

"Bow the rod to him!" I yelled. This is when you must give line to a fish—when it jumps—or the extra tension created by the jump can allow a fish to throw the hook. Jeff knew this and was doing it. The fish had its body sideways to the boat, making it feel extra heavy. Jeff pumped the fish rhythmically for ten minutes, gaining about half the line back. Then the fish picked up speed and took line back out.

"Big Bull Mahi," Wayne said once he got a good look at it. The fish was an electric turquoise now.

"It's a fifty-pounder!" Wayne said loudly. "One of the largest I've seen this year." The mahi pulled hard sideways for another five minutes. Jeff, able to get line in with extra effort, had his arm and shoulder muscles working hard. The fish was tall in front and more tapered toward the tail, more so than most other fish, so when it turned sideways it felt like two fish were on the line with the extra resistance! When the fish got near the boat, it began swirling in circles, emitting bright turquoise flashes.

Ian had the long gaff ready—a six-inch-wide cadmium-plated hook on a pole. He was in the port corner at the back of the boat. Jeff stayed in the fighting chair, keeping medium pressure on the fish. Ian missed with the first swipe of the gaff. "Aim below the front end of the dorsal fin!" Wayne yelled to him. Ian got it on the next swipe, quickly lifting it up over the gunnel and into the boat.

The fish jumped off the gaff and went wild. "Keep your legs off the floor!" I yelled to Jeff. The mahi was still hooked and flipping circles in the boat—a dangerous time with any big fish. Jeff was kneeling on the fighting chair—I was halfway up the ladder to the upper deck. Ian was in the middle of the action behind the fighting chair, swinging a wood club at the jumping fish—like a baseball player trying to hit a fast, rotating curve ball—he missed it three times before scoring with a direct hit. And that was it.

The fish was big; five feet long. We got good photos of Jeff holding it before its color faded. Then we laid it flat on a hundred pounds of ice in a large cooler with its yellow tail hanging out. Wayne turned the boat around and started back on course at trolling speed—seven miles per hour. Ian reset the outrigger lines with fresh flying fish; I did the same for the two stern lines. Then it was back to fishing—I sat down in the fighting chair.

"Trader Jacks could make two hundred fish sandwiches from that mahi," Ian declared. "Brilliant job, Jeffrey!"

"Thanks for your skilled assistance," Jeff replied, smiling big.

"I reckon Ian needs practice with the old club," Wayne shouted down from the upper deck, laughing. Jeff and I laughed too.

"Excuse me, Mr. Captain, Sir. There's no limit to the number of misses in cricket, only that I eventually make a hit," Ian quipped. "It's not like baseball!"

Trolling for big fish in the ocean gives a man time to think. Meeting Wayne was no coincidence. Had we gone to the correct parking lot and met Pa the day before, we would have missed Wayne; Pa would have arranged transportation back to our car.

Once again, as many times in the past, opportunity presented itself and our frequencies harmonized—good vibes prevailed. I called it Soul Steering. Shamans in the Amazon knew there were no coincidences. Promoting positive experience required steering. I knew we would have a good day fishing. Now it was my turn…

"I was sitting in the fighting chair when Wayne yelled down: "We're showing mean fish at 1,500 feet over 5,000 feet of water" Mean translated to awesome in Kiwi.

Jeff went up top to look at the sonar screen, it read the depth at 5,200 feet. The fish, V-shaped on the screen looking like birds flying, were congregated between 1,400 to 1,600 feet deep, well off the bottom but nowhere near the surface! Wayne didn't know what they were, tuna maybe. Periodically, a large V-shape would appear around fifteen feet deep—big predator fish? We trolled for an hour, running parallel to the island; north to south, then turned east. We could clearly see the surf breaking on the reef that formed the lagoon around Rarotonga. Ian reached into the beverage cooler and brought out two Steinlager beers from New Zealand and presented them to Jeff as a prize. "You might want to share one with your Dad, he's been skunked so far." Ian whispered, deploying some Kiwi humor. Both Jeff and I relaxed, thinking about his big mahi over a brew.

The sky was blue and the only clouds were in a line along the far western horizon. They looked like whipped cream; an inch high at arm's length. "Rain again tonight," Ian predicted. Another hour went by. The wind had shifted and it was calmer now. Wayne put on an Eagles' CD.

We were in the middle of the South Pacific, as close to the middle of nowhere as you could be, listening to *Take it to The Limit One More Time.* The pointed mountains of Rarotonga were completely green with tall coconut palms lining the beaches in front of them. The sand was golden in the sun, highlighting the absence of any activity. *This was Hawaii a hundred years ago,* I thought.

These islands were as far south of the equator as Hawaii was north of it. Rarotonga, at twenty-six square miles and a population of eleven thousand, was the largest of the Cook Islands. It was just behind us now as we trolled east toward Tahiti.

"We saw a blue whale right about here, two weeks ago, Ian said. "Huge."

"Largest animal on the planet," I said. "Did you ever see..."

"*Wham, Wham!*" the rod in front of me buckled and line raced off its reel. I quickly grabbed it and pushed the drag lever forward, pulling hard two times to set the hook. Then I reset the drag for the fight and put the rod's butt end into the swivel cup in the crotch of the fighting chair. The fish took line out and raced west, straight out from the back of the boat.

"This is a bullet fish!" I shouted. Ian came over and checked the drag position, making sure it was reset correctly. I held the rod at forty-five degrees and didn't reel for at least ten minutes while line was speeding out. The reel's drag was giving line perfectly.

"You gotta love those Penn reels," Ian said, standing by me. "The new ones run as smooth as silk polishing a crystal ball." The rod had a good bend to it. This fish was a living torpedo, pure muscle. "It's a nice wahoo, great eating."

"A nice ono in Hawaii," I said, excitedly. Ono meant sweet and good to eat in Hawaiian.

The rod pounded hard meaning the fish was shaking his head as he swam.

"*Wa-Hoo!*" Jeff yelled out at the top of his voice, celebrating how the fish got its name. Jeff had never liked calling a wahoo an ono. It was a long, sleek, silver-blue torpedo, a major predator in tropical waters.

"Let him run, he can go a long way! They're able to swim fifty miles an hour and weigh up to two hundred pounds!"

Wayne shouted down. He had slowed the boat to limit putting extra pressure on the fish. "This is a mean one!"

"Wahoo have razor sharp bones in their mouth instead of teeth—if they get slack they can turn and bite any leader off," Ian reminded me.

The fish kept bolting out to sea. What endurance it had. After another ten minutes at full speed, I could feel he was starting to slow. I started pumping the rod to try and turn him, but line kept going out. All the action so far had been straight out from the back of the boat—mostly just me holding the rod and letting the fish zing-out line.

"This fish is heading to Tonga," Jeff informed us.

"He's got a thousand miles of open ocean to go," Ian reminded him.

"Should I tighten the drag a bit?" I asked Ian.

"No!" was his short answer.

"When he turns, he's either gonna come racing at us or go sideways," Ian explained. "Reel like hell if he comes at us." The fish took out more line and was back to full speed. Wayne adjusted the boat to keep the fish at the stern. I just had to keep the line tight; couldn't imagine what it would have been like to catch such a fish three thousand years ago—it would have fed an entire tribe of the first Polynesians. They had to settle for spearing small fish with sharpened bamboo in the lagoon. Humans have changed significantly since then, but not these fish! Wahoo were fully evolved well before any human souls found this place. I had caught several ono in Hawaii, but not one this big.

"I hope he stops before Tonga or we'll run out of line," I joked." There were about four-hundred yards of 130-pound monofilament remaining on the spool. I was pumping with the rod and getting line back sporadically. After another fifteen minutes of pumping and reeling, the fish made a sweeping turn and came directly at the boat. He wasn't feeling resistance anymore—he was charging the boat at full speed.

"Reel like hells on fire!" The captain yelled down.

I reeled and guided the line onto the reel's spool as fast as I could—my right arm was a spinning blur. My left thumb was bleeding from guiding line. I had two football fields of line to reel in.

"He seems to be hooked well," Ian said, using binoculars. I was excited to get this guy in the boat.

The wahoo hit solidly above the boat's propeller with a loud thud. We were all astounded. He had attacked the boat!

"That fish is mad at us! Enraged!" Ian yelled as he grabbed the long gaff.

"He hit the boat trying to kill it!" Jeff exclaimed. The fish was still very much alive and swimming in a circle at the back of the boat. It was snapping its razor-sharp jaws at the leader. I stood up and held the rod high to keep pressure on the fish while guiding it toward Ian. *Could this fish be intelligent enough to be mad?* I wondered.

"Heads up everybody, this guy can bite!" I yelled out, as I guided the fish toward Ian.

Ian was ready with the gaff. "Got to be careful with this one!" he yelled from the port corner of the boat. Then he reached deep in the water with the gaff, pulling up fast and gaffing the fish a foot in front of its tail, not the best place. With the gaff, deep in the fish's flesh, Ian hauled it out of the water straight up over the gunnel and into the boat.

It flew off the gaff instantly and went crazy like the mahi. But this guy could take a foot or hand off, or worse. Jeff was up top with Wayne. I kneeled on the fighting chair, holding a seat cushion in front of me. Ian was swinging a longer club, an aluminum baseball bat! With the wahoo flipping and snapping, he hit it square on the head in midair on his second swing, and then again after it hit the floor.

"Seventy-pounder," Ian said, "Wahoo!" The fish was six feet long, metallic blue on top, silver below with vertical lavender bars along its length. It just fit into the cooler with the mahi—two tails were hanging out now.

"Nice job with boat control, Wayne!" I shouted up to him. Then I saluted Ian: "You looked like Mickey Mantle in the World Series!"

"Thanks—nice job getting that fish!" Wayne shouted back. "I reckon Ian needs to give up cricket and switch to baseball!

Back at the dock, Ian cleaned the fish. Both were considered outstanding table fare, and there were monster slabs of boneless fish meat. We asked Wayne if we could donate them. He immediately said "Yes—not a problem." We'll call the city office in Avarua tomorrow; they will take care of getting the meat to the needy. Trader Jacks has a big freezer; the fish will be hard as rocks by morning."

We had done this on other trips when it was impractical to ship the meat home. I was happy they would arrange the details. We paid Wayne and gave Ian his tip.

"Until next time!" Ian said, bloody from cleaning the fish.

"Thanks for getting lost hiking across the island," Wayne added. "It's *All Good.*"

Everyone was smiling as we waved goodbye while walking to the car. I felt good about the day—we'd had a great adventure catching fish that would help provide nutrition for needy locals. Jobs in Rarotonga were scarce if not connected to tourism.

We drove back to the Edgewater Hotel and cleaned up. All we'd had for lunch was the beer, peanuts, and a deli ham sandwich that we brought on board, so we were hungry. It would be a special night at the hotel, with dinner served outside under the stars along with genuine Cook Islands entertainment. It appeared Ian's rain forecast would not happen—the whipped-cream clouds on the western horizon had disappeared.

The Edgewater Hotel was in the northwest corner of Rarotonga. From our room, standing on the deck, we faced west. The reef, with surf constantly breaking on it, was two-hundred yards out from the beach. The constant drumming of the waves was hypnotic. At night, Orion was lying on his side near the northern horizon and the Southern Cross was high above. For pre-dinner entertainment, my son serenaded the ocean with a ukulele I'd bought him on our first day.

For two hungry fishermen, the buffet was exceptionally inviting: a twenty-pound tuna had been lightly seared and laid out on banana leaves; barbequed pulled pork prepared island-style smelled terrific; tantalizing baby lobsters had been skewered with local onions; marinated mahi was bathed in coconut sauce *and fresh memories;* local sweet potatoes were topped with melted marshmallows; Polynesian coleslaw was tossed with papaya and mango; and local veggies on the salad bar looked fabulous. Most of those dining were older, European hotel guests. I could hear bits of German, Dutch and French. Americans were in short supply.

Immediately after dinner, the entertainment began. We had dined outside with the ocean in the background and the performers between us and the ocean.

Shirtless young men with red flowers woven into palm leaves around their heads wore white seashell skirts with banana leaves. They started playing long drums that lay horizontally on the ground, synchronizing their beats with each other and the pounding surf behind them. Young ladies wore pink-flower head-wreaths with black bikini tops and carmine-red garland skirts. The dancing—"ura" as the natives called it—was high energy, much faster than the hula in Hawaii. It started with the ladies swirling in circles before the men joined in. They wove in and out between each other and began singing in Rarotongan, the Cook Island's version of Maori: *Tane and vaine, tane and vaine, ura, ura, ura.* Translated: *Men, and women, men and women, to dance, to dance, to dance.* It was special; we were watching the evolution of young Polynesian souls in the new millennium.

After the singing and dancing, Jeff and I took a walk on the beach. For being the rainy season, it was a clear night. The rainy season in the South Pacific was only slightly wetter than the dry season; the rain comes and goes all the time. The sand was moist in front of the calm lagoon where small fish were jumping and eating insects.

Tomorrow would be our snorkeling day. Coral heads were right offshore in the lagoon and easy to find. They provided shelter and food for multi-colored reef fish—nature's aquarium.

We ate a tropical breakfast: scrambled eggs with mahi accompanied by sweet local bananas, papaya, local bread, and Kona coffee.

"This coffee is from three thousand miles north," I remarked.

"Big ocean," Jeff replied.

"They don't make 'em any bigger," The waiter said; he had heard us as he refilled our coffee cups. He was a young New Zealander.

"How long have you been working up here?" I asked him. The Cooks were north of New Zealand.

"Just since January—summertime in New Zealand. I'm back to school later this month."

"What are you studying?" Jeff inquired.

"Oceanography."

"Plenty of that down here," I noted.

"Yes sir, there is! My name's Ian, I'm from Auckland."

"Our mate on the charter boat yesterday was an Ian," I remarked.

"That was my Dad! I'm a junior."

"Small world," I said.

"Big Ocean," Jeff added.

Ian was free to talk as most other guests had eaten already. I had been to New Zealand on business, so it was interesting to talk to young Ian. He gave us specific instructions on where to go snorkeling. The best spot: a fish sanctuary!

"He told us it was across the road from a shop called The Fruits of Rarotonga," I repeated to Jeff.

"I heard it, Dad," Jeff reminded me he could still hear. Redundancy was a habit of mine that usually was unnecessary. But it may have saved me a couple of times.

"Just want to be sure," I confirmed. "I don't want you to miss the best snorkeling the South Pacific has to offer!"

With Jeff driving the rental car, we turned right, leaving the hotel heading south about eight miles. We found the fruit shop and parked across from it. There was a shallow area in the lagoon called *Raui* by the locals. It meant: "Not to be touched." We were just ahead of a sign that read: "Fish Sanctuary. Take No Fish. Only Observe."

"Thanks Ian!" Jeff said out loud.

The water was eighty-two degrees and clear, the tide was out. We could see the coral heads off-shore; all were an easy swim away. I spread a large towel on the beach. We sat on it and put our snorkeling equipment on. I had brought high-quality masks and fins from home for both of us—I never trusted rentals. Nothing's worse than a leaky mask or loose fins! It was always worth the effort to bring them along.

There was a slight haze to the water from the pounding surf, but less than when the tide was in. The lagoon was five to fifteen feet deep where the best coral could be found; twenty feet maximum near the reef. It was important to start snorkeling where it was shallow and go slowly—starting around three feet deep—then head deeper when you could clearly see the bottom. This was to avoid stepping on stonefish. They warned us about them at the Scuba Diving Center in Avarua the first day. Stonefish are poisonous and perfectly camouflaged, looking like an encrusted rock or a lump of coral. They're brown or gray with red or yellow spots and mostly stay on the bottom. These fish are native to the Indo-Pacific and can kill you. They sting with spines in their dorsal fins that inject a potent neurotoxin. You don't want to step on one! The hospital in Avarua always has anti-venom on hand, and you need to get to it fast if stung. Hot water helps destroy the venom and can be used as first aid; vinegar reduces the pain. But anti-venom is a must.

We got to the first large coral head in about eight feet of water. The diversity of fish was amazing. Hugging the bottom was a huge blue starfish at least three feet in diameter! Jeff saw it first. This was the largest starfish I'd ever seen. It moved slowly, probably looking for a dead fish to eat. We treaded water for several minutes watching it.

Right at the surface, just beyond the starfish, we saw long, thin trumpet fish, colored yellow with flashes of silver. Their mouth was one-fourth the length of their body! If you unwound a brass trumpet and laid it out flat, you would have a facsimile of a trumpet fish—well, almost.

Trumpet fish are ambush-hunters, waiting to eat small fish that leave the protective folds in the coral below. They suspended near the surface, moving only if we got close. When I pointed at them they moved a foot or two.

Two large Moorish idols, shaped like angel fish, were feeding below us. Brilliant yellow with black stripes, long snouts, and streaming dorsal fins; they swam around purple coral humps, pulling their snouts in and out of crevices while probing for food. A Picasso triggerfish followed behind the idols. It had a light blue head and lips, a dark blue band beyond its head, a red spot above its pectoral fins, and a golden-yellow triangle pointing in from its tail—like it had been splashed with a rainbow of paint. Indeed, nature got help from Picasso when designing this fish. It made me think of the Hawaiian name for trigger fish: *Humuhumunukunukuapua'a.* There is a restaurant in Maui that will give you a free drink if you can pronounce it!

Jeff was swimming ahead of me and had just made a surface dive to one of the coral heads. We were in fifteen feet of water. I snorkeled above him looking down—he was pointing to something behind the coral head. I swam forward and saw it—a giant parrot fish at least four feet long! This was the largest parrot fish I'd seen in all my years of Scuba diving and snorkeling.

The parrot fish was a fluorescent blue and green, punctuated by its red lip. Jeff was far enough away so he didn't disturb it. The fish was eating coral, biting chunks off, and crushing them in its jaws. Then separating its food—the organic polyps—from the calcium carbonate frame of the coral. Carbonate dust blew out its gills as it ate. This guy had a mouth that could crush rocks—coral was the same as the mineral calcite.

Jeff came up and cleared his snorkel, blowing hard to get the water out. We continued making numerous sightings of tropical reef fish, an ichthyologist's dream. Their pictures and names were all on a waterproof Mylar card back on the beach towel. We turned toward the reef as a school of Crevalle jacks—big, powerful twenty-pounders—swam under us. I felt for my diver's knife in a sheath on my left ankle, double checking it was there.

Jeff would surface-dive deep to investigate strange animals and wave me down if he saw something unusual; hoping for a big octopus. We were snorkeling on the surface over twenty feet of water not far from the reef. As the fish got bigger over deeper water, the thought of sharks entered my mind. We'd had a good swim, but it was time for dad to go in—my favorite son (my only son!) was now my favorite guide. I followed him to the beach. No stonefish were sighted!

We had a late lunch at Trader Jacks—we liked the place. After lunch, we had time to do some relaxing, look around the tourist shops and take a slow drive around the island. There were locals selling seashells that I wanted to look at. Unusual specimens. Also, it was enjoyable to have discussions with the locals; many were transplants from New Zealand like Wayne and Ian.

We finally ran into Pa at Trader Jacks! It was my fault we didn't connect with him for our trek across the island. We did start out in the wrong place! A half mile away was the correct trail, the one with a sign in the parking lot. Pa was amazed we made it to the needle going the wrong way...

Western Wall in Jerusalem

9

Conundrums in Jerusalem

Walls That Divide

Prologue:

For over sixteen centuries Jews have been praying in front of the Western Wall in Jerusalem. Slips of paper, prayers, and holy notes are stuck into crevices between the blocks; plants grow out of other separations such as the magical and poisonous Henbane with its yellow flowers. Standing, facing The Wall, men dressed in long black coats, black hats, and black beards, pray. Some pray louder than others. It's the Wailing Wall to them, their Kotel. Behind it is the Temple Mount, the holiest of holies in Judaism; where Jews believe God found the clay to make Adam. There's a famous tradition among Orthodox Jews: Pray daily at The Wall for forty days for a single request, and your request will be granted. Moses prayed for forty days at Mount Sinai, obtaining direction from God for the Ten Commandments.

The Western Wall supports the west bank of the Temple Mount. Massive cubical blocks of limestone comprise the ancient wall, built twenty years before the birth of Christ. What you see today is one-eighth of the original wall, terraced slightly to add strength.

The Wall's blocks show great age—some are dislodged enough to hold bird nests. Brown and amber colored blocks alternate with ivory and gray but show golden yellow on clear days in the setting sun.

Behind The Wall is the Muslim Quarter. Ever since the Six-Day war in 1967, when Israel won control of East Jerusalem from Jordan, there has been sporadic terrorist activity at The Wall and the plaza west of it. Prior to that, what is now the Western Wall Plaza was a labyrinth of narrow alleyways between poorly constructed buildings.

Under Jordanian rule, slum conditions developed, and Jews were harassed and charged to pray in a small thirty-meter section. The Israeli army, after defeating attacks by Jordanian forces, bulldozed the slum area—known as the Moroccan Quarter—exposing The Wall, creating the open plaza, and allowing anyone to pray for free. In 1968 Israel compensated the Arab people who had been displaced and helped them relocate.

The Western Wall area is sacred to three religions. For the Jews, it's where the world began and where Abraham bound his son Isaac. For Muslims, it's where Mohammed ascended to heaven. And for Christians, it's where Jesus spent the last weeks of his life. It has been a focal point of religious disputes for centuries.

Israel, 2002

The police—two men and two women in blue uniforms—quickly formed a semicircle in the center of the plaza, facing The Wall. They knelt and aimed their semi-automatic pistols at The Wall, just below the men standing on top of it. These men, heads covered in black cloth, were throwing bricks and stones straight down at the men praying. One of the men praying was hit by a brick on the side of his head. He stumbled to his knees, rubbed his head where it was bleeding, put his prayer book under his coat to keep the blood off, then stood straight up and went back to The Wall to pray. Most of the others praying did not move; they kept praying, but with louder voices.

Army soldiers in olive green materialized fast and began taking positions behind the police, standing and aiming their automatic rifles high on The Wall. "Fire at their feet!" the captain ordered his soldiers in Hebrew. Rapid automatic fire ensued and we could see the brick throwers jumping to avoid bullets. Some bullets hit the top edge of The Wall, throwing dust and making cavities in the ancient limestone.

I was astonished; it was surreal. I ducked down on one knee, ready to run somewhere. But where? I instantly became totally aware, looking at the frightened people around me. *Brat-tat-tat, brat-tat-tat,* more gun fire...

"*Rubber bullets*!" An older lady shouted to me. She was huddled down with the tour group under a stone arch, up a stairway, and to the left of The Wall. I got down on both knees and started talking to her. I had forgotten I was in the tour group! My brain was doing strange things. . .

People down in the plaza were running in different directions. Several tour groups took cover under other arches. Each tour guide held up a flag with a number on it designating their group. The older lady and I were in group five.

"Be calm everyone, the Israeli Defense Force and the police have things under control!" Abbie, our tour guide, yelled out. More automatic fire erupted; the police did not shoot, only the army. Two younger women in our group started screaming. Abbie, holding her flag high, moved over to them, hugging them. Abbie was a young, attractive Jewish girl who grew up in Tel Aviv. She spoke several languages and was a superb tour guide.

Hoping Abbie was right about the situation being under control, I said to the older lady, "I'm Stanley from Minneapolis."

"And, I'm Jill from London," she said. "You're an American lad for sure! First trip to Israel?"

"Second. And you're a Brit for sure."

"That I am, for seventy-two years..." A loud explosion interrupted her. We could feel the vibration and see smoke behind us near the Jaffa Gate. Everyone covered their heads. The two younger women screamed again. A different group of soldiers in brown uniforms was standing out from where the explosion occurred. The entire tour group was frightened—that was the gate where we had entered the plaza. Abbie was listening on her VHF radio.

"It was a controlled explosion!! Supervised by the IDF bomb squad. Somebody left a shoulder bag unattended. The IDF blew it up!" Abbie told us.

"Standard Operating Procedure: Leave a bag alone, boom, it's gone," Jill said.

"Wow, this is intense!" I could smell the unmistakable odor of detonated nitro-explosive. Jill, a dedicated Catholic, had been to Israel often. She felt more at home here than in London. I appreciated her comments, they provided additional understanding. She told me to look up at a yeshiva outside the plaza; I could see six large glass pillars filled with fire burning on water and topped with metallic Stars of David.

"Each one of those represents one million Jews killed during Hitler's Third Reich in World War II," Jill explained. "These pillars are controversial; the liberal Left in Israel hates them. The conservative Right sees them as fitting reminders of the holocaust."

The masked Arab men had disappeared from the top of The Wall. I hoped their feet hurt like hell. Senseless terror! The explosion had blown up a lady's shoulder bag filled with brightly colored cosmetics, creating red, blue and purple chips of concrete that penetrated the containment barriers the soldiers had brought to surround the bag. The blue police and green soldiers conferred in small groups while their commanders talked on radios. The plaza was empty except for them. After the soldiers gave the signal, the tour groups recomposed and returned to the open plaza. Abbie took control of ours.

"Let's go back to The Wall one more time," Jill said to Abbie.

"Jill wants to go to The Wall one more time—is that okay with everyone?" Abbie pointed to The Wall about fifty meters away. Everyone agreed.

"When Jesus walked past this Wall, he was thirty-three years old and The Wall was fifty-two." Jill spoke to everyone, providing perspective. Israeli police were close, watching The Wall, so we stayed back. Looking up at the top of The Wall, I saw nobody. Straight ahead, I could see the same Orthodox Jews still praying, including the one hit by the brick. Above them were several small lizards running around. *Holy lizards*? I wondered.

And above the lizards were swallow nests with baby birds. I was glad we came back a second time.

Next on the tour was the Christian Quarter. This was my first time, and Jill was excited about being here again. We walked out of the plaza through the now-calm Jaffa Gate and onto David Street, a narrow alleyway with flower shops and religious stores. It continued east to Muristan Road, which we took north to Souk El-Dabbagha and then to the Church of the Holy Sepulchre. Old Jerusalem, open to the world, surrounded us as we stood in the courtyard of the church.

"This church, with its chapels and shrines, commemorates the Crucifixion and burial of Jesus Christ. Within it and next to it is the site of Calvary, where Christ was crucified," Abbie explained. "Its two blue-gray domes are behind what looks more like a castle than a church."

Patchy patterns reflected its age, from the light sandiness of the tower, to darker shades matching those of the Western Wall. Cubical stone construction with arched, barred windows was used. There had been an obvious need for security.

"You just have to stare at it awhile—feel its age and history—before going in," Jill said. "This is where Christ was crucified, buried, and resurrected."

This church of the Holy Sepulchre, like all of Jerusalem, had experienced much torment and destruction over sixteen centuries. It was built by the Roman emperor Constantine around AD 330, rebuilt after its destruction by the Sultan Hakim in 1009, restored by the Catholic Church after the Crusades, then a disastrous fire in 1808 and an earthquake in 1927. Quite a history.

Upon entering the church, we were directed to Stone of Unction, or Stone of Anointing. This, it is believed, was where Christ's body was anointed and wrapped after His death. The stone we were looking at dated from 1810, replacing the original that had been destroyed in the fire. Its *location* was holy! The tour group surrounded it. Jill and two other women knelt, made the sign of the cross, and kissed the gray limestone rectangle—red and orange with discolorations and worn smooth from kissing and touching. The rest of us touched it before moving on, reminding me of people kissing the foot of Saint Peter's statue in his basilica in Rome, which was also worn smooth from being kissed and touched.

We moved away from the Stone of Unction with Abbie guiding us to the Greek Orthodox altar where, under glass, was an outcropping of rock believed to be from the site of the Crucifixion. It was noisy and crowded, not quiet and somber as one might expect. We had to wait our turn to see it as there were many guides holding up flags...

"Abbie, please tell everyone how the Jewish people view Christ," Jill asked. "Us Christians believe He was the Son of God."

"Many Rabbis believe that Jesus was a special person; not the son of God, but an enlightened person who provided a good example for how to live a holy life. He is called Yeshu in Hebrew." Abbie explained.

"There has been much debate about this. Modern Rabbis appreciate the significance of Jesus," a young man wearing a yarmulke (skullcap) said.

"It comes down to whether you accept the New Testament or the Old Testament." A man wearing a Chicago Cubs hat joined the conversation. "New is for Christians, Old for Jews." The tour group was becoming animated.

"It really comes down to faith and holding true to your beliefs; you've got to *believe,*" Jill said. "We may regard certain details differently, but we all believe in salvation through God." I found Jill, as a dedicated Catholic, surprisingly open- minded.

"But many of us believe quite differently from what you believe. We don't believe in the trinity or communion." A Jewish lady from New York joined the discussion.

"There was a time in Sunday school in the 1950s when the nuns told us you had to be Catholic to go to heaven. Other Christian faiths didn't qualify," the man wearing the Cubs hat said. "I felt really sad for my Lutheran friends back then!"

"And eating meat on Friday was a mortal sin, equal to killing somebody!" A woman in sunglasses exclaimed. "But fish were okay to eat. Some Pope declared it a sin to help Italy's fishing industry. Martin Luther cleared things up."

"Many things have changed," Jill said. "The Catholic church has stopped teaching most non-scriptural commands and now follows New Testament scripture as a priority."

"Not completely," the woman in sunglasses said. "Catholics still believe in Purgatory and that you have to be baptized to go to heaven. And then, there's limbo for babies who die before being baptized. What kind of nonsense is that?"

"What faith are you?" The young man wearing the yarmulke asked her. He was Jewish, visiting from Brooklyn.

"I'm Lutheran, Christian of course." she answered, and took her sunglasses off to look at him. He was tall with thin arms and legs and had a pale complexion, and emanated a certain sincerity.

"But I have Lutheran friends, and they're baptized. We never discussed purgatory." Jill was thoughtful.

"Sure, but Lutherans are taught that baptism is not an absolute requirement to get to heaven. Finding faith in God through Jesus is the priority," the woman answered, holding her sunglasses.

The man in the Cubs hat spoke up: "Regarding purgatory; we've been taught that it's where you pay off debts for sins that were forgiven but not enough penance was done. Also, if you died with only venial sins that were unforgiven, no problem, you just went to Purgatory for a while, then off to heaven. If you had unforgiven mortal sins, forget it, you went straight to hell. I'm Catholic and this is what they taught us in Sunday school."

"Do you believe it?" The young man wearing the yarmulke asked him.

"Not really, I mainly believe in the Ten Commandments."

"Then you are Jewish like me! Mosses was one hundred percent Jewish and God gave him the Commandments." Everyone laughed. "And what's a venial sin if I may ask?"

"Some nonsensical infraction, like swearing!" A stately, gray-haired man declared, beating the Cubs-hat man to an answer.

"There's nothing in Scripture that mentions purgatory or limbo that I know of. We Lutherans believe you go directly either to heaven or hell when you die. There are no intermediate stops," the woman said, interrupting the levity while putting her sunglasses back on.

"And many Catholics still believe that when you're dead, you're dead until the last judgement," The Cubs fan added. "I don't believe it, but I was taught it."

"That's not a point of emphasis in American dioceses anymore. The modern Vatican realizes it has been ambiguous on many topics. Once again, let Scripture rule," Jill said. "Many priests teach that your soul is judged when you die."

"Look at some of the craziness in Judaism, like not eating pork because it's dirty and unholy. That only made sense before we learned to cook it enough to kill the parasites!" A yet-unheard-from-woman exclaimed.

"That craziness depends on how orthodox you are! I have friends who go to the synagogue every Saturday, and then go have a BLT for lunch!" The Jewish lady from New York said.

"They're a lot like me," the Cubs fan said. "Where I'm half Catholic, your friends are half Jewish!" There was more laughter.

I was in a state of total amazement. *Where else in the world could you have this discussion?* I wondered. *We're now talking about degrees of Catholicism and Jewish Orthodoxy!* That's a bit like arguing you're only partially pregnant, but refreshing nevertheless. The world has certainly changed from my bubble-gum days.

Standing next to Abbie, who was watching for our turn to go to the altar, I could tell she would continue to stay out of the conversation. I had been mostly listening, fascinated by the civility of how things were going. I was trying to think of something to say that might add meaning. Then it hit me…

"Who was it that said: 'God is a comedian playing to an audience that's afraid to laugh?'" I asked, but couldn't remember the philosopher. I knew it wasn't George Burns.

"Voltaire!" The young man wearing the yarmulke said. "And it's "*too* afraid to laugh."

"Thanks for the correction," I said. "Smart man."

The conversation went on until it was our turn to view the rock outcropping and the altar. Our tour group had a remarkable diversity of individuals; I was impressed with them. It was an interesting example of how to dialogue on different beliefs. Abbie, holding flag number five, led the way through the crowds.

We viewed the altar and the outcropping relic. Jill took the most time looking at it; it was certainly something to ponder and respect. For Christians, it was very real and holy.

Inside the church, it had the feel of an old castle rather than a cathedral. One had to consider its age and all the disasters it had survived. The walls, unlike outside, were clean and warmly lit. We climbed stairs that brought us to the Tomb of Jesus Christ. There was a polished marble slab that covered the original stone that he had been laid out on before burial. We all touched the marble slab, even the Jewish people. The burial site was close by.

"Do you believe in Jesus?" Jill asked me.

"I've been up and down on it my whole life. Today I do, twenty years ago, I didn't."

"What changed your mind?"

"Once I saw hard evidence of the other side, the spiritual dimensions, with good fighting evil, just like we saw here today at The Wall, then I knew there had to be supreme guidance for balance, and Jesus beat all his competitors for my vote. I reasoned that where there's evil, there must be good. Or everything would be evil and totally out of balance. Good translates to Jesus."

"What was some of the evidence, if I can ask?"

"Proof of demonic possession and that exorcism works; verified electronic communications and video evidence of spirits; young children who had near death experiences and, after revival, could tell information they had no way of knowing before, like passwords, combinations for safes and locations of hidden valuables. Conversations with authentic mediums that reveal previously unknown information; and, personally, from shamans I've met in the Amazon and Belize who could summon spirits, levitate objects, and confirm that good and evil spirits exist. It has been a project to sort this out. There is much bogus information; strict vetting is required. There's order and disorder in the complex spirit world, as there is here in the physical world. The arrival of Jesus to bring hope for our salvation amidst such chaos makes the most sense. He died for our sins but also to qualify for our faith in him. We all suffer in our lives; some more than others, but everyone suffers. As Hemingway said: 'All stories told long enough end badly.' Christ died a horrific death at age thirty-three to save us and prove he was worthy of our devotion and love. Whether his Father created the universe is of no significance to me. '*The Source*' may be above Jesus, so what? At the least, he's a benevolent, eternal spirit that helps humans fight evil and gives our souls the chance of First Class Residence in the afterworld."

"Thank you for that!" Jill said. She had tears in her eyes. "I didn't need any affirmation. I have strong faith in what I believe, but many others who sit on the fence line of belief need to hear you! You should write these things down."

"Many have already written it," I noted.

"But most of those writers didn't travel the world like you have; fifty different countries! You have perspective!" She and I had talked about my travels back when we were huddled down by The Wall. Her comments made me think.

The next day I was floating like a cork in a giant soup-bowl of chlorides: The Dead Sea. Like in the Great Salt Lake in Utah, you can read the newspaper while floating on your back, keeping both your head and feet dry. The Dead Sea, at fourteen hundred feet below sea level, is the lowest spot on Earth. It's thirty miles long, nine miles wide, and one thousand feet deep with a salinity of thirty-four percent, about nine times saltier than the ocean. Jordan borders to the east, Palestine to the west. The thing to do is float in it and enjoy the hyper-salinity, then finish with a therapeutic mud bath. It's a good place to do some deep thinking.

I thought about another wall I'd seen earlier in the day, one separating the territories from Israel proper. The portion separating Bethlehem from Israel was formidable; huge rectangular solid panels over forty feet high, painted gray with barbed wire on top. They extended as far as the eye could see. Not ancient but modern, built by Israel. At the Wall's base, up to ten feet, there was continuous graffiti. Nobody was praying at it! Our tour guide said it was necessary to keep Israel safe.

This border wall was about fifty percent completed in 2002. It would be over four hundred miles when finished. For the most part, with some exceptions, it followed the "green line" of the 1949 armistice, agreed to as Israel's border by the U.N. at the end of the Arab-Israeli war. It separates Israel from the territories—much of it defines the western border of the West Bank.

Israel does not provide the same level of security in the territories that it does in Israel proper. For example, tours can go to Nazareth safely, but no guarantees to Bethlehem. Nazareth is in Israel. Bethlehem is in the territories. Yesterday, the bus tours to Bethlehem were stoned, causing cancellation of part of our tour today, giving us more time to float in the Dead Sea and think, and talk. A few from yesterday's group were on this tour. Jill and Eli, the young Jewish man, were floating next to me. He had switched from the black yarmulke to a tight-fitting, yellow swim hat; I almost didn't recognize him.

"So, there are walls and there are walls. In 1968, I went on a student tour that included Berlin," I said to them while kicking my toes in salty bubbles. "The wall separating east from West Berlin was very much in place. It was a keep-in wall; the one we saw today was a keep-out wall. Reagan put an end to the Berlin wall—I'm not sure anyone can do the same here."

"Not anytime soon," Eli replied. "There are implacable differences in ideology between Muslims and Jews, as you know. Still, many Jewish people support the idea of a Palestinian state provided peace is guaranteed. One major problem is Gaza—it's not connected to the West Bank. To make a Palestinian state, there would have to be a road through Israel, or land transferred from Israel, to connect the two. Right now, any car with a yellow Israeli license plate driving through the territories gets stoned. You're okay with a blue Palestinian license plate."

"Didn't Israel offer to the give back ninety percent of the West Bank in exchange for guaranteed peace?" I asked Eli. Jill was floating between us and listening.

"Yes, but the Palestinian Authority wanted ninety seven percent and a piece of Israel for a road that would run from Gaza to the West Bank. Israel was willing to do this! But then the issue of getting back East Jerusalem came up. Israel won control of East Jerusalem after the Six-Day war in 1967. It was filthy and in tatters—Israel cleaned and fixed things like water and electricity, then annexed it in 1980. Today, East Jerusalem is part of Israel, not the territories," Eli explained.

"Can you imagine Jerusalem turning into Gaza?" Jill said. "All of what we saw yesterday was in East Jerusalem!"

"It will never happen," Eli said. "Even Jordan and Egypt don't want that to happen. They get a share of the tourist business Jerusalem creates. There's no tourism in Gaza."

My God, the Palestinians refused ninety seven percent of the West Bank which belonged to Jordan before 1967! And they only had to guarantee peace?" Jill said in disbelief.

"And Israel agreed to give land for a road through Israel!" Eli reminded her. Jill kicked her feet hard in disgust, unintentionally spraying Eli and me with the Dead Sea.

"A serious situation with no obvious solution; five U.S. Presidents tried to fix it!" I said, shaking the chloride solution off my head.

"I'm sorry!" She apologized.

"He can take it! He's waterproof in that yellow swim hat," I said pointing to Eli. Jill laughed.

"How to guarantee peace is a real problem. The Palestinian Authority operates separately from Hamas, right?" I asked Eli.

"Absolutely. You can talk with the P.A. sometimes but not Hamas, they are blue-blooded terrorists," Eli asserted.

"America has to stand as Israel's strongest ally!" Jill said.

It was time to change the subject. Eli raised his feet up almost touching his head while keeping both dry, and asked, "You're a scientist, tell me, what's holding us up?"

"Chlorides," I said. "About nine times more than in the ocean; sodium, magnesium, bromine, calcium, and potassium chlorides. Hypersaline, we biochemists say. The only life in the Dead Sea are salt-tolerant bacteria on the bottom. So, it's almost dead, but not completely." The water was hazy and calm with a turquoise hue.

"Knowing that, we can now seriously enjoy it," Eli said. "That's what's in those bath-salts packages they sell in the gift shop."

"I'm going to buy some," Jill said. "Use them in baths at home." We were watching people on shore painting themselves with mud from the Dead Sea. We paddled over and joined them.

"This is pure, gray, salty, sterile, chloride mud!" I said. We filled our hands with it and covered our bodies. When the sun dried it, I felt like a marble statue. Maybe a robot. Then when I moved, my mud-coat cracked. It was an unusual sensation. I felt like C-3PO in Star Wars, with broken arms. We applied more mud and allowed it to dry.

"Does this really cleanse our pores, or skin?" Jill asked.

"That's what they claim," I replied. "It will certainly reduce the population of bacteria on your skin."

After we had enough mud cleansing, we shuffled like robots over to a row of freshwater showers outside the gift shop. The water was cool and felt good. There were long-handled brushes provided as it was a bit of a challenge to get all the mud off in a public setting. A cleansing experience for sure! After we put our street clothes on we went into the gift shop to look around. Stopping in front of a postcard rack, I picked out one that showed the Western Wall at sunset. All three of us stared at it.

"There are good walls and there are bad walls," Eli said.

"But none should come between souls!" Jill said.

I nodded in agreement. . .

Postscript:

I flew back to the USA the next day, taking El AL to New York then Delta to Minneapolis. The security at Ben Gurion airport in Tel Aviv was something to behold. They check everybody and everything twice. If you look suspicious, you may get checked naked! All baggage and cargo were opened and checked by at least two inspectors. All travelers are asked a list of questions; get smart with them and you don't fly. The process made me feel safe, a necessary inconvenience. It's why everyone here has good odds of living another day.

In retrospect, it was hard to take a neutral stance on the conflict. Arabs hate Israel and Israelis for many reasons; religion is only one of them. Much of the hate centers on the fact that Israel is a democracy. There's no female discrimination. The economy doesn't depend on oil. Individual freedoms exist, people can sing and dance. And security is hard to penetrate. All in glaring contrast to other countries in the Middle East.

Shaman's mask — Belize jungle

10

Two Shamans
Life-Saving Secrets in Belize

Prologue

Doctor Nigel Jones met Carlo Santi in Belize in early 1980. Jones had just graduated as a naturopathic doctor. Previously, he had earned a PhD in Plant Science at a leading university in England. His interest was in herbal medicine. Santi, at eighty years old, was in his prime as a natural healer; he practiced outside the small town of Roaring Creek in western Belize. He was a shaman's shaman.

It was a good time for the young Englishman to meet Santi and learn herbal medicine from the expert—the old shaman realized it was time to share his knowledge. There were at least a thousand species of medicinal plants in Belize and Santi knew and used about half of them—the ones that truly worked! It was the goal of Nigel Jones to earn the respect of Carlo Santi and become his apprentice; he believed the shaman knew how to cure cancer. But Nigel would have to earn his stripes in jungle medicine first.

Belize, December 1981

Four British soldiers were in an army jeep moving fast through the rainforest—one was a medic. They drove on a narrow road, crossing the New River at Crooked Tree, and then through the wildlife sanctuary to the Goldson Highway. It was black-dark as they wove and slid on the muddy road.

"It's over thirty-five miles to the hospital!" the soldier driving shouted.

"Go fast!" Patrick Brady, the medic, yelled back. The old jeep's suspension springs were a literal noise machine on rainforest roads.

"Tell me again what happened—details," Brady asked the older of the two men in the backseat.

"We got into the smoke," The older soldier told Brady. "We were camping out on assignment, built a camp fire, then started coughing. We moved and the smoke followed us. Then the itching started and the pain in our throats. We used canteen water to wash our arms and legs, but it made things worse!"

"Looks like you got into poisonwood smoke," Brady, told him. He had seen this before but not as severe; usually from someone who had contacted tree sap from a poisonwood tree. Smoke inhalation was more serious and affected the whole body.

The younger soldier, Leonard Finnegan, was showing symptoms of shock. He was dehydrated, sweating profusely, and had blue lips. Brady tried to get him to swallow water but he kept choking on it. Both men had red rashes over most of their exposed skin: arms, legs, feet, and face. Bleeding lesions penetrated the rashes. The medic gave them shots of epinephrine and checked their blood pressure—Lenny's was dangerously low at 70/40. "Go as fast as you can," he ordered the driver.

The driver pressed the accelerator to the floor and the old jeep came alive, vibrating and throwing clumps of mud. "She's not built for speed!" the driver shouted.

"Just get us there!" Brady retorted. It was a Vietnam-era jeep with a canvas top and no windows. Humid air whistled past them with the roof flapping.

"How are you doing?" Brady asked Oliver, the older soldier.

"I think me needs another shot of that Epi stuff!" Oliver begged. "The frickin' wind makes the itching unbearable."

"In ten minutes, I'll give you another five hundred micrograms," Brady told him. Reaching back from the front seat to the two suffering soldiers in the back, he applied hydrocortisone cream to the most severely affected areas. It was the last of the tube. "Why didn't they put two tubes, or four, in the bloody med kit?" He mumbled to himself. "Government stupidity." Patrick Brady was almost through his last tour of duty. He loved medicine, but he'd had enough of the military. As a young man, only twenty-two, he had already served old England for four years—providing first aid in various jungles. He planned to go medical school after his discharge.

Brady called the hospital on the jeep's VHF radio, alerting them to the situation and that they were about an hour away. It was raining now and they had to slow down. Both men were in serious pain, sweating, dehydrated, and shivering. Lenny was in the most trouble.

The E.R. doctor was waiting with Doctor Nigel Jones at the doors of the City Hospital when the jeep arrived. Two female nurses had gurneys ready. They laid each man flat on his back, feet elevated, and rushed them through a hallway into a treatment room. It was an old hospital, founded in 1820. Warm and humid inside, just like outside, it smelled of pine-scented floor cleaner. The treatment room was small, with flickering fluorescent lights. The nurses began cutting the soldier's clothes off, using long tongs to remove strips of it. They started applying the liquid solution Dr. Jones had brought, using sterile camel hair brushes. The young E.R. doctor had called Nigel immediately after talking to the medic on the radio. Jones' apartment was close to the hospital so getting late calls for help was not unusual.

"What happened?" The ER doctor asked the medic as they crowded into the treatment room. The driver stayed outside.

"They were camped in the wildlife sanctuary at Crooked Tree and used poisonwood for a campfire. They got into the smoke—it enveloped them," Patrick Brady replied, and explained the treatment protocol he tried to follow. It didn't take much poisonwood smoke to severely affect a person.

"Get the younger soldier on a ventilator!" The ER doctor ordered the older nurse. "Start saline IVs on both men and bring me the methyl-steroid syringes." The younger nurse kept applying Dr. Jones' solution to the rashes.

"Use more solution!" Jones had to yell over a rattling window air conditioner that was blowing hot air.

"Unplug that stupid thing," the ER doctor ordered. Brady pulled the plug.

"How long ago did this happen, Patrick?" Dr. Jones asked Brady, calling him by his first name after seeing it on his medical case.

"About six hours ago, including the drive," Brady answered.

Dr. Jones had taken over the application of his solution. Its effectiveness decreased when it was applied late—sooner was better than later. Jones applied large amounts, pouring it on and using soft brushes to direct it, alternating between the two men.

Lenny's seriously-low blood pressure started to increase as the saline entered his circulation and Jones' solution took effect. Oliver was itching less and had stopped shivering. "I feel a bit better," he said.

"What's in that solution?" Brady asked Dr. Jones, amazed to see how well it was working—the men were improving. Oliver's vitals were back to normal while Lenny's were showing improvement.

"There's a tree called the gumbo-limbo, and its sap is an antidote for poisonwood," Dr. Jones explained. "It's often found growing near poisonwood trees. Animals know this and will eat gumbo bark if infected. The solution is made by boiling gumbo-limbo sap in water with herbal emulsifiers."

"Brilliant! They should have taught me that in training!" Brady was mad. "I could have helped these men hours ago."

"Governments don't approve natural treatments," Dr. Jones replied. "Rainforest medicine is regarded as voodoo. You and I need to talk sometime. Oliver told me it's your last tour of duty and you're planning to go to medical school?"

"Yes, that's my plan, when I get back to the U.K."

Brady was helping apply the solution while they talked. Dr. Jones was glad to see him involved.

Belize, April 1982

A few months later, Nigel Jones was snorkeling around Ambergris Caye; a large island off the Atlantic coast of Belize. It was a calm, blue-sky day and the sea gently lapped over the barrier reef. On his belt were a dozen sample bottles for collecting algae specimens. Certain toxic algae were potential candidates for his research. The water was crystal clear over a forest of staghorn coral twenty feet below. He sensed some activity to his right, toward the reef.

The green morays were huge, six-footers. These giant eels were weaving and swimming like snakes in and out of the staghorn coral. Nigel snorkeled over them; he had never seen this many large morays together. There were twelve of them, emerald-green with long, ribbon-like bodies and heads like snakes with serrated teeth. They had no pectoral fins—no "hands" like other fish—so they had to keep moving. They swam by making undulations that ran the length of their bodies. Colorful reef fish were darting around trying to avoid them.

On the deep side of the coral, out toward the barrier reef, were four scuba divers—one was an instructor. When they came out over the coral ridge they were instantly surrounded by the eels. The instructor gave the group the stop sign, motioning them to tread water. Then he gave hand signals for them to adjust their BC vests for less buoyancy so they could suspend with their arms folded! Nigel was astonished; he knew the eels were poisonous. He stayed on top of the water and moved sideways to avoid being directly over them.

The eels were everywhere. One of the young divers was filming them when, suddenly, one bit at the silver ring on his left hand. The diver dropped the camera and shook his hand violently. The eel wouldn't let go. Blood gushed from his hand as the stubborn green ribbon undulated wildly. Frantically, he kept shaking his hand trying to get the eel off. This caused the eel's double set of teeth to penetrate deeper. The diver punched at the eel with his right hand while screaming in pain through his air hose. More blood. The instructor quickly grabbed a knife from his ankle sheath and slashed the eel, cutting into its midsection. The eel pulled loose, and it was bleeding now—other eels began attacking it. The instructor pointed up and all four divers surfaced fast. They could do this safely since they were no deeper than thirty feet.

Nigel swam over and told them he was a naturopathic doctor and pointed to shore. He and the instructor helped the wounded diver swim. All three had to kick hard. Nigel had both his hands cupped around and pressing on the diver's hand to get compression. It was some distance to the beach so they had to use their snorkels. The other two student divers followed them.

"The pain! Stop the pain!" The young man shouted after he took his mouthpiece out, kneeling on the beach. Nigel kept compression on the bleeding hand while the instructor called for help on his emergency radio. There were no other people on the beach.

"There are toxins in their mouth mucous," Nigel told the wounded diver. "I know it hurts." Nigel could feel that two fingers, the little and ring finger, and part of the hand, had ripped open when the moray pulled away. Morays have two lower jaws with teeth curving in and a spare set in their upper jaw. When they bite and the victim tries to shake or pull back, serious damage can occur.

"Get four bags of ice and a beach towel!" Nigel ordered the two other student divers. "Leg it!" They ran to the old grocery store on the road that led from the beach. Nigel took his bright yellow tee shirt off and wrapped it around the young man's hand. The man yelled out in pain.

"Hold this tight with your other hand. The pain will stop when the ice gets here.

What's your name?" he asked the young man.

"Teddy, Ted Schultz."

"Good, strong name!"

Nigel quickly cut a piece of rubber air-hose off one of the scuba tanks.

"Okay, Teddy, you have to be strong for me now!" Nigel gave him the piece of rubber hose and told him to bite down on it.

"An ambulance is coming from San Pedro," the instructor confirmed. "Should be here in thirty minutes. What can I do to help?"

"Several ounces of ground red pepper will help stop the bleeding. GO FAST!" Nigel yelled. The instructor ran to the store. *Why didn't I tell the other two to bring pepper with the ice?* Nigel was mad at himself.

Nigel was using an air hose as a tourniquet on Teddy's arm—the bleeding was hard to control and he was worried.

Nigel relaxed the tourniquet for a few minutes—just long enough to keep the arm from turning blue—then retightened it. He reminded Teddy to keep pressure on his hand; the yellow tee shirt was red with blood.

All three divers came back from the store, each carrying something. Nigel grabbed the jar of cayenne pepper and told Teddy it was going to sting. He unwrapped the tee shirt. "Bite the hose now," he commanded as he poured red pepper on the wounds. Teddy screamed while biting on the hose. "Fill that towel with ice!" Nigel shouted. They poured four bags of crushed ice on the beach towel and carried it over to Nigel. It sagged from the weight of the ice as they held it by the corners.

"Lay it flat on the sand," Nigel instructed.

"Put your hand deep in the ice," Nigel told Teddy. Teddy's eyes were watering and he was sweating. "Deeper," Nigel loosened the tourniquet. The ice was turning red above the buried hand. Nigel poured more pepper on the red spot in the ice and pulled the towel corners up, making a sack. Then told the two student divers to hold it shut as they sat by Teddy.

The instructor called on his radio to check the ambulance. Nigel tightened the tourniquet and started pressing on acupressure spots on Teddy's body with emphasis on his feet and head. He had to lessen the pain and prevent Teddy from going into shock.

Moray eel bites are toxic. Hemolytic toxins in their mucous glands clot and destroy red blood cells in the victim. The pain hits immediately as the curved teeth act like barbs on a fish hook, preventing prey from escaping. In addition, bacteria and fungi in an eel's mouth can cause serious infections.

All five men rode in the ambulance to the clinic on the island. When they arrived at the small clinic, the divers holding the ice-sack with Teddy's hand in it helped him into a wheel chair and pushed him into clinic where the attending nurse was waiting.

"The doctor is on a house call—he'll be here shortly." The nurse looked apologetic. "He knows you're coming."

"Bad moray eel bite; from a big one," Nigel told the nurse. "He needs a saline IV with pain medication and antibiotics right away, as soon as you're done checking his vitals."

"Yes, Dr. Jones." She knew Nigel from previous assistance with patients. The clinic staff always listened to him, just like at City Hospital.

Teddy was conscious, sweating and in pain, but not in shock. Another nurse unwrapped the towel and started cleaning his hand. "He will need many stitches," she said, just as the clinic doctor walked in. Dr. Juan was already in blue scrubs. "Hello, Nigel," he said as he went over to look at Teddy's hand. "Hello, Juan," Nigel replied.

"Looks like the cayenne and ice slowed the bleeding down. Good work, Nigel. Shark?"

"Big moray."

"How much blood did he lose?"

"I estimate three pints."

"That's borderline for shock!"

"Rosita," Juan called to the taller nurse. "We better switch the IV to high viscosity saline."

"Tell me the details—what happened?" Dr. Juan inspected the wound. Nigel let the instructor tell the story. Juan examined the hand carefully while listening.

"The little finger is gone, bones are crushed and its ninety percent severed, holding on by a flap of skin," Juan reported. "We can save the ring finger." He instructed the two nurses to prep for stitching and anesthetize the arm. We can't delay, it has been over two hours; If we don't move fast he'll lose the ring finger and hand function. There's no time to boat him to Belize City."

"I agree, Juan," Nigel replied, as the nurses got things ready.

"Nigel, do you have the ingredients for that herbal, antifungal potion of yours? The one containing jackass bitters and grapefruit seeds?"

"Yes, back in the lab in Belize City. We're on the same wavelength." Antibiotics only control bacteria, big morays have toxic fungi in their mouth, too. "I'll take the wave runner and be back ASAP," Nigel said. Wave runners looked like snowmobiles and ran on top of the water—fast!

"Do it!" Juan urged. "Many of the fungi down here are resistant to all three classes of antifungal drugs,'' he explained to the others. "Dr. Jones' potion stops fungi in their tracks!"

Nigel put his hand on Teddy's shoulder to show his concern. The pain medicine was working, and he had avoided shock. "We have three worries: toxins, bacteria, and fungi. The first two are under control. I'll be back shortly with medicine that prevents fungal infections. We're giving you the Full Monty!"

"Thank You," Teddy said, with tears flowing, knowing he had lost a finger.

Nigel ran out to the dock behind the clinic, got on the big Yamaha wave runner, and sped off, gunning it to fifty miles per hour in less than a minute.

Belize, July 1983

"There are old mushroom hunters and there are bold mushroom hunters but there are no old, bold mushroom hunters. All wild mushrooms are poisonous." Doctor Nigel Jones told the ecotour group as they crouched down holding their magnifying glasses to look at a mushroom cluster. Guiding in the rainforest provided supplemental income for Nigel Jones. He was tall and muscular with blonde hair looked more like a Malibu lifeguard than a research scientist.

Dr. Jones continued his commentary: "The edible ones contain trace amounts of low-grade toxins that most people tolerate.

Also, many of the low-grade toxins denature during cooking. But, I would never eat a raw, wild mushroom of any kind. They make your liver and kidneys work overtime. *Don't touch these!*" He pointed to the cluster on the ground the group was studying.

"How poisonous are they?" an older man in a safari hat asked. Kneeling was a challenge for him as he looked through his magnifying glass.

"Very! They have no name and are quite common-looking with gray stems and Chinese hats, but very poisonous. The shaman, Carlo Santi, uses a Mayan hieroglyph to designate them: an ocean wave inside a circle."

"What's considered very poisonous?" A young lady with a ponytail asked.

"When less than ten milligrams can kill a two-hundred-pound man!" Nigel emphasized.

"Is this mushroom one that Carlo Santi uses on people?" She asked. The question caused Nigel to pause. He knew Carlo had told other shamans about the "ocean wave in a circle" mushroom as treatment for serious viral infections. But using toxic mushrooms for other treatments, specifically cancer, was never mentioned!

"Sometimes, but only in extremely low doses," Nigel clarified.

"Is it found throughout Central America?" The man with the safari hat asked.

"As far as we know, it's only found here in Belize." It was one of the eight toxic mushrooms Carlo used to treat cancer and the only one Nigel showed on tours. He had made Nigel promise to never mention the other seven.

Nigel showed the tour group these common-looking mushrooms to emphasize the need to be cautious. There were many edible varieties of mushrooms—various shapes and colors—sold as food in local markets, but they were farmed from known parentage. These gray killers could easily confuse a mycologist, not to mention an ecotourist.

The group moved on through the rainforest, going one by one on the narrow trail passing a variety of medicinal plants and trees. They were south of San Ignacio below the Mopan River on a trail known to shamans. It was thick rainforest that got over one-hundred inches of rain a year, mostly between May and November; a period called the *high season*.

"Here we have a mushroom called the Amethyst Deceiver," Nigel commented, admiring nature. "It's a real beauty; dark indigo stalks a foot high and topped off with translucent lavender umbrellas." There were ten of them perfectly illuminated by sunlight streaking through the trees.

"Wow," the lady with the ponytail was impressed. "They redefine purple!" She was studying mycology at the University of Wisconsin and was taking photos to show her professor. She was specializing in mushroom toxicology and was interested in which mushrooms were dangerous.

"Can you eat it?" The man wearing the safari hat asked.

"Some of the locals do, but I don't recommend it. This mushroom accumulates arsenic from the soil—look up!" Dr. Jones said loudly. Ten scarlet macaws flew overhead making rapid shallow wing beats while squawking and screaming at the tour group. They were large red-feathered parrots with yellow and blue wings and tails, flying one-by-one.

"Marvelous birds!" the lady with the ponytail observed. "Each one looks to be four feet long!"

"They can eat poisonous fruits, unlike other birds," Dr. Jones added.

"How can they do that?" the man with the safari hat wondered.

"Ornithologists aren't sure, it may be because these macaws eat a lot of clay, and clay detoxifies poisons. Shamans use it to detoxify people," Nigel suggested.

"Can these parrots eat poisonous mushrooms?" the lady with the ponytail asked. The birds were out of sight now but you could still hear them.

"Good question…I don't know. Maybe," Dr. Jones replied. "They live for fifty years!" Carlo taught that for every poison in nature, there was an antidote somewhere; you just had to find it and learn how to use it.

Nigel's time in Belize with Carlo Santi and other natural healers was providing remarkable insights into nature medicine.

Belize, June 1984

Carlo Santi was a true Mayan bush doctor, born and raised in western Belize; a natural healer who had perfected the power of herbal medicines. Carlo had Mayan heritage but you wouldn't know it at first glance; he usually wore a white shirt, sunglasses and a baseball cap. But without the hat and glasses, looking at him straight on or in profile, he was identical to stone sculptures found in the Mayan ruins. He'd inherited their long nose, flat forehead, and large lower lip. At eighty-four he easily passed for seventy.

Carlo's healing knowledge had been shared with Nigel Jones over the last three years. Something told him this exceptional young man was different. Carlo heard his inner voice, his spirit voice, which told him to share everything with young Doctor Jones. It was hard for Carlo to teach all of it. He didn't have the right words in English to explain the medical and botanical science of his work—he spoke English and Spanish using common words. When he first met Nigel, he was impressed that the young man was both a people and a plant doctor, ND and PhD; skilled, dedicated, and trustworthy.

Carlo worked out of his home, a small wooden house with a thatched roof and no electricity or tap water. He had five-gallon buckets of water brought in from town and purified it with drops of bleach; three drops per liter. This water was used for washing and cleaning. He filtered rainwater for drinking and medical use. If he was treating someone with a viral infection, they were told to add five drops of oregano oil to each liter of drinking water—and drink only this water until the virus was gone. "Viruses hate oregano," he often said.

Behind Carlo's brother's house was a remarkable garden of mushrooms and medicinal plants, each identified with stones bearing Mayan hieroglyphs, all growing under Carlo's guidance. The mushrooms served special purposes; those he used most had not been scientifically classified and had no names. Thus, the need for the hieroglyphs.

Many of his treatments required combinations of medicinal plants with or without mushrooms; Carlo called it co-therapy. Mushrooms were a type of fungus, not a plant. It was important to harvest medicinal plants at the correct time; the leaves and roots needed to be chopped properly and set out to dry. Plant cells, millions of them, had to be broken open and exposed to sunlight to enhance their medicinal power.

Nigel helped Carlo with the gardening and exploring the rainforest for new species. Carlo's success was insured by the garden; it allowed him more time with patients and less time searching the rainforest.

The Cure for cancer was perfected over seven years and worked for many different cancers—it was kept secret by Carlo mainly to prevent improper use. He had no financial ambitions but knew others would. He just wanted to cure people. Nigel Jones was the only other human being that knew the formulas. Carlo's treatments for other diseases were shared openly with locals and fellow shamans.

The Cure was something he had discovered *from a patent* seven-years earlier. In August of 1977 a young woman with pancreatic cancer came to Carlo for help. He treated her with a diet that strengthened her immune system and her body's ability to fight cancer. It was an anti-cancer diet of vegetable soup containing large amounts of turmeric accompanied by drinking two liters of lemon tea per day to alkalize the body; it was one of his procedures for treating cancer. For many it worked, for some it didn't. Pancreatic cancer is a killer and required special attention.

It was not the practice of shamans to track the progress of patients by scheduling follow-up appointments. Most of the time there was a long line of people waiting to see the best shamans and little or no paperwork after a visit. It was up to the patient to come back so he didn't see the woman with pancreatic cancer again until she returned two months later.

"I'm well," she told him. He recognized her immediately.

"You're a strong woman. The soup and tea helped your body cure itself," he said confidently.

"No, they didn't—a mushroom cured me! The turmeric soup and lemon tea helped after the mushroom, not before."

"Tell me more," Carlo said.

"I'd been eating the soup and drinking the tea for two weeks after seeing you. I felt better for a week, then got worse. My husband had picked some mushrooms that we eat all the time. I was very sick and not hungry so I only took a small bite of one, just to please him. It hurt my mouth and throat so bad; I started to sweat, it was hard to breathe. He tried a small bite and had to spit it out. He knew then he had picked the wrong mushrooms."

"What did you do then?" Carlo asked, listening to every word.

"I had to lie down—I thought I was dying. I fell into a deep sleep for many hours, then woke up the afternoon of the next day feeling better. I ate more of your turmeric soup and drank more lemon tea and went back to bed for another night. The next day I felt very good. The pain in my left side was gone and my energy was back. That was six weeks ago."

She looks as healthy as a race horse, Carlo thought to himself. His head was spinning. He had helped other less serious cancers with turmeric soup and lemon tea, but it usually took months to work. That toxic mushroom had done something powerful.

It took Carlo several years to perfect the mushroom treatment, using methods not scientifically accepted. Often, he had to make several changes in a patient's treatment at the same time, and of course, had no placebo controls. He could feel and smell the difference between colon and liver cancer or between other cancers and sense the overall condition of a patient, then select the correct treatment. Carlo did not use any scientific instruments to diagnose a patient. His five senses were the scientific instruments!

The most important requirement was to decide which mushroom extract to use on a patient. He had eight different toxic mushrooms to choose from; all were growing in his brother's backyard. Microgram quantities—millionths of a gram—activated a person's ability to fight cancer. It was an extremely powerful effect.

He would use a safety pin to test them: First, he would prick a mushroom with the point of the pin, then prick the patient's arm and examine the reaction; if it looked like a large mosquito bite that was a good indication. The faster the reaction the better. This, plus his intuition, provided guidance as to what mushroom and dose to use.

Somehow, minute amounts of these highly potent mushroom toxins—well under a lethal dose—woke up the immune system with a jolt. Once awake, the immune system was moderated at just the right level of activity with synergistic effects from the turmeric soup and lemon tea. For people, allergic or not responding to either of these, backups were required. Carlo had them.

Nigel knew the formulas, eight of them; each used a different mushroom. Knowing which formula to use on a patient was the mystery. This was where Carlo's intuition and sensory perceptions came into play along with the safety pin test. Nigel had watched him treat cancer patients. He knew Carlo did not know how to teach his intuitive skills—he didn't have the words. But it was clear that selecting the right mushroom at the right dose involved a complete understanding of each patient's condition.

"How does it work?" Carlo asked Nigel. He didn't know what was happening at the molecular level—only that it worked.

"I have a theory, Carlo, but I need to run lab tests to confirm it. I'm going to express mail to England the frozen blood samples I've kept from patients, for analysis."

"Don't use too much science." Carlo's wisdom was speaking.

"Just enough," Nigel said winking. It was easy to sense their mutual respect.

Nigel believed that specific white blood cells—the "Special Forces" of the immune system—were being super-activated by the mushroom toxins, boosting their cancer-cell killing power. That was the first action. The shock of the toxin also caused the activated white blood cells to work synergistically with the turmeric and lemon. That was the second action. Basically, Carlo's secret treatments powerfully awakened specific cells in the immune system and boosted their function.

Once the lab results came back, Nigel knew exactly what was happening. Dr. Nigel Jones now had a medical name for Carlo's cancer therapy: "I'm calling it *Extreme Macrophage Activation—E.M.A.,*" Nigel told Carlo. "*E.M.A.* is how *The Cure* works!"

"What's a macrophage?" Carlo asked.

"It's the immune system's biggest white blood cell, the body's Number-One cancer killer. It looks like an amoeba, with long sticky arms that attach to and kill cancer cells. Macrophages in your patient's blood samples were more numerous and larger, and had more sticky arms compared to those from cancer patients on chemo!"

"I knew it had to do with blood cells." Carlo, excited, slapped his leg with his hand. "Tell me more."

"These macrophages are always around in our blood and tissues; cancer cells can deactivate them. Also, cancer cells can masquerade as normal body cells so macrophages can't recognize them as the bad guys. Your secret mushrooms wake macrophages up, big time, allowing them to override these limitations. They ring a molecular fire alarm!"

"So, I'm really stimulating the body to cure itself!" Carlo exclaimed. "Yes, you are!" The young shaman was happy for the old shaman.

"You are a smart young man, very talented and trustworthy. I have shared my deepest secrets with you. I discussed only one of the eight mushrooms with other shamans, the one for treating a serious virus. What you just explained to me could seriously endanger you. Nobody outside Belize pays any attention to me—I'm just an old shaman peddling snake oil. But with you, it will be different."

"Please don't worry about me. That's for me to do. I still have a lot to learn about *E.M.A*," Nigel said...

In late 1983, Nigel made a special effort to watch what Carlo did to diagnose and prepare a patient for treatment. Several days prior to administering a mushroom toxin, Carlo would restrict food and have them drink plenty of water and alkalizing tea. Then he'd check their urine and either increase or decrease the amount of alkalizing tea, and after several more days, reexamine them, checking for changes in pulse, eyes, kidneys, muscles, and nerves—then repeat the safety pin test. This would confirm when to start the treatment and what mushroom to use. Nigel helped with the process and the scheduling of follow-up appointments.

This was all part of the learning curve for Carlo and Nigel during the years it took to perfect *The Cure.* Luck was on the side of the young woman with pancreatic cancer seven years prior—her husband had "accidentally" picked precisely the *right* toxic mushroom for her cancer. He must have had guidance from The Source. There are no coincidences…

London, 1985-1993

In early 1985 Nigel had to leave Belize and return home to London. His parents had been killed on the M3 in a terrible car accident. The family business that his brothers and sisters depended on was collapsing in his father's absence. His dedicated help was required.

He prayed for Carlo. It was hard to keep in touch because Carlo couldn't write and had no phone. At various times Nigel arranged a phone call through people he knew in Roaring Creek. Carlo would tell him how well *The Cure* was working and that he missed his apprentice—who he now considered a young shaman!

After the Jones' family business was sold in 1992. Nigel returned to Belize in '93 to celebrate Carlo's ninety-second birthday. He could hear his Soul Voice…natural medicine was calling him back. He had become quite disappointed in what was happening in England. EU regulations promoted prescription drugs that replaced simple, low cost treatments. Anybody with an infection was prescribed antibiotics. Kids with problems in school were treated with antidepressants. New diseases were being created and named: people whose legs moved at night were prescribed medication as were those who got tired during the day. And for those with minor aches and pains, they were diagnosed with fibromyalgia and given drugs.

In Belize, things were changing too. Attempts to evaluate medicinal herbs were underway—samples were collected and sent to the National Cancer Institute for testing. Those in the know understood that the last thing the NCI wanted to discover was a cure for cancer; rumors of local cures in Central America forced them to show interest for political reasons. There were some lab successes with rats and mice, but that's when the plug got pulled. Going too far with non-patentable natural treatments was not advisable; they put the highly profitable chemo treatments at risk of disappearing! So, cancer was still very much alive and kicking in the U.K. as the Number Two killer—second only to heart disease.

Belize, December 1998

The ocean pounded over the barrier reef. West of the reef were islands called cayes of which Ambergris Caye was the largest. The town of San Pedro was at the southern end of it, a short boat ride from Belize City on the mainland.

Black frigate birds were feeding on small fish that had been wounded on the reef. Nigel focused his binoculars on them, "Red bellies on the males, white ones on the females," he said, describing them.

"So, you've become an ornithologist as well as a shaman." Pat Brady was impressed. Patrick Brady, the medic Nigel had met during the poisonwood-tree incident, had left the army, and Belize, in 1983. He went on to become an oncologist, an MD specializing in cancer research. He'd stayed in contact with Nigel and knew the stories about Carlo Santi and other healers.

"I'm just a rookie shaman at best, but no orny. I'm lucky if I know a dozen birds." They sat at a table outside the Conch Shell Inn on Caribena Street in San Pedro watching tourists walk around in swimming suits. When a gust of wind blew the beach hat off a young lady, Brady was up in a flash to retrieve it, smiling as he put it back on her head.

"She's got a smashing bum," he said to Nigel.

"There are a lot of smashing bums around here! Still single?"

"Aye, still single."

"Cheers then!" Nigel toasted Patrick.

"Cheers back to you!" Brady, held his beer up, while looking at Nigel. "San Pedro hasn't changed much in seventeen years."

"More tourists," Nigel remarked, putting his binoculars down. "Everyone is either an ecotourist, scuba diver, or a Mayan-ruin expert. The growth has been both good and bad for Belize. More tourists spending money but less virgin rainforest."

"Where did that scuba diver get bit by the moray…Teddy, I think was his name?" Brady asked.

"North of here about twenty miles, just inside the reef in twenty feet of water."

"And he recovered well?"

"Yes, quite well; with only one lost finger, the left pinky. His hand function returned to normal. There was so much healing like that to do here; it was continuous."

"He was lucky you were there! It's amazing how you have integrated plant science with naturopathic medicine and shamanism. You must be the only one who has!" The ex-army medic took a drink of his beer.

"Maybe, I'm just sorry I had to leave Belize, had to tend to the family business—it was critical. As the oldest sibling, it required my fulltime effort."

"It was meant to be; the time wasn't right! When I tell the other doctors in Banbury I know an English shaman named Nigel with a PhD and ND, they just stare at me in disbelief."

"Cheers again," Nigel took another drink. Brady did too. "Like that Belkin beer?"

"It's good, I never had it in the military. We mostly drank Guinness. Glad those medic days are over."

"I'm glad you came!"

"So am I, it didn't take much convincing to get me to leave England's cold December rain behind."

"Besides its nice weather, how is England these days?"

"It's in trouble, it needs to get out of the EU. Socialism is killing the economy."

"Margaret Thatcher was famous for saying: "Socialism stops working when you run out of other people's money," Nigel quipped.

"Right, and Ayn Rand added: "You can ignore the truth but you can't ignore the consequences of ignoring the truth." Both men looked over at the beach where other ladies were chasing hats.

"What about you, Patrick? Where do you want to be in the future?" This was somewhat rhetorical because they had discussed the possibly of working together on the phone.

Patrick took a long drink. He was thinking of his first thoughts—deep thoughts—that he'd had when Nigel phoned him several weeks ago, suggesting a meeting in Belize. Patrick Brady, MD was involved in a research project with a group of doctors focused on improving diagnostic procedures for cancer. He was four years younger than Nigel and low man on the doctor totem pole in England, so Patrick was unable to use his talents to their full extent.

"I got a group of doctors to make an investment, matching mine from selling the family business. There's money now. Private money!" Nigel explained.

"See. The timing is right now," Brady remarked. "I can be here drinking beer with you and it might change my life. We couldn't do it earlier—I was in med school and you were running the family business.

"Time has a way of sorting things out, doesn't it?" Nigel acknowledged.

When did the old shaman die?"

"December of 1994, he was ninety-three."

"Remarkable! Did you two keep in touch after leaving Belize?"

"A few times by phone thanks to friends in Roaring Creek. He had no phone. I came back in 1993 to celebrate his ninety-second birthday. I had a premonition. He was tired, couldn't talk long, told me he was ninety-nine and had one more year to go. But that was a joke he'd used for years. When anybody asked him his age he would answer: 'Old—probably ninety-nine.'"

He did talk about the government projects and developments to protect and classify medical plants in Belize. And reminded me to keep the mushrooms secret. I've told only you and one other," Nigel added.

"And I have absolutely kept it to myself," Brady assured him. "Are the mushrooms alive and well?"

"You bet! They're growing in both indoor and outdoor gardens on my farm in Costa Rica."

"Carefully managed by that retired botanist?"

"Yes, and he's in good health. I don't think I ever told you he was my major professor for my Ph.D., Dr. George Becker."

"He's the one-other?"

"Yes."

"Brilliant," Brady acknowledged. "So, here we are in 1998, back in Belize, seventeen years after the poisonwood event, four years after Carlo's passing. Do you think you know how to do what Carlo did?"

"A qualified 'yes,'" Nigel answered. "Carlo had eight different formulas. They all involved activating macrophages in the immune system starting with a microgram shock dose of mushroom toxin. There's one exception, like I explained on the phone last month. I know them well."

"What's the exception again, some algae strain?"

"A toxic strain of red algae I isolated in 1982. Ten nanograms of its toxin increase macrophage activity fifty times!"

"That's smashing. Does George know how to culture it?"

"Yup. We have it frozen in ampules right now."

"What don't you know?"

"How to diagnose and assess a patient the way Carlo did. How he used his intuition and senses to decide which formula to use on a patient. What pretreatments help? I ignored these at first; I thought of them as redundant shamanism. They're not. We need to use scientific instruments and a lab to guide the process! I need a medical-research doctor's help. Do you know one?"

"I'm here in Belize, right? Didn't come to see the green morays..."

"Want another beer?" Nigel asked him, smiling with relief.

"Aye!" Brady said. Nigel raised two fingers when the waitress walked by, she nodded and brought two bottles of Belkin.

"You understand the dangers?" Nigel tested him. "The big pharma war-machine is for real."

"I do," Brady said. "I sure do. I've thought it through. We must avoid the men in black! Your farm is still in the mountains, right?"

"Yes, with loyal locals and a retired sheriff from Arizona providing security."

"And there's virgin rainforest behind us?"

"Yup, and it comes complete with keel-billed toucans and jabiru storks,"

"That makes three of the twelve birds you know. You might fancy becoming an orny someday after all." Brady suggested. "Later, of course!"

"Maybe," Nigel chuckled.

Brady stood up and looked out past the beach and the reef, taking a slow drink of Belkin. He had just made a life-changing decision. Both men sat silent for several minutes, looking out at the blue water washing over the reef.

"Helping humanity is risky!" Nigel knew taking risks for the right reasons was part of life.

"But humanity needs a cure for cancer!" Brady affirmed. "We must pull out all the stops!"

"We'll be using Mayan hieroglyphs for identification, you'll need to study-up."

Brady laughed and took a deep breath: "Just tell me what's next."

Nigel's blue eyes sparkled with elation, like rays of sun on a rolling ocean. He paused for a moment, wiped the table with a napkin, took a notebook out of his pocket, opened it to page one, and slid it to Brady. "Here's the plan for launching *The Cure* in Costa Rica, and then the world…"

Postscript:

This story was the result of my experience with several professional shamans and a competent naturopathic doctor. The names, times and some of the places have been changed to protect the people involved. And, by the way, I saw the garden!

Author and Sekhar at the Taj Mahal

11

By a River in India

Divine Architecture Presents Options

Prologue:

There's a river in northern India called the Yamuna. Its waters originate in the Himalayas and are sacred for Hindus. They believe that bathing in this river cleanses the soul and frees the body from the torments of death. The Yamuna runs for over eight hundred miles and passes through the city of Agra on its way south. Genghis Kahn drank from it in 1206.

Between 1630 and 1653 a magnificent building was constructed on the south bank of this river in the city of Agra. It's truly a mystical place and an architectural love story! But the journey to it was an exasperating experience. But it was worth the stress and discomforts to find a spiritual oasis of peace and beauty.

Next to the river an old man washed his cattle with a push broom, brushing dry mud off their backs and flanks. They were large, gray oxen with wide horns that resembled those of Cape buffalos in Africa, but these animals had been tamed by castration and centuries of domestication and worship. The old man brushed them clean.

Not far from this man, two young boys pulled on a rope tied to the neck of a goat that wouldn't move. The old man yelled something to them, and they dropped the rope and walked on. In a short time, the goat began following them. Women upriver from the old man stood in the water and washed clothes, beating them on sandstone slabs held up with rocks. They were all dressed in brightly colored clothes. Nothing worn by any one woman matched anything worn by any other woman. When they finished, they piled the wet clothes on old bicycles and went home. It was hard to believe, but all the bicycles had flat tires and they had to walk them.

Agra, India, July 1996

It had been a grueling business trip—three weeks of driving in central India was no picnic. The heat and truck exhaust was overwhelming. Old trucks belching black diesel exhaust moved slowly on roads clogged with traffic. Exhaust spewed directly onto the road. Two lane roads made it impossible to pass, so people in cars behind trucks gambled with suffocation. The trucks waited in line to get into towns, and there was no way to get around them; some were disabled with their drivers trying to make repairs. The trucks carried everything imaginable: mystery goods covered with dusty tarps tied down with ropes. Some carried local people too, it was not unusual to see fifty or more sitting in the back of a truck, on boxes, on each other; hanging on any way possible.

Trucks carrying pigs and chickens were mixed in with those carrying people and goods—many of the animals were dead. It was hot and dry and the air carried a fine brown dust that didn't settle quickly. It covered the trucks and roads; you couldn't get away from it. Breathing through a wet cloth helped, and we did. This was India, and travel by road was tough going.

I was with my Indian business partner, Sekhar Dash, who was based in Hyderabad. Sekhar and I had become good friends over the last four years and often scheduled a tour or relaxation time after finishing our work. This was one of those times. We flew from Bangalore to Delhi and hired a car and driver to take us to Agra; it took six hours to get to our hotel. Tomorrow would be a special day, we needed to leave the hotel at 4:00 am.

We arrived early, before sunrise, which was important. A trace of wood smoke in the air carried breakfast aromas from vendors outside the entrance gate. Hot lamb, chicken kebabs, grilled eggplant, and fried plantain were the main contributors. We saw the food stands as we walked through the parking lot to the Great Gate. Our hotel had provided hot cereal, Kati rolls, and tea for an early breakfast—even so I was tempted by the lamb kabobs at the stands! But we had to keep moving.

The entrance, called the Great Gate, was a red sandstone building about seventy-five feet high with a large entry arch. Above it, we could see eleven small domes in a row between two towers in the dim light coming from the food stands. It was dark in the predawn and black inside the Great Gate building. Straight ahead was another arch with something framed by it, very faint but large and directly outside! We walked through the arch and came out into grassy emptiness. There were no lights, no moon, no stars, just an ethereal darkness. The grass had to be the start of the garden. In the distance, a fuzzy outline of a structure was barely visible. Was that it? Had we seen an optical illusion in the arch? We could barely make out the start of a walkway but proceeded straight ahead. Slowly, as I was prone to tripping in the dark, Sekhar walked behind me on the paved path. It was the first visit for both of us. I could sense his excitement. I was excited too…

"The power must be out! I feel like an American who had lived his entire life in Arizona and never saw the Grand Canyon," he whispered to me. A few people were shuffling behind us now. *Here in this place,* I thought, *it's fair to equate a natural wonder with a manmade wonder.*

On our right, we could barely make out the rectangular water channel where the guide book said it would be. We followed the walkway to a central square where fountains spewed water toward each of the four cardinal directions. *Their pumps had power?* I thought. We could see the water from the fountains as the darkness was slowly giving way to that special time called first light.

It was then that the main dome was no longer imaginary! It was, indeed, a reality as it became a luminous giant pearl. Then a rose. The Taj Mahal was rubbing its marble eyes and waking up on a cloudy morning. For the first time, Sekhar and I could see it clearly.

Already beautiful in the low light, its domes and minarets would soon brighten. Our timing was perfect. As the clouds cleared, the Taj's pearly-rose domes morphed into golden-yellow as the sun took control. We stood on the reflecting pool bridge—halfway to the Taj Mahal from the Great Gate—and watched the Taj change colors. Its ivory marble glistened modestly now, resisting the glare of the sun with thousands of inlaid gemstones. The gems formed swirls of flowers in mystical patterns; sapphires from Sri Lanka, amethysts from Persia, carnelian from Baghdad and jasper from Punjab. They became alive with the rising sun.

Sekhar and I walked the smooth marble terrace surrounding the Taj in our socks. The 390-year-old marble terrace was clean and smooth, patterned with squares and rectangles like a giant puzzle. More optical illusions appeared; round columns imbedded in the walls of the Taj were not round but flat marble rectangles rising to the ceiling. They were engraved with designs that tricked the eye. We walked completely around the famous mausoleum until we got back to our starting point overlooking the garden.

The two of us sat down on the terrace and stretched our feet out. We leaned against one of the four minarets that towered high at each of the four corners of the terrace. The minarets represented the four great Emperors of the Mughal Dynasty, including Shah Jahan, the builder. They tilted slightly away from the Taj so if they ever collapsed they could not fall on the building. *What love and ingenuity was put into this masterpiece of creation,*

I thought. Jahan was more than a builder, he was a dreamer and a lover of the woman he adored. The Taj Mahal was his gift to her.

It was quiet on the huge terrace and, amazingly, we were mostly alone. I thought for a moment of my shoes in the care of two shoe-tending ladies on the steps coming up from the garden. There was no deposit receipt. If they were taken by mistake and gone, could I find a pair my size in Agra? I felt in my pockets for my passport, wallet and hotel key. Touching them reassured me and I finally relaxed. Idiosyncrasies; I had to remind myself I was in India, not Brazil or Argentina.

Below the terrace, the garden came alive. The morning sun began to brighten it. A few men swept the walks around the reflecting pool, which created a second—upside down—Taj Mahal. A perfect inverse image of it; two were better than one.

The walkways and water channels intersected at the center of the reflecting pool, making a large Greek cross that divided the central garden into four square sections between the Taj and the Great Gate. Each of the four were further divided into four more sections and crosses. Four was the most sacred number in Islam, the Greek cross was an ancient emblem of Christianity. Interesting combination!

It was warm and calm with more tourists arriving now. It felt like a summer morning when I was a teenager—that youthful energy that drives excitement was alive in me. Thoughts of the horrible road trip disappeared and I relaxed even more. Sekhar sat quietly with his eyes closed, sleeping peacefully. I examined the meticulous symmetry and bold beauty of the famous mausoleum towering in front of us. It defined perfection.

When we imagine a special place that we have never been to, our minds create an impression of it that can be hard to match. When we finally get there, we often find ourselves disappointed in some way. We may know the place from books and movies, or from someone telling us about it, but until we've been to it, we can't know it. When I stood beside the Taj Mahal, it exceeded anything I ever imagined it to be.

"Can you imagine the Grand Canyon?" I asked Sekhar, nudging him. I had to say it again and nudge him again.

"Grand Canyon...imagine it?" He said, in a groggy voice. "Hardly can, even though I've seen pictures of it. Hard to imagine it in three dimensions, or its changing colors, or the smell of its cliffs cooling off after a rain, or the birds that fly over it. I know this now after seeing the Taj Mahal for the first time; my imagination can't put in all the details!" We talked about such details, ones that held the magnificence of an experience. It was easy to shut our eyes and talk, we both dozed this time.

He died in jail," Sekhar announced, waking up suddenly and breaking the silence.

I wasn't sleeping, just daydreaming. I had to think for a minute. "The Emperor Shah Jahan?" I had read about him in the guide book. Sekhar nodded.

"In Agra Fort," Sekhar pointed in the direction of the red sandstone fort down river.

"His oldest son put him there," I remarked.

"The Mughals were like that. They were Muslims."

"You don't have to be a Muslim to do your father in," I pointed out.

"No, but when you have as many sons as he had the odds are against you."

"And probably extra bad if you're an emperor loaded up with treasure," I quipped.

"He was," Sekhar asserted. "With his grandfather's treasure."

"That's how he could build this for her," I said, looking up at the Taj.

"Can you imagine it?" Sekhar said. "He wanted to build another one across the river—a black one!"

"Hard to imagine. The beauty of just one is hard to comprehend."

The sun moved higher and the Taj became brighter. The east faces of the minarets dazzled in bright yellow, they had no inlaid gemstones to buffer the sun, so their brightness contrasted with the more subdued illumination of the Taj.

Inside the Taj Mahal were the tombs of Emperor Jahan and his wife, the empress Mumtaz Mahal, his third wife but first love. She died giving birth to their fourteenth child in 1631. Totally distraught by her death, he created the Taj Mahal to honor her. It took twenty-two years, twenty thousand workers, and one thousand marble-carrying elephants to create it. Today, it's a mausoleum for the world—the eighth wonder—stunning in its ivory-whiteness by the river!

"Think about it: the world's most perfect building, built for love, not for religion, government, business, or ego!" I exclaimed, thinking deeply.

"Yes, very true!" Sekhar agreed. "But there was a tie to religion that involved Mumtaz. Notice how the Taj is larger and grander than the mosque," he pointed to the three-domed mosque next to the Taj. "Nothing should be greater than the house of Allah."

"Well, the Taj certainly is," I said. "I think old Jahan worshipped Mumtaz a tad more. He probably felt Allah could do with a break from all the heavy- duty praying he gets five times a day. There was only one Taj, and it was for her."

"The Mughals were that way," Sekhar said. "They didn't take Islam literally. They made some adjustments. Jahan wanted to combine the world's religions into one for her. In fact, the Taj Mahal is an architectural blend of Hindu arches, Islamic domes and a Christian cross at the very top!"

"That's food for serious thought!" I admitted.

"The Emperor Jahan believed there should be one religion for everyone—Muslims, Hindus, Christians, Jews, everyone. The idea started with his grandfather Akbar, who dreamed of a divine faith with justice. He believed the Koran was unjust and that God would never write an unjust book. He abandoned Islam before he died." Sekhar explained.

"You are quite a student of this all. I'm impressed."

"Do you believe Allah is God?" Sekhar asked in a serious voice.

"I believe over a billion people believe Allah is God," I replied.

"Do you know there are ninety-nine different names for Allah and all of them are inscribed on the Taj?" Sekhar asked me.

"Never knew that," I replied. "Sounds contradictory to Islamic doctrine. It would be worse than having multiple names or pictures of Muhammad."

"It was another adjustment made by the Emperor Jahan to let people know: The Taj Mahal is reformed Islamic doctrine!" Sekhar asserted. "Do you believe in God?"

"I believe in God but I'm not sure any religion has it right. New evidence points to Jesus, I lean that way," I replied. Do you believe?"

"Yes, but not in a religious way. Religion has been the source of humanity's ills! Look no further than Islamic terror today! The world needs another Emperor Shah Jahan to make adjustments!"

"Somebody needs to rewrite the unjust parts in the Koran." I understood how troublesome this would be.

"Very difficult to do," Sekhar lamented. "Muslims believe it's the words of Allah, and you can't change them."

"There are moderate Muslims who are open-minded about this; I know some." I said. "They don't believe in polygamy, execution by stoning, female genital mutilation, honor killing, or male superiority—to name a few. They believe the Koran has been corrupted and misinterpreted."

"Maybe it has. It depends on which Imam is running a mosque; a radical or a moderate," Sekhar asserted.

"And the worldwide trend appears to be toward the more radical types! But I'm no Imam expert. I've only met a couple."

"Radical Imams proliferate in Pakistan," Sekhar added. "They interpret the Koran literally and derive their version of Sharia law from it. That includes wife-beating, polygamy, clitorectomies, and other medieval horrors like you mentioned—key tenets of their version. Changing this will require major adjustments!"

"The moderates I know don't live by those tenets of Sharia Law, they live under U.S. constitutional law. Some may pick and choose aspects of Sharia, but many disregard it completely. And they significantly outnumber the radicals!" I could tell Sekhar was testing me.

"But those Muslims don't have the guns and bombs that the radicals have! If ten percent of the world's Muslims—a low estimate—live by strict interpretation of the Koran and Sharia law, that's over one-hundred million to worry about," Sekhar added.

"Reformation is what Islam needs, like Christianity and Judaism had centuries ago: A major reformation, starting with organizing the moderate Imams! The big question is, can it be done without massive killing—without World War III?" I asked.

There was no response from Sekhar. The muffled sounds of tourists walking around in their socks, speaking in low volume as if in church, blended with river sounds to create a hypnotic effect. As time passed, both of us dozed in the bright sunshine again. I woke up first and jiggled Sekhar.

"Let's get up and walk around," I suggested.

"Yes. Good idea," Sekhar responded.

We stood up and began walking in our socks once more. The marble floor of the terrace had warmed up; I should have brought thicker socks. We went inside the Taj and saw the tombs, then outside to see the Mosque, then back to the Taj and the garden. The calligraphy and engravings on the front face of the Taj were remarkable, the product of skilled artists.

The sun was fully out now and the Taj marvelously illuminated. Birds unfamiliar to me flew high overhead; large white birds with wide tails. They dove around and through the open tops of the minarets, then swooped down to the terrace and back up until they were over the Taj's great dome. Half of them flew through the arched openings under the lesser domes before joining the others that were now over the garden. A remarkable sight. Then they were gone as quickly as they had appeared. I felt my consciousness jolted; where did they come from and where did they go?

Strangely, the birds made me notice passages from the Koran on the Taj Mahal. They were inscribed in the marble between the flower patterns in bold, black, Nashk characters of lines and swirls. "These were the favorite passages of the Emperor; the good words that came first in the Koran," Sekhar explained. It was known that the more punishing and radical passages came later and trumped the earlier passages. It was something the emperor Jahan didn't accept. His grandfather Akbar had instructed him as a young boy that Allah wouldn't allow such distortion of his words."

A tour group of older German couples walked past us speaking with a Bavarian accent. The tour guide, a young Indian boy who spoke German, pointed to these passages from the Koran. An older man walked away from the group. He had his hands behind his back and held his right wrist with his left hand, looking like a construction inspector. He walked over to the wall facing the river and looked down, where local people were working, then he looked up at the Taj Mahal, the side facing the river. The young Indian tour guide kept an eye on him while continuing to explain the Koran passages.

Two weeks earlier a young Muslim man from Pakistan had attempted to blow himself up with plastic explosives while on the same tour. The explosives failed to detonate and the man was arrested. Nothing was said to the press. Had the explosives detonated at least thirty tourists would have been killed or seriously injured, including this young tour guide. The guide had been criticized for not being more observant.

"Radical Muslims want to blow up the Taj." Sekhar was upset.

"Do you understand German?" I asked Sekhar.

"No, but I know what he's telling them about what we talked about in the car yesterday. He's talking about the young Muslim that had plastic explosives strapped to his legs under his pants, and that the fuse fell out before he could light it. The guide could get in trouble for telling this."

"Failed explosions don't make the news," I said.

"No. Tourism would suffer," Sekhar replied.

"Who's behind this?"

"Radical Muslims from Pakistan. They hate what the Taj stands for: beauty, love, and unity. Hindu arches that harmonize with Muslim domes and the Christian cross. Unthinkable for them." Sekhar reasserted.

"The young boys with explosives tied around their waist don't hate this beauty, they don't even recognize it. They have been told the Taj is an old stone building that contradicts Allah.

They hate because they have been taught to hate. They are profoundly poor with nothing to do and no place to go; easy to radicalize." Now I was distressed.

"That's right. And the teachers of hate, radical Imams, operate thousands of Islamic schools where only the Koran is taught—nothing else. And the parts that call for killing nonbelievers, infidels, and apostates are glorified. The young boys rock on their knees chanting killing words and think about the promise of seventy-two virgins." Sekhar lamented.

"What's the solution? Is there a solution?" I asked him.

Another tour group came by, Japanese tourists this time. They were dressed well; the women in expensive dark-colored dresses and the men in business suits. They didn't look comfortable in the bright sun. The men walked ahead of the tour guide and were talking fast and motioning frequently with their hands to each other. Two of the younger men photographed the Taj with their Nikon cameras, then moved away from the group toward the riverfront overlook. The women walked with the guide but did not seem to be paying attention to what he was saying as he pointed to the black swirls and lines that represented the Koran passages. They moved by faster than the German group and the guide did not seem bothered by the two that were away photographing.

"Those good words in the Koran, what exactly do they say?" I asked Sekhar.

"They say the soul must be at rest to return to God and be at peace with him. They also speak of love and justice."

"And these passages are superseded by the more violent verses

"That's right." Sekhar nodded. "Some theologians say it's because Mohammed didn't get enough pagan converts with the good words, so he had to resort to distortions and threats. Killing infidels was at the top of his list!"

"So, the Japanese and German tourists are infidels like us, and the shoe tending ladies, and the Hindu women washing clothes by the river, and the old man brushing his cattle, and the two boys with the goat—all of them. Meaning there are at least five billion infidels in this world! I noted.

"Reform, reform, reform—it must happen, the poison must be cut out of Islam from within by moderate Muslims! They have to group together, world-wide, and prevent their children from being radicalized." Sekhar's face showed red with emotion.

"I agree, it has to start with the children, the challenge will be how to keep them out of radical schools and mosques," I said, emphatically. "Then get them to accept the rest of us as part of God's creation."

"Meaning Sharia must be rewritten, corresponding to adjustments made in the Koran," Sekhar declared.

"How can that happen?" I asked him.

"It needs to start somewhere, like with support from the U.N.," He suggested, testing me.

"Won't happen—the U.N supports strict Sharia," I stated sadly.

"That's because of the Arabs, it won't happen with them in control,"

"So how does it get started?" I asked him.

"I believe it needs to start here in India, away from Pakistan. The Muslims here have Mughal blood in them; they would make the required adjustments. Not all at once, but methodically." Sekhar sounded hopeful.

"Wow, a world model for moderate Muslims and new Islamic law. A global revelation!"

"Yes, civilized law!" Sekhar exclaimed. "It can be a new start for Islam! India has a billion people and a big army with guns and bombs to defend the idea. And it's a democracy! Many Hindus would support it. Today they would, not yesterday. Muslims killed millions of Hindus many yesterday's ago. . ."

"That could force the U.N to change!" I was excited. "Or maybe we need a totally new U.N.—one with a different charter!"

I could tell Sekhar had purposely engaged us in this tough dialogue on Islam. This discussion needed to be had around the world! I would write it down! Millions of moderate Muslims are endangered, and billions of non-Muslims.

We walked back to the stairs that led down to the garden and our shoes. We sat down and put them on. I was happy mine were still there—it was a needless worry. I tipped the ladies who had watched them. The garden ahead of us was bright now in the afternoon sun with many people walking around. A great diversity of people, it was easy to spot Muslims and Hindus, Christians and Buddhists. They all looked human. I glanced back at the Taj Mahal, all white now in exquisite splendor, and saw that the white birds were back, flying high over the great dome of the building built for love.

"A good omen," Sekhar said, pointing to the birds.

Down by the river the old man was gone as were the clothes-washing women. It was too hot now to wash cattle and clothes. The two boys were swimming in the river. The goat was with them and seemed to be happy in the water. I was happy too—for them and for the strong possibility that goodness would prevail.

45-pound Musky caught by author using Lenny's method

12

The Smile of Death

Life and Death in Ojibway Country

Eagle River, Ontario, 1970

The Indian had watched his grandmother drown when he was a young boy. She was old and in poor health, unable to work or enjoy life. She had become a burden on the family. So, she decided to drown herself in the river that flowed from the lake, over the dam, and into the far north where he had never been.

He remembered her not as an old woman in poor health but as a healthy, vital woman full of energy and kindness and love of life. Some of his favorite memories were of her fishing for walleyes with a hand line, always catching more fish than his father, and of her setting traps in the clean-white of winter in special places she knew. She would smile and sing those old songs—Ojibway songs. These memories were the best part of the boy's life. In his dreams, he could feel her hands smoothing the birthmarks that covered his face and arms, massaging them to the rhythm of her songs. He remembered the songs well—they told of a spirit world that was good and went on forever. A world that gave credit for a life rich with love and experience. A world filled with happy souls.

Fifteen years later:

The big fish suspended effortlessly in the clear water, her brown-spot camouflage made her invisible. Forty feet below, walleyes chased mud minnows on the bottom of the lake. Instinctively, the big fish could reduce her buoyancy, sink slowly, and eat walleyes. But she had eaten this morning, and now the warmth of the sun was speeding her digestion. Fanning her pectoral fins for stability, she stayed high in the water in a rock cradle by an island.

The Indian cast the lure into a rock cradle that was off the end of an island surrounded by large rocks. He reeled it back to the boat after each cast using a slow jerking technique that alternated with dead stops where the lure didn't move for several seconds. Big muskies were attracted to such a retrieve! When worked properly, the lure looked like a wounded fish that would be an easy meal, one not requiring an energy demanding chase.

It was a lure his father had made; a flat piece of cedar wood painted black that was one-foot long and had two large hooks. On this day, fishing alone, the Indian had removed the hooks. His intension was *not* to catch a musky, only to find one. A big one! It was common for muskies to follow lures before attempting to eat them.

So, the Indian was just exploring for muskies—cousins of the northern pike, only larger. There were muskies over seventy pounds in the lake; World Records! Large muskies had various feeding spots that they visited. By mid-summer they preferred rocky reefs near deep water that had current. If weeds were close, the spot was even better. A "spot" was a specific place in the lake, it could be as small as a single rock or many yards in diameter. Each musky had its own itinerary—wind direction helped determine the spots that were visited on a given day. Big muskies preferred wind-blown spots that gave them odds on finding fish to eat. But muskies moved around; the longest the Indian ever saw the same musky on the same spot was three days. The lake was huge—thousands of acres—and had myriad hideouts.

He worked the lure in specific patterns at different speeds, flipping and popping it on the surface, followed by dead stops; waiting a few moments, then starting a zig-zag motion. Muskies were carnivorous—they preferred fish but also ate frogs, rodents and baby ducks. The Indian was fish-smart. He soaked his wood lures in fish guts overnight, reasoning that just resembling a fish was not enough; they had to smell like one, too. Big muskies often followed lures with their noses just inches away; no fish smell, no bite.

The Indian kept casting at the rock cradle at the end of the island, trying different actions with the lure. Then he moved the boat away from the rocks, over deeper water. He did this quietly using a paddle, not the motor. On a cast, out beyond the cradle while reeling the lure slowly in a zig-zag motion, a five-foot shadow followed deep below it. The Indian got down on his knees, thrusting his fishing rod deep into the water up to the reel, to the same depth as the shadow. The giant fish, now visible, turned and followed the moving lure; the Indian could see its wolf-like head and large red tail. It was a huge musky! At that moment, before the fish tried to eat it, the Indian pulled the lure up and into the boat. Even without hooks, he didn't want the musky to bite the lure and feel that it was made of wood. Muskies didn't get to be five feet long by being stupid. The Indian would come back later with fishermen who would pay extra to catch a big musky. Hooks would be on the lures!

"Big fish. I know where you live," he said in Ojibway. He paddled away from the island before starting the twenty-horsepower motor. It was time to head back to camp and find fishermen. He would use the extra money to buy beer. The Indian liked beer…

It was a ninety-minute run back to the fishing lodge where he worked as a guide. He thought about the fish. It was big—he would see only three or four this size in a good year! The Indian would get a one-hundred-dollar tip if the fish was caught by a client, fifty dollars if the fish only followed. It was a calm July afternoon, the sixteen-foot Lund boat was making a symmetrical wake with a bald eagle following it, checking for wounded fish. This eagle recognized the Indian who often threw it a northern pike that had mistakenly eaten a musky lure. "No pike today," the Indian told the eagle. It understood and flew off.

He turned the boat west passing a long island that was shaped like a net from the air and then veered north, past a flat rock full of seagulls and into another large basin with a hidden reef in the middle—an invisible rockpile the size of a semi-truck that was only one-foot under water at its shallowest. The Indian knew most of these killer reefs on the lake. If you hit them going fast they could take your motor off and sink the boat! He enjoyed scaring clients by running close to such a reef, then pounding his foot on the aluminum hull as he swerved abruptly. "Big rock!" He would shout, faking a hit. Clients would cringe and shudder. He only did this to fishermen who didn't know the lake.

North of the hidden reef, he passed three islands that guarded the entrance to a wide channel. It wove its way west then north across a match-line on the map that divided the lake in two sections: north lake and south lake. The boat's wake disrupted a family of loons in the calm water. The Indian swerved to miss them, but the male got up, flapping and doing a mad dance while making sharp, staccato loon sounds. He wasn't happy his family had been disturbed. The female just rocked in the wake with a small fish crosswise in her mouth.

Just beyond the loons were several islands in the main channel. The middle island had a small wooden cabin that held specific significance for the Indian, but it wasn't pleasant for him to think about that island. He had lived there for three years with his wife and kids in his young days, as he referred to them. He always looked at the opposite shore when he passed the cabin.

He was steering the boat straight north now and was about a third of the way to the fishing lodge. Ahead was another hour of islands, bays, and hidden rocks. He could do this run blindfolded–it was automatic for him. A form of Ojibway meditation took hold of his soul at these times.

Lenny Martin was the Indian's name. He was short, skinny, and strong. When cleaning walleyes for shore lunch with a group of fishermen—on some nameless rock on some nameless island—the birthmarks on his face and arms blended with the nature around him. The rocks on the lake were from time's childhood, billions of years old. Their scattered reds and purples mixed with browns and grays matched Lenny's camouflaged body.

He kept the boat on a course that averaged north. In the distance, he could see Pine Tree Lodge.

Thirty miles from the big fish, Lenny tied the boat to the gas dock at Pine Tree Lodge, known as PTL. Guests were clustered outside the lodge around several Weber grills, frying walleyes and drinking Labatt's beer. Elaine Parker, owner and Commander in Chief, was in the kitchen cooking beans and potatoes to go with the fish. Dinner would be served outside at PTL—a shore dinner—on the beach surrounded by white pine trees. The mild breeze from the west was bringing in fresh air from Manitoba.

The lodge and its twelve cabins faced south looking over the north lake's largest bay. Elaine's husband, Harold, had passed away fifteen years ago. She ran PTL with local help and used a yellow pad for her paperwork. Elaine lived in Madison, Wisconsin during the off season, November through April. Most of her guests returned year after year; she was a mother and grandmother to them. Young children who had come with their parent's years ago now came as adults with their families. Most guests were from the Midwest but not all—California, Texas, Pennsylvania, and Hawaii were well-represented. PTL was a special place.

Lenny was talking with several fishermen on the dock by his boat.

"Lenny saw a giant musky!" A fisherman named Sam said.

"Very big," Lenny said, matter-of-factly.

"How far from here?" Frank, another fisherman, asked Lenny.

"About ninety minutes when no wind," Lenny answered.

"How big is big?" Sam asked.

Lenny looked around. There were six men on the dock now. He went over to a six-foot man, put his hand on the man's chin and pointed to the ground with his other hand.

"Holy guacamole, that's over sixty inches!" Frank declared excitedly. The world record was sixty-two inches. He took a long drink of his Labatt's.

"I don't believe him," one of the walleye fishermen said. Sam and Frank were musky fishermen and they knew it was possible. In the 1960s this lake produced two such fish that were never officially weighed but were over sixty inches.

"Bigger than me," Lenny reaffirmed, he was two inches over five-feet tall. He noticed that the disbelieving walleye fisherman was short, too, and couldn't believe a fish bigger than him was in the lake.

"How much will it cost?" Sam looked at Frank who silently lipped "one-hundred."

"One hundred dollars if you catch, fifty dollars if only follow," Lenny specified. "World record more."

"Canadian?" Sam checked his wallet.

"U.S. dollars. Green money," Lenny replied. Normally, guides got twenty-five dollars a day for walleye fishing, musky guides got fifty. Frank and Sam discussed it. They were both betting men and often went to Las Vegas together. Iowa boys.

"Tell you what, Sam, whoever catches the fish doesn't pay; the other guy pays the hundred bucks," Frank wagered Sam.

"Get ready to pay!" Sam grinned, taking a drink of his beer. Lenny could smell the beer. Every man on the dock was drinking a beer.

"What time tomorrow?" Frank asked Lenny.

"Not tomorrow—fish active now!" Lenny insisted.

"Mother of Mercy," Sam exclaimed. Neither of them had eaten yet!

"We gotta go!" Frank was anxious. "It's now or never. A hot, *active* monster fish takes priority over eating." Sam could see *hot* fish frying on the Weber grills, luscious walleyes, but no time for them. *Hot* had just been redefined.

"Ten minutes!" Lenny ordered. Both men ran back to their cabins to get jackets and gear. It was 6:30 p.m. and would be dark at 10:00. Elaine came out of the lodge and handed Frank a lunch bag, knowing they hadn't eaten. "Ham sandwiches, chips and soda pop," she said. "Thank You!" Frank smiled, grabbing the bag as he headed to the dock. Sam was already in the boat. "Catch a big one!" Elaine shouted.

Lenny had the motor running. Frank handed his tackle box to Sam and got into the boat with his fishing rod and the food. Lenny, wishing he had a case of beer along, put the motor in gear and headed south. Elaine did not allow her guides to drink beer when guiding. Lenny could still smell all six bottles that were open on the dock. He would have negotiated a lower price for catching the fish if a case of beer could have been included.

The boat skimmed through the water smoothly, but slower now with three men. The Indian wished he had the Alumacraft boat with its forty-horsepower motor—the one he used when guiding for the other lodge. The PTL boats were fine for walleye fisherman who fished close to the lodge; musky fisherman fished all over the lake. A forty-horse would have made a big difference with three in the boat. More push, more speed. The other lodge was run by a half-Indian named Lester who had different rules: Lenny could take out all the beer he wanted provided he paid for it. Being Indian meant the Ontario Provincial Police—the OPP—didn't bother you much.

Lenny cruised through the main channel, swerving to avoid the same family of loons as before. This time the male, apparently in a better mood, stayed calm. Then they passed the several small islands that came before making the sharp left turn where the channel opened wide. Frank pointed to the small island that hid the cabin where Lenny once lived with his wife and kids. He remembered Elaine talking about it a few years ago; it was not a good story and you had to ask her to tell it. Lenny looked straight ahead when passing the island—the small deserted cabin was hard to see, hidden behind trees. You could see it if you knew where to look. Lenny didn't give it a glance.

Sitting backwards looking at Lenny, Sam took notice of his extensive birthmarks. He had not thought much about them in the past, but with the sun shining on Lenny, they stood out. Frank had told Sam on their drive up from Iowa about the horrible names guests from other lodges had called Lenny: Moss

Face, Franken Face, Dung face and worse. It was mostly men from Illinois who'd stayed at a certain lodge. A dangerous mid-lake reef was near that lodge, a good walleye spot. When Lenny guided for walleyes he would fish several deep rock-humps around it. The lake was full of underwater rock-humps; knowing which ones held fish was the key. Lenny out-fished the other boats—not something guests from that nearby lodge appreciated. Sam just shook his head. There were some real mean SOBs in this world.

Sam was ten years older than Frank and both were divorced. Frank, at fifty-five, had more energy, and he could cast twelve hours a day. Sam liked to mix in trolling, but with trolling you couldn't see follows and seeing follows was a big part of musky fishing. Muskies were famed for their wary and cautious nature; old Wisconsin guides called them "the fish of ten thousand casts." Lenny had disproved this in Canada by fishing with lures that smelled and moved like real fish. He would stop a lure in front of a following fish, let the musky get a good whiff, then slightly twitch it and get ready for an explosion when the fish hit. He had watched many suckers and ciscos—common baitfish in a musky's diet—flop and splash near the surface, stopping momentarily to rest, only to get inhaled by a musky. The musky was instinctively conservative with its energy; a fish or lure that had been moving, then stopped suddenly, was an energy-saving meal! The Indian figured the musky was a fish of one or two thousand casts, when you knew how to fish for it.

They were now beyond the three islands that guarded the entrance to the main channel, well out in the middle of the big expanse of water with the hidden reef. In the calm, Lenny didn't have to hug the shoreline; he could head east through the middle of the open water, the shortest route to the fish. When viewed from where they were on the lake, the far-east shoreline—a five-mile-long expanse of forty-foot trees—looked only a quarter-inch high. This was big water!

Lenny stopped the boat in the open water after Frank grabbed the lunch bag.

"Time for short break." Lenny put the motor neutral, he was looking at the position of the sun.

Frank opened the bag. The ham sandwiches looked good—thick cuts of ham with lettuce, mayo, and mustard between slices of Elaine's home-made bread. She knew they both liked mayo and mustard.

"Coke or Dr. Pepper?" Frank looked at Sam.

"Take what you want. No difference to me," Sam shrugged his shoulders.

"I would prefer a rum and Coke but will default to a Coke." Frank handed two ham sandwiches, a bag of chips, and the Dr. Pepper to Sam. He offered Lenny a sandwich, but Lenny was already eating a cold walleye filet that he had wrapped in foil. Lenny thought, *what I really need is a beer.*

A large flock of seagulls found them, dipping and diving and calling to each other. Frank opened one of the extra sandwiches and started throwing pieces of it at the birds. Some were sitting in the water and others flying. They gobbled up every morsel and called louder, bringing in more comrades. Then Frank fed them his potato chips and more birds appeared out of the blue.

"Now look what you've started," Sam said, not willing to share his chips with the birds.

"It's all part of fishing." Frank grinned. Sam shook his head.

They were about thirty minutes from the big fish, confirming it took longer to get there with three in the boat. In his imagination, Lenny could still smell the beer the fishermen were drinking on the dock at PTL. In one of Lester's boats he would have had several Molson by now.

Lenny switched his thoughts to his grandmother. She was old and had lived her life well—it was time for her to leave. She could choose any day; she chose a warm August day. It was something she had been thinking about for quite a while and knew it was her time. It was unpleasant to think about at first, but then became easier when she realized her sons understood how to help.

Lenny recalled how elegant she looked in her favorite powwow dress that day; her long hair—still mostly black—ran down her shoulders. She stood waving to her family and friends that had gathered to watch her leave. Smiling to them, she then walked into the river, beyond the dam, and sat down in shallow water. Several eagles flew above her, looking for wounded fish coming over the dam. She was smiling her best smile now while looking up at the eagles in the blue sky. She hummed the melody of one of her favorite Ojibway songs while two of her sons gently moved her into deeper water. The third son, Lenny's father, placed a heavy rock in her lap and stepped away. She smiled at them and raised her hands up, pointing at the sky.

Underwater, she inhaled slowly, filling her lungs with water. This is what the Ojibway elders had told her to do. Her eyes were wide open as bubbles rose from her nose and mouth. There was no panic, just a look of surprise as the cool water entered her body. But then, after a few moments, fully alive, her expression changed from surprise back to a smile. The skinny little boy with the ugly birthmarks was sitting next to her, holding his breath. It was part of his education to watch. She touched his face and arms, rubbing his birthmarks, still smiling. As she slowly faded—there was no pain, it was like going to sleep. She was entering that world she had described to the boy, the world her mother had described to her. It was the place she had dreamed about often, the place where your body was young again, with no disease; a place with new colors and wonderful music that enlivened the soul. The best of her experience and love from her life on Earth was with her. Lenny couldn't stop watching. She was the only person he truly loved.

Suddenly, he was pulled up and out of the water by his father. "You have watched enough, boy. *Remember it!*" He would remember it often whenever he drove a boat on the lake.

They were thirty yards from the island with the rock cradle. Lenny would not fish since there were two fishermen with him; he would with only one. He gave them instructions. Frank was told to cast off one side of the boat, Sam off the other. Both would use the flat wooden lures Lenny's father made, one was black and the other white. Frank flipped a silver dollar he had won in Vegas. "Call it," he said. Sam called heads. Heads it was. Sam picked the white lure. Both lures were in a plastic bag of walleye guts that gave them an authentic fish odor. Lenny told them to set their drags tight and set the hook hard when a fish hits the lure.

"Pull back hard, two times. Reel fast, don't give slack. Loosen drag when fish is close. Hold thumb on line for more pressure. If fish jumps, lower rod. Keep reeling." Sam and Frank new all this, but it was good to hear it again. Lenny's vocabulary had suddenly improved!

"Cast *there*!" Lenny pointed toward the rock cradle, a semicircle of large rocks just under water. Frank made the first cast, Sam followed. Frank's lure landed right in the rock cradle. He immediately started retrieving it in a fast zig-zag pattern near the surface. Sam's cast landed ten yards left of the cradle in deeper water—he let the lure sit motionless until the ripples were gone. Then, slowly, very slowly, he pulled the white lure down a foot and let it surface, allowing the ripples to disappear again, then repeated the sequence. Frank's second cast was fifteen yards to the right of the cradle over deeper water. When it hit the water, he repeated his fast zig-zag retrieve. Sam's lure was only halfway back to the boat, hardly moving, quivering in the water. Both lures left a trail of fish-gut juice.

A dark "log," deep in the water, swam under Frank's lure. "Here she is!" he said in a loud whisper. "She's huge!" The late afternoon sun illuminated her golden body as she moved higher in the water—slowly.

"Her eyes are the size of my silver dollar!" Frank exclaimed.

"Keep lure in water. Move it slow. Make big circle." Lenny told Frank. The fish was too big for the figure-eight pattern most often used on a follow. It wouldn't be able to turn sharply enough to follow the two circles of an eight. Sam did not get distracted—his lure was ten feet out from the boat—he stopped reeling and let it quiver. The big fish kept following Frank's lure that was making a five-foot circle in the water, running about a foot deep. About halfway around the circle, nose on the lure, the fish disappeared. "She's gone," Frank said, astonished. "No!"

"Fish not gone! Cast more—reel slower." Lenny instructed Frank, knowing the fish was still around and being cautious. Sunset was in thirty minutes—moon rise had just occurred. The absolute best time to awaken a big musky! Their timing was perfect. Sam kept his lure quivering about five feet off the bow; he was ready to reel in and cast a second time. He could smell the fish guts on the lure that was lying motionless now, next to the boat. Something told him to give it one more twitch…

Sha—Boom! The water exploded as the giant fish smashed the white lure, hitting the side of the boat while going vertical, drenching Sam with a bucket of water. Sam instinctively tightened his grip on the rod and pointed it at the fish.

"Set hook!" Lenny yelled. Sam pulled back hard and reeled, but the reel's spool didn't turn, the tight drag held. The rod buckled and jolted Sam. Quickly, he turned the star-drag toward himself a half-turn to lessen the drag. He could feel that indescribable pulsing resistance to movement that only a big fish can produce. It was like pulling on a heavy spring nailed to a wall—your pull got an equal pull back. In those first seconds, nobody—fish or man—was going anywhere. Then, after a few more seconds, the drag reluctantly gave line and Sam could feel the mass of the musky. The fish, head shaking violently, straightened and torpedoed out in half-leaps creating a mountainous wake. Everything was tight—the monofilament line sang soprano notes.

"Keep less pressure on her. Back off the drag some more!" Frank instructed. Sam turned the star-drag toward himself only a quarter turn. The fish was running straight out from the bow and taking line. Lenny pulled the outboard motor up; the fish had moved them into open water. He grabbed the paddle and positioned the boat sideways to the fish to slow her down. Frank was in the middle. Sam stayed in front. *The fish was pulling the boat!*

"Did you see that jump when she smashed the lure? She was completely out of the water—vertical. She's over sixty inches!" Frank shouted, infused with excitement—he could see it was a record-class fish. Sam was cool and reasonably collected. He held the rod high and let the fish run, staying even with her for ten minutes. For every ten feet of line reeled in, she took ten feet back out.

"She almost fall in boat," Lenny said, while putting on an old pair of leather gloves. Sam wasn't listening…he was paying attention to the fish. Dripping wet from her jump, he kept his rod bent at a forty-five-degree angle, holding it high while slowly bringing in line. His quality equipment was making a difference. Sam had bought the Ambassador 7000 reel and the seven-foot Fenwick rod in Florida the previous year; a gift to himself celebrating his retirement. Tarpon fishermen were catching two-hundred-pound tarpon with the same equipment.

Sam felt like he was trying to pull a blanket away from eighty-pound bulldog. Suddenly, the fish turned and headed directly toward the boat. No longer feeling the resistance, she re-energized—swimming normally now and moving fast.

"Reel fast!" Lenny shouted.

"Keep the line tight," Frank advised. Sam reeled fast and kept the line tight.

When the fish saw the boat, it skyrocketed again, this time landing back in the water sideways with a splash that drenched Frank and Lenny. "Beats going to a water park," Frank gurgled, belching water.

Sam was smiling! *Everyone* was wet now. He reeled in the slack line after the jump. All the action was now around the boat. The fish sideswiped it and surged forward, feeling the unnatural aluminum metal with its entire body. There would be no debate about its length or girth; Sam, Frank, and Lenny saw it up close. The lure's front hook was in the corner of the musky's mouth—the back hook was hanging free. Just one hook was holding the fish! *Thank God Lenny used extra- strong hooks,* Sam thought.

Lenny changed places with Frank so he could get next to Sam and grab the fish. He got down on his knees next to Sam. "Bring her to me head first," he told Sam while pulling his gloves tight. Sam could manage the fish now. Finally, his heart was pounding—Sam moderated his excitement and kept his emotions in check until he knew the fish was ready to be boated. Lenny reached for the fish, grabbing her under a gill plate but not in the gills. He attempted to lift her up but he needed to be a foot taller; he got her halfway out of the water before the glove on his left hand came off and he lost his grip. He held her for several seconds right at the boat. It's giant wolf head with silver dollar eyes and mouth full of spiked teeth was fearsome. Frank and Sam saw it clearly—then she was gone!

In moments of despair, the silence can be deafening. A few quiet seconds passed.

"*Slam Bam, Slam Bam*"; she was not gone! She was under the boat caught on something, slamming the bottom of the boat with her big tail. Thumping continuously, rocking the boat.

"The fish is still on!" Sam and Frank yelled nearly at the same time.

"Put rod deep in water!" Lenny shouted. Sam leaned over the side and did just that. He had the rod in the water up to the reel – he didn't want to lose this fish. He gingerly pushed down on the rod, giving it small jerks; *Slam Bam, Slam Bam,* continued. Then there was a metal scraping sound and another *Slam Bam.* Seconds later Sam couldn't feel or hear anything, nothing. No thumping, no resistance, no splashing. Gone, all gone. He reeled in the lure; the front hook that had held the fish was bent straight out. The rear hook that was hanging loose was also straightened. It must have caught under the boat on the keel or a rivet. That made it possible for the fish to exert extra leverage on the hook in its mouth. Sam knew he had just lost the all-tackle world record musky! The three men sat in total silence...

"Sam, you caught that fish." Frank broke the silence.

"Not really, we didn't boat it," Sam lamented.

"But Lenny did grab it, if only for a few seconds. That's the way they release tarpon in Key West—in the water. They don't bring them into the boat! They grab the leader and shake the fish off. A rivet did that for you! We had it! It was a perfect release. You caught it—the world record! I can say I was with the man who caught the world-record musky!" Frank hugged Sam.

All large muskies are females; forty-five inches is considered big for a male. This fish was a record fish at sixty-three inches—one inch taller than Lenny—and had a thirty-inch girth.

It calculated to be seventy-one pounds! Twenty ounces over the sixty-nine-pound, eleven-ounce all-tackle world record caught in Wisconsin in 1949. It had been a very special day in the fishing world. Both man and fish had won!

Frank and Sam each gave Lenny one hundred dollars, two fresh Benjamin Franklins; they'd just had the fishing experience of their lives! Frank had cancelled their bet. His lucky silver dollar was better suited for measuring musky eyes than winning bets. Lenny thanked them with his famous smile of broken teeth; he would drink beer this weekend. The sunset was rich with a full spectrum of dark reds and purples as they headed back to PTL. A mile west of the rock cradle, where the water was calm and cool; two bald eagles flew over their lake.

Lenny thought about the beer he would drink this weekend with his friends in Kenora, on Lake of the Woods—a million acres of musky water. The lake PTL was on covered sixty-eight-thousand acres. By comparison, a three-thousand-acre lake in northern Wisconsin, the birthplace of musky fishing, was considered large. These Ontario lakes were in a different class.

The previous day had been a perfect day for Lenny; he'd held the largest musky ever caught and had earned two hundred dollars that he would spend on beer with his friends! It was time to celebrate.

It was a Saturday afternoon when Lenny went into one of the bars where fellow Indians spent their time. Some of them lived in apartments upstairs. Country and western music was playing but he never liked it; he liked his grandmother's songs. He had learned to associate various country and western songs with his grandmother's Ojibway songs and trained his brain to hear her singing them instead of the song that was playing. It usually took a half dozen Molson, his favorite Canadian beer, to activate the process.

He ordered two Molson and pulled out one of the U.S. hundred-dollar bills to pay. Shorty, the bartender, was not surprised. "Fish money from the Americans?" he asked. Lenny nodded.

"How big was it?"

"Bigger than me." He put a thumb and index finger on his head one inch apart, meaning one inch taller than he was, his favorite way of measuring a fish.

"A big one!" Shorty said. Lenny grinned.

Soon his friends started showing up. They heard he was in town and that he'd caught a big musky—this meant he had money! Lenny ordered Molson for everybody.

The beer was easy to drink and more friends showed up. It reminded him of when he was young and bought beer; he had always been generous with his beer money. There were plenty of fish to catch. Money was swimming in lakes.

In those younger days, he even bought beer for his wife's boyfriend. Lenny had stopped living with her except on occasions when everybody was drunk and they all slept together. He and the boyfriend got into fights often. Once it was because the boyfriend wore one of Lenny's favorite shirts. Lenny's broken teeth were reminders of those days. The time he lived in the cabin with his wife and kids was something he didn't like to think about. He raised his hand and Shorty brought out two more Molson.

The bar was filling up with people: Indian men, American fishermen, hookers, locals, kids, and dogs. Several dogs drank beer off the floor, lapping it up whenever it got spilled. It kept the owner's wife from having to mop. Lenny was well into the Molson when Tiny came in and forced himself onto two bar stools next to Lenny. The stools belonged to a couple who were dancing. There would be no moving Tiny. He was a huge man, 350 pounds. He punched Lenny on the arm, announcing himself—they had been friends forever. Lenny said nothing. He raised his hand and Shorty brought Tiny two Molson. Lenny pointed to the money piled in front of him, mostly Canadian change from the U.S. hundred-dollar bill. Shorty took two dollars from the pile. Tiny drank the first bottle fast. Lenny was mentally converting a Johnny Cash song to one of his grandmother's songs. He would talk to Tiny when the song was over. Tiny knew this.

When the two of them started to talk in Ojibway they also used English words when there were no equals in Ojibway. They recalled going to the powwows as kids. In those days powwows were mostly about playing games and having fun, now they were about politics; like how the Indians could get more money from the government. Tiny was completely on government support, and rightly so given his disabilities. But most of the other Indians in the bar didn't deserve it. That was Tiny's thinking. Lenny didn't care, his money swam in the lake. He told Tiny that his best times were when his grandmother was here. That was over thirty-five years ago. Today he lived alone; even his two boys didn't visit him.

"Ever see Nancy?" Tiny asked.

"Has new boyfriend—moved to Winnipeg." Lenny said.

"What about the boys?"

"One works at paper mill in Dryden—doesn't come to Kenora. The younger one lives with Nancy." A Dolly Parton song played and Lenny paused to translate it in his head. He could hear his grandmother's sweet voice. He would buy her a beer if she were here. She liked beer, but only one bottle. Tiny was watching young girls dancing while listening to Lenny and Dolly.

How would it feel to drown? Lenny wondered. He saw his grandmother drown. Her eyes were open, still smiling when her arms floated above her head, right when his father pulled him away. But was it that way for others? Did others smile? How could he imagine it?

He thought about it again: Maybe it was like drinking beer; being very full of beer, then drinking more beer until it ran out your mouth and made you wet. But you kept drinking, barely able to swallow anymore. Then urinating, and drinking so much that you were urinating constantly and drinking constantly until your urine was pure beer. Totally full and wet with beer, you never stopped drinking; endless drinking. You would be timeless and weightless like a fish after ice-out in spring, slow and half asleep. Then, in your tiredness and wetness, without another thought in this world; your soul would smile forever.

Five years later:

"What's that guide's name, the one with the birthmarks?" Larry asked.

"Lenny Martin," Elaine said. "He doesn't guide for me anymore."

"Why not?"

"He's drunk most of the time now. He used to be a good guide. He hangs out in Kenora."

"He still guides for Angry Bear Lodge. I see him on the lake sometimes," Jim said. Larry and Jim were fishing buddies, regulars at PTL. They were sitting with Elaine Parker at her kitchen table, a place where discussions from trivial significance to vast, worldly importance had been taking place for decades. She was the boss, but also everybody's mother and grandmother; short, smart, sweet, and neat. She had been down every road in the resort business for over thirty years.

"Elaine, tell us the story about when their baby froze to death in that cabin," Jim asked her.

"It's a horribly sad story," Elaine said. "Lenny and his wife Nancy were living in that small cabin on that island in the main channel—you both know where it is. They had three kids; two boys and a four-month old baby girl. It was late October and a severe cold front had come down from the north. The older of the two boys was told to take care of his brother and the baby when Lenny and Nancy went out drinking in Dryden. It got late and they didn't make it back to the cabin. The kids fell asleep and the fire in their wood stove went out. It got down well below freezing! The boys were huddled under a wool blanket by the stove and the baby must have rolled out from between them onto the wood floor. The cabin was on cement blocks so the cold wind got under it. The warped wood floor boards had gaps where it could blow in. The baby froze to death! I don't think she had a name yet."

"My God," Larry mumbled, it was hard for him to talk.

"There's more," Jim said. He'd heard the story before.

Elaine continued: "The older boy couldn't go for help because his parents had taken their boat across the lake—over twenty miles—and left it at the Indian reservation on the east shore. No fishermen were around in late October. The kids were stranded on the island."

Elaine paused. "You guys want a beer?" They nodded yes, entranced and disturbed by the story. She went to the refrigerator and took out two Labatts for them. Elaine never drank alcohol when PTL was open, May through October.

She got back to the story, "The warden arrived at the island late that morning. Nancy had called him from the reservation. She couldn't start their boat and Lenny was still drunk. It was already cold enough for ice to form along the shore. The warden didn't know what to expect. When he saw the baby on the floor he immediately examined her; she had no pulse and was blue and motionless. He tried mouth-to-mouth resuscitation, but it was too late. The younger of the two boys was crying and pointing to her. The warden—distressed to say the least—spoke to the older boy, but it was hard to get him to talk.

"The warden looked around and noticed several empty vodka bottles in the other room. It was a two-room cabin. He suspected that the boys may have been drinking, which would have explained why they didn't wake up if the baby cried. Blankets were on the floor in the main room along with a box of stale donuts, two fishing rods, and a pair of old boots—not much else. The boys had restarted the fire when they woke up. The warden put it out and took the boys and the baby to the reservation. That's as much as I know," Elaine said sorrowfully.

"Horrible. Unbelievable," Larry was shocked.

"I think about it every time I fish around that island!" Jim added, still disturbed.

"We never heard anything about further investigations. It wasn't smart to gossip about it back then! Indians were treated differently in the 1970s; certain 'events' were ignored by the authorities. The cabin was abandoned. Still is today," Elaine finished. "Keep this to yourselves."

Lenny, drinking a Molson at the bar in Kenora, went back in his mind to a fish he'd caught recently. It was important for him to remember the details of catching truly big fish—the "Big Girls" he called them. The ones over forty pounds.

He was thinking about last week when he hooked a forty-five-pound, fifty-five-inch fish while guiding a young man who had never fished muskies before. The beer helped him focus his thoughts; but uncharacteristically, he drank it slowly in small amounts.

Lenny fought the fish first, making sure he'd hooked it well, then handed the rod to the young man. "Keep reeling," he told the man who could immediately feel the power of the big musky. He had never experienced what it felt like to reel one in; a twenty-four-inch northern pike was his biggest fish—until now! Lenny knew the musky was hooked well; both treble hooks were deep in its lower jaw. The big fish fought hard, making several jumps and a deep run. Then it bulldogged around the boat. The man controlled the fish well, doing whatever Lenny told him to do. They had been on the deep edge of a weed bed and had drifted into thick weeds during the fight. The fish had tangled in long green cabbage weeds and then got into a mat of brown coontail weeds, thicker yet. "Reel slow and steady," Lenny told the man while reaching for his pliers and gloves. The fish was in the middle of the weed mass and could hardly move. "Do you want to keep fish?" Lenny asked the man. "No, let it go." Lenny was happy to hear that. In his younger days, he would have automatically clubbed the fish. "Pull fish and weeds to me." The man followed Lenny's order.

With gloves on, Lenny reached into the weeds near the fish's head, glad both trebles were in its mouth. When he could see the gill plates he reached with his left hand into one, beneath the red gills and into the front corner of the gill plate. Then squeezed hard avoiding its sharp teeth by not reaching in too far. The fish shuddered and squirmed—the weeds kept it from swimming. "Move rod over; hold it tight," Lenny ordered as he started to peel weeds off the fish. The fish tried to swim, but couldn't. When its head was clear of weeds, Lenny, with the pliers in his right hand, unhooked the fish then slid it over the gunnel into the boat.

"*Come here!*" Lenny shouted. The man, mesmerized by the ordeal, came over to Lenny. "Hold fish," Lenny said to him. Lenny took the man's right hand and showed him where to grab and squeeze the lower lip of the fish, outside its mouth. The man followed orders and did this, then reached under its belly with his other hand and held it up. It was a beautiful musky. He could feel its muscles quivering and wanting to swim. Lenny had the man's camera, hoping he remembered which button to push. He framed the fish and snapped the bigger button on the front of the camera.

"*Into the water!*" Lenny said. The man carefully slid the fish into the water. "Good release—fish did not get hurt!" Lenny said happily. They watched the fish shake itself for a few moments; free of weeds, hands and the stinging hooks, it was a glistening golden torpedo in the sunshine. Then, with a strong tail kick, it disappeared deep.

After decades of guiding and many hundreds of muskies caught, only thirty-three had exceeded forty pounds! Lenny remembered each one of those Big Girls. In Canada, he considered a trophy musky to be any one over twenty-five pounds—it was impossible to remember all of them. But the one he remembered most was over seventy pounds—he had released it five years ago for a guy named Sam.

"Lenny. Lenny! Tiny said loudly. He tapped him firmly on the shoulder. He had just arrived and was accustomed to having to jolt Lenny to get recognized. "Are you translating a song?" Tiny pushed two bar stools together and sat down on them while he waited for Lenny to answer. It was not difficult to recognize Tiny.

Finally, Lenny shook his head. "No."

"What then? You were in your trance." Lenny grinned when he recognized Tiny, and put one finger up for Shorty to see—one bottle of Molson for Tiny. Lenny had stopped ordering two beers at a time.

"Where were you? Tiny wanted to know.

"Pulling weeds off a big musky," Lenny finally answered.

"That was a nice one," Tiny remarked. The picture of the forty-five-pounder was in all the papers from Dryden to Kenora. A fish over forty pounds was always news. Lenny grinned when Tiny showed him the picture in the *Dryden Observer*.

"Ronnie will be here in about an hour," Tiny had to do a lot of convincing to set a meeting up. Both Lenny and Ronnie, the older son, had refused to meet for the longest time. They had blamed each other for the fate of the baby. But Tiny persisted.

When Ronnie walked into the bar, he sat down on the other side of Tiny, which kept 350 pounds of flesh between him and his father. He ordered a Pepsi.

Tiny showed the Dryden paper to Ronnie who hadn't seen it. He looked at it carefully. "Was it a money-fish?" he asked, looking past Tiny at his father.

"One hundred-dollar fish," Lenny answered. A touch of pride showed in Lenny's eyes.

"That's ten hours of overtime at the mill," Ronnie said, taking a sip of the soda, he didn't drink alcohol anymore. He was fair complexioned and thin like his dad, but taller. Lenny hadn't seen his older son in years.

"How long have you worked at mill?" Lenny asked his son. The paper mill in Dryden was the number one employer in the area.

"Three years."

"Do you see your mother?" Tiny spoke up.

"Not often—she's in Winnipeg. Every time I see her she has a new boyfriend."

"Where's your younger brother?" Lenny knew what the answer would be.

"Still living with her. Not working, same as her." Ronnie finished his Pepsi. Lenny put up his hand and Shorty brought over two Molson and another Pepsi.

"Only number two today," Lenny held up the beer and toasted Tiny. It was after 6:00 p.m. and remarkable it was only Lenny's second beer of the day!

"You should go fishing with your father," Tiny told Ronnie.

"I don't think so." Ronnie answered.

"He drinks less beer now," Tiny informed the young man.

"Three a day! No more," Lenny proudly proclaimed. My goal is zero! A government nurse is helping me…"

"What changed you?" Ronnie asked him.

"Your great-gramma," Tiny said, not sure Lenny would answer.

"She's been dead a long time—why now?" Ronnie wondered, showing more interest.

"She's not dead; her soul's alive in my head. She's singing now," Lenny added.

Ronnie didn't respond; his father's answer had surprised him.

"She told him to stop drinking so much," Tiny explained. As Lenny's best friend, he had told him to stop many times, or at least slow down. "Lenny didn't listen to me, but he did listen to your great-grandmother!"

"Recently?" Ronnie asked.

"In June, and again last week," Lenny said.

Ronnie had tears in his eyes.

"Life has been a rough ride for your father. You should go fishing with him," Tiny encouraged Ronnie. "Life is short." Ronnie was in deep thought. He had been drinking vodka that night many years ago, but he never admitted it to anyone. Both he and his father were to blame for "Baby."

The three of them sat at the bar looking out at Lake of the Woods. Nobody said anything for some time…

Finally, Lenny broke the silence. "I can take you fishing." Ronnie looked at his father like he had as a young boy.

"On Lake of the Woods?" Ronnie asked.

"On the secret lake," Tiny replied. Not sure Lenny would tell him.

"On Eagle Lake?" Ronnie asked, excited. "For musky?"

"*Yes!*" His father answered. "On Eagle Lake! For musky! Your great grandmother is singing now…and smiling."

Postscript:

I have been to Canada, fishing mostly for muskies, every year for over thirty years. Usually in July. I have fished with many different guides on different lakes, but Eagle Lake in Vermilion Bay, Ontario is my favorite. This story combines aspects of my experience and stories I had heard over those years.

Open market in northern China

13

A Mystery Virus in China

Microbe Hunters in Action

Prologue

Dr. Harold Perkins MD, PhD was the lead scientist in a U.S. pharmaceutical company that specialized in antiviral medicine. At age forty-five he was in his prime and had experience treating viral infections with natural, non-drug, medications. His company sent him to northern China to investigate a viral skin infection spreading in the north that Chinese doctors were not able to treat. Professor Guangsheng Chang, Chung, as he liked to be called, was a professor at a leading University in Beijing who had experience in virus research. Dr. Perkins had met Professor Chung in Hong Kong at a microbiology conference several years ago and admired his scientific expertise and practical knowledge, past and present. When the Chinese government invited Dr. Perkins to come to China to help solve the skin infection problem, he asked for Chung to be his advisor and interpreter.

Harbin, China — August 2002

Chung was a small man in his 70s and quite fit for his age. He had learned English from American G.I.s during the Second World War. He was thin, fair complexioned, and wore glasses. As a young boy, sitting on a hill above Nanking, he witnessed the slaughter of Chinese civilians by the Japanese Imperial Army. Hundreds of thousands perished in Nanking in 1937. Befriended by the G.I.s during the war, they became Chung's heroes. His most trying challenge was not the war, but to survive the "dark-days" under Mao Zedong from 1957 to 1976.

"Professor Chung, tell me what it was like under Mao." The two scientists were sitting together in a teahouse in Harbin in the north of China. Chung lit up a Marlboro and according to him, smoking was his only bad habit. He liked American cigarettes.

"Well, Dr. Perkins, I can tell you they were horrible, treacherous times. Still, today, after much telling of it, my twenty-five-year-old daughter doesn't believe one word. She never experienced it. Mao is a national hero to the young; the older Chinese know the truth about him. After Mao's death in 1976, massive propaganda covered up everything."

Dr. Perkins listened intently. A lovely young Chinese girl dressed in a brilliant red silk dress refilled their tea cups. It was 3:00 p.m. and tea time, a formal event in upscale teahouses in China's big cities. The green tea they were drinking was made from young leaves that opened first in the morning—these produced the finest tea.

"What about daily life? What did the average person go through?" Dr. Perkins was more than curious now.

"Very difficult," Chung said. "Everyone was on a food ration: three kilos of rice per month, 250 grams of cooking oil, no meat unless you killed something. There were no restaurants during the Cultural Revolution from 1966-1976. People in their 80s were sent out to work the fields. Books were burned and professors killed; the Voice of America was broadcast into China, but anyone caught listening went to jail. Kids were taught to spy on their parents and destroy any property not posted as government-owned. Permits were required to travel anywhere except for kids under sixteen—they could move around and destroy things."

"Sounds like the worst of bad nightmares. Where were you when this was happening?"

Chung took a drag on his cigarette and paused for a moment. "I escaped to Hong Kong in 1968. I was thirty-nine and very lucky—my parents and brother did not survive. They were cremated and their ashes used for fertilizer. Human ashes were kept on piles next to rice fields, the wind blew them around and created a haze that fertilized the fields."

"My God! We were never informed of this in America." Perkins knew some of what Chung was saying but not these stark details. "When did Nixon come here?"

"Nixon came to China in 1972 and opened the door a crack. Mao agreed to a small crack. Deng Xiaoping took over in '78 and ruled until his death in '97. Deng's most famous quotation was: 'It's better to be poor under socialism than rich under capitalism.' Many things opened up after Deng died."

"How many died during the cultural revolution?" Dr. Perkins stirred several drops of manuka honey into his tea.

"Mao killed 78 million people. More than Hitler and Stalin combined. He's enshrined in formaldehyde in Beijing as a great leader of the people. All you can see of him is a large white head—looks like a bleached basketball—a red robe covers the rest of him. His picture hangs everywhere in China," Chung explained. "Propaganda works."

Perkins sipped his tea, deep in thought: The great majority of Americans have no idea how horrific evil can be when it emerges from a government out of control. Communism on a large scale promised murder on a massive scale!

"This skin virus; tell me more about it." Perkins looked at Chung. He had read the translated reports but wanted a firsthand explanation from the professor.

"It started like shingles two years ago, mostly up here in the north. But, unlike shingles, the rash doesn't go away and the nerve pain never stops. In the few patients where the rash did go away, it came back in a short time. Nerve inflammation is severe and very painful. Chinese doctors have tried both Chinese medicine and western drugs. Nothing works. The virus appears to shut down the immune system. And it can be contagious! All the doctors up here want to hear your suggestions."

"I understand. If it's shingles caused by the *Herpes zoster* virus, it can lie dormant and reactivate anytime. Various types of stress can cause reactivation. With shingles, we've been successful at treating the rash, but nerve pain may continue in some people for a longer time. We might be dealing with a mutant virus here that persists to a greater extent."

"In your letter, you said you wanted to visit some hospitals treating infected patients. The Chinese government has approved your trip. All patients will be in isolation, but you can speak with the doctors and medical assistants who are treating them," Chung explained. "We start tomorrow. Tonight, we eat Chinese food at a Harbin noodle restaurant near our hotel."

Professor Chung had taken the train to Harbin from Beijing; Dr. Perkins had flown in on China Air. Harbin was 780 miles northeast of Beijing and 250 miles south of the Russian border. It was best known for its remarkable International Ice Festival every winter. And winter was serious in northern China. The festival is massive with building-sized ice sculptures of castles and pagodas that go on for blocks, lit up with a plethora of lights. But that's in winter. It was a warm summer day outside.

Harold and Chung walked from their hotel to the Dong-Wong noodle restaurant. It was small compared to big restaurants in fancy hotels, but there was still the bustle and clamor that all Chinese restaurants have. The head server recognized Professor Chung and directed them to a small table where they would be least affected by the noise. Servers were pushing carts around stacked with various noodle and dumpling specialties in fiber baskets.

"Well, Professor Chung, I'm officially in China!"

"Yes, Dr. Perkins, you are here. I hope you like noodles and dumplings, because they are the house specialty."

"The aromas are delightful!" Harold was hungry.

"The dumplings are stuffed with different foods;" Chung instructed, "mushrooms, chestnuts, pine nuts, corn, shrimp, pork meat, or combinations. I don't think you would like those stuffed with fish eyeballs or grasshoppers."

"Probably not," Harold said, smiling. "But the others sound good, except for the pine nuts."

"There are many pine nuts here in the north. Everything organic in China is tested for edibility. Pine nuts pass the test. All animals are eaten except bats!"

"Because of superstitions?"

"Yes."

"What's your favorite dumpling dish here?" Harold asked.

"Mushrooms with corn and cumin," Chung answered eagerly. "Number two favorite: shrimp with chestnuts." All the dumplings looked plump and fully stuffed with whatever was selected.

"Both sound good. Let's have them with a Chinese beer," Harold suggested. Chung signaled one of the ladies pushing a cart, she came over. He spoke to her in Mandarin, then she put two fiber baskets in the middle of their table along with chopsticks and two small plates and smiled graciously. The beer came warm in green bottles, 640 ml, with the labels washed off. Harold had second thoughts about ordering the beer!

After the satisfying dumpling meal, Chung ordered his favorite dessert for them: Flour puffs stuffed with sweet bean paste. It was different but tasty, a mild-beany sugar kick.

They walked back to the hotel after dinner. Chung mentioned there would be a government official with them tomorrow; standard operating procedure in a communist country. The government created jobs this way, keeping track of people by hiring 'officials' who monitored everybody. Officials even monitored officials! This was the way communism worked; spying at all levels was a multifaceted business in China. Old professors who interpreted for American scientists were near the top of the need-to-monitor list. Knowing too much about any one thing was not a good prescription for longevity. Absorbing this gave Dr. Perkins pause; it got his soul's alarm bell ringing.

Their hotel was a three-star; the four-stars had been booked months in advance. There was no such thing as a five-star hotel in Harbin. Water was turned off from 7:00 p.m. to 7:00 a.m. and, when on, had a brown tinge and sulfur odor. Toilets did not flush well; the lever had to be pumped up and down several times like in England. Walls were thin and *activity* in adjacent rooms was easy to hear. The beds were hard and the pillows made of rubber. Nevertheless, Dr. Harold Perkins slept well.

The two met for breakfast at 7:30 a.m. Harold did not even try to take a shower in the foul-smelling water. He slapped on a heavy dose of shaving lotion and dressed in a suit and tie, knowing he would be scrutinized. Chung wore yesterday's clothes: brown pants and an open-collar gray shirt. The hotel provided steamed rice and green tea for breakfast. Tea leaves were added to boiling water in your cup and the lid was used to hold them back as you drank. The cup was hot and hard to handle. Harold held it with two fingers at its very rim, then inhaled the steamy tea mist as it evaporated. Everyone in the dining area was Chinese except Harold Perkins; the hotel staff called him "Mr. Harold."

As they went by taxi to the first hospital, Chung lit a cigarette and offered one to Harold, calling him "Mr. Harold," for a touch of humor.

"No thanks." Harold laughed. "The 'Mr.' prefix on my first name is amusing."

"You don't smoke?"

"Nope, never did."

"I got the habit from American G.I.s during WWII. I buy them with my taxi money."

"Taxi money?"

"The government gives me taxi money to go to the university, so I walk instead and keep the money! American cigarettes are my only pleasure now."

At the entrance to the hospital Mr. Lee was waiting for them. He fit the classic government stereotype: short, round-faced and middle aged with jet-black hair. His stern expression was accentuated by a pair of extra-thick glasses.

Harold introduced himself, then they walked together with Chung following to a large conference room filled with doctors in white coats. "You need give talk to doctors, before see patients," Mr. Lee explained. He spoke English, but not as well as Chung. Harold Perkins had been expecting this. He could see a large whiteboard on the wall that, with Chung translating, was all he needed. He was introduced to everybody as Dr. Perkins, the lead scientist at a Wisconsin company called A.V. Biotechnology. They had all read the antiviral studies Dr. Perkins had supervised in the U.S. so the Chinese doctors referred to him as "The American Doctor."

Harold had learned from prior experience that when his comments were to be translated, he would need to speak in short declarative sentences, then pause for translation. Dr. Perkins walked over to the lectern and began:

"*Ni Hao,*" he said loudly, waving his right hand." Then said it again, "*Ni Hao.*" Chung translated, "Hello. Hello." Everyone laughed, even Mr. Lee.

"We are going to talk about new strains of probiotics that have antiviral effects." Chung continued to translate. "Probiotics are living, beneficial bacteria that improve bowel regularity and stimulate the immune system. Our company has patents on using specific probiotic strains in rotation; we do not use more than one strain per day. Their main effect is to stimulate the antiviral capabilities of the immune system. They do this by stimulating the body's T-cells. Each probiotic strain stimulates a different type of T-cell. Rotation of probiotics is important to prevent competition with each other. Our probiotic strains are totally non-toxic and have no adverse reactions. How much they can help treat a viral infection, like the suspected shingles virus in this epidemic, depends on several factors." Chung translated clearly as Dr. Perkins continued…

The presentation went on for two hours, longer than Harold expected. Chung, besides translating, was answering questions and creating dialogue among the doctors. He had thoroughly studied A.V. Biotechnology's literature and reports.

After the presentation, they visited the patient containment area. They could not go inside but could see patients through glass windows and talk with the doctors. There were twenty-two patients being treated. All had severe, fluid-filled red blisters covering more than their waistlines and backs, the most common locations affected in conventional shingles. Many of these patients also had blisters on their arms and legs, upper chest, forehead, and around their eyes. Over half of them had been in containment for over six weeks. Cold compresses and opioid drugs were used to control pain—steroids had only a marginal effect on reducing inflammation. There had been at least forty cases of suicide connected with the epidemic! One of the attending doctors had contracted it. He was taken to a different hospital.

Harold asked basic questions of the staff that had assembled outside the containment area. "What were the patient's home living conditions like?" "Was there overcrowding or poor sanitation?" "Did they eat moldy food?" "How many had chickenpox as children?" And so on… The staff conversed with each other before anyone answered, seniority playing a role as to who spoke first. Surprisingly, they did not have such information except for two patients who remembered having chickenpox.

"Clearly, this is unlike any shingles we have seen in the USA," Dr. Perkins noted. Chung had been translating, but some doctors understood enough English to follow most of what Dr. Perkins said.

A tall, thin woman in a crisp white lab coat joined the discussion. "My name is Doctor Olga Zhou." She reached out her hand and Harold gently shook it. They smiled at each other. "I'm half Russian and half Chinese," she admitted. "It's not so uncommon anymore."

She had been at the presentation and was now with them outside the containment area. Dr. Zhou—maybe thirty years old—had short, dark hair, Nordic eyes, and an unblemished, round face. There was no need for translation; she spoke English well.

"It tested as *Herpes zoster*, the shingles virus." She held up the report.

"Could it be a mutant strain?" Dr. Perkins questioned. "One that has learned to severely depress the immune system, or a conventional strain activated by something else?

"Their T-cell counts are very low." She pointed to the patents behind her in the containment area. "Do you think your company's probiotics can help?"

"Did you get the samples we shipped air express in dry ice?" Dr. Perkins asked.

"We have all the probiotic samples that were sent. They arrived frozen."

"That's good to hear. To answer your question: I don't know. But we have helped many patients with conventional shingles in the U.S. and U.K."

"Before your visit, we had intended to try your probiotics on the most serious patients. But we decided to wait for you and get specific details. Thanks for coming so soon! Your lecture was very informative. These new probiotic strains are harmless, correct?"

"Yes—that we know for sure. No adverse reactions. Whether they can help here is the question." Harold had a positive feeling that the probiotics would help. However, it was very disappointing they didn't have more information on the patients' histories.

"Then we must do the test!" She said fervently. The other doctors conferred for several minutes. It was well known she was a brilliant, young internist and obviously they agreed with her, but she didn't have seniority! The senior doctor looked straight at Dr. Zhou, his wisdom working overtime. After a long suspenseful minute, he nodded to her, giving his approval to do the test. "This would never happen so fast in the USA," Harold mumbled to himself.

"It's lunch time. Can we have lunch and discuss details?" She asked. Harold looked at Mr. Lee and Professor Chung. Lee had just listened until now. In fact, he had disappeared for some time during the lecture.

"Yes, we can," Mr. Lee answered, looking at Chung, wondering why he was needed anymore. This was government business and Dr. Zhou spoke English! Harold sensed this and was quick to introduce Chung to Olga, mentioning how valuable Chung's scientific advice had been while giving a serious look to Mr. Lee. He wondered why Chung hadn't introduced himself earlier. The order of things like that was different in China.

They had a simple lunch in the hospital cafeteria, steamed white rice with a healthy assortment of boiled vegetables: turnips, parsnips, kohlrabi, and Chinese cabbage—vegetables not commonly eaten in the US anymore. Sugared tomato slices were for dessert along with green tea.

During lunch, Dr. Perkins outlined his idea of how to do the test and Dr. Zhou made her suggestions. After an hour, they were done and test parameters had been agreed to. Half the patients would be treated with probiotics and half would not. They would start treatment tonight. The treated patients would not be harmed by the probiotics, but may or may not be helped by them. Dr. Perkins had to repeat this as a necessary disclaimer. Quickly after saying it, he looked at Chung and Dr. Zhou with an expression of confidence, nodding with a smile.

"We have other hospital visit," Mr. Lee said. "We go now." Harold and Chung followed his orders. Lee walked ahead of them to the taxi stand next to the hospital.

"Let him pay," Harold whispered to Chung, "Save your taxi money!"

The second hospital had thirty-two patients in confinement and would wait for a preliminary report from Dr. Zhou before running a test. Dr. Perkins reminded them that success depended on the ability of the probiotics to colonize intestinal surfaces and increase the activity of a patient's T-cells. This could happen quickly, in a few days, or it may take up to two weeks or more. Each patient was different. He wanted to be clear on this. Professor Chung summarized in Mandarin.

Harold and Chung took a taxi back to the hotel while Mr. Lee took a different taxi; he lived outside Harbin.

"Chung, I'm going crazy with all my names, Dr. Perkins, Perkins, Mr. Harold, The American Doctor… lets you and I agree to settle on Harold."

"Okay, Mr. Harold," Chung said. Harold had a good laugh again, "Your same joke got me twice." It was welcome levity.

They discussed a schedule of events. There was little else Harold could do for the patient's other than offer advice when it was needed, which could be done by phone. Harold had Olga Zhou's private phone number so they could stay in touch daily. The Chinese government wanted him to remain in China during the tests. For the evening, Mr. Lee had organized a dinner at a large Chinese restaurant. Attending would also be ten government employees from the local communist party. "Let's think about tomorrow—I have an Idea," Harold mentioned to Chung.

In the taxi to dinner, Harold suggested they investigate several small towns and villages, looking for clues.

"We could go all the way to Jixi. I know it well." Chung was there last year.

"Excellent. We seriously need to understand what's causing this epidemic."

"What about Mr. Lee?" Chung asked.

"We'll hire a car and a driver. I'll tell Lee we're doing some touring while waiting for test results and will call in daily. He doesn't need to know our mission." Professor Guangsheng Chang and Dr. Harold Perkins shook hands. "We're doing well together, Professor." Just as I had expected. Their taxi pulled into the restaurant's circle drive.

The restaurant was immense: a large circular, central, area with over one hundred tables, every one filled. Red carpeted floor, huge windows with golden drapes, twelve large chandeliers hanging above, and dozens of waiters and service personnel moving quickly. What was indescribable was the blend of voices, aromas, bright lights, and clanging utensils—raucous discordance Chinese restaurants are famous for.

A man dressed in a black suit conversed with Mr. Lee, then led the three of them to a separate room with two large, circular tables, each with a Lazy Susan in the middle. Waiting for Dr. Perkins and Mr. Lee were ten government bureaucrats—nine men and one woman. Entertaining foreign guests was the only time they ate out in style. Mr. Lee made the introductions in English, leaving out conjunctions and prepositions as usual. A large picture of Chairman Mao hung on the wall behind him.

The drinking didn't start until they all sat down. An older lady wearing an elegant red robe came in holding a tray with a decanter on it, filled to the brim with a clear liquid. There was a small glass in front of each guest, the lady filled them with the mysterious liquid. Harold thought it might be a local wine akin to Japanese sake—Chung knew better.

Mr. Lee stood up, held his glass high and bellowed, "To good Chinese whiskey!" then shouted, "Gum Pay!" and drank all of it. The government bureaucrats drank in synchrony with him. Chung looked at Harold, their glasses still full. Quickly, they held their glasses up, said "Gum Pay," and drank. The liquid was pure poison, like high proof vodka spiked with acetone and ether! It numbed the esophagus and made you dizzy. It was a sacrilege to call it whiskey.

"Again!" Mr. Lee commanded. The lady refilled the glasses and everyone drank again.

"I feel dizzy," Harold said to Chung, sitting next to him.

"Good Chinese whiskey," Mr. Lee repeated, smiling demonically at Harold.

"If you say so," Harold replied, wondering if any smile from Lee was better than none. Harold had to eat something quickly to neutralize the two ounces of poison he had just imbibed.

Servers started bringing in food. Multiple dishes were placed on the Lazy Susans, which took up most of the table space. Everyone had a small plate in front of them, a pair of plastic chopsticks, and a small soup bowl with a ceramic spoon. In the center of each Lazy Susan was a huge bowl of soup from which servers started filling everyone's bowl.

"Fish-head soup," Chung told Harold.

Several small heads, one eye showing on each, were floating in Harold's bowl. "It tastes better than it looks," he said to Chung, after sipping some of the broth then pushing it aside.

"I will tell you about the food." Chung adjusted his eyeglasses while looking at Harold then grabbed the rim of the Lazy Susan and started turning it, pointing to various dishes: "These are boiled peanuts; this is grilled snake; here are pickled chicken feet, fried peppers, spicy tofu, raw octopus, jumbo prawns, fried pig intestine, and black beans." It was hard for Harold to show enthusiasm. The prawns looked okay. He started with a few swollen peanuts, which were quite good but hard to catch on a moving Lazy Susan with plastic chopsticks. Anyone could rotate the Lazy Susan. The servers brought tiny saucers and filled them with different sauces. The government employees ate ravenously. Snake dipped in spicy soy sauce seemed to be a favorite.

Everyone was served a bowl of plain white rice that they piled other food on top of, then held it close to their mouths, and using chopsticks, shoveled it in. They all went back to grab more food on the Lazy Susan with the same chopsticks.

Harold was astonished. It was a double dipping party! "I can't believe this!" he mumbled to himself. He grabbed his bowl of rice and started eating it plain, using his soup spoon; he didn't eat anything from the Lazy Susan! This made Mr. Lee smile. At the end, they were all served green tea in small ceramic cups and deep-fried flour buns sprinkled with sugar. Harold asked for seconds on the buns.

After the meal, everyone stood up and started walking around, holding their liquor glasses. The lady in the robe came back with another bottle of the clear alcoholic liquid and filled everyone's glass. Harold looked very concerned. He would have to drink with them or they would be insulted. He needed government support—without it, forget doing business in China. But more of that poison and he would pass out, maybe die! Chung motioned Harold to come over by him. Chung was standing next to heavy burgundy curtains covering a large window. Harold came over and Chung whispered something that made Harold raise his eyebrows! Then Chung elaborated.

One of the higher-ranking government employees under Mr. Lee, who knew some English, came over holding the decanter of liquor. He saw that Harold's glass was full, so he refilled his own and got ready to toast, looking Harold in the eye. Harold, with the curtains behind him, remembering what Chung told him, held his glass high, and watched the man carefully. At the exact moment the man said "Gum Pay" and threw his head back to swallow, Harold shouted "Gum Pay!" and did the same, except he threw the liquor over his shoulder into the curtains. It worked perfectly. The curtains got the poison, not Harold. He had to repeat it three more times and did it flawlessly. Then he stood, unwavering, and smiled at the employee, who introduced himself as the entertainment official.

"Dr. Perkins can drink!" the official announced loudly, and everyone cheered. "We must use his probiotics!"

Chung winked at Harold.

The next morning, they were in a taxi heading in the direction of Jixi in the far northeast corner of China. It was 225-mile drive from Harbin to Jixi and there would be villages along the way to investigate. Beyond Jixi was the Russian border. There were indications the epidemic may have started is this area.

They had a good driver, his name was Wang, a short thin man who wore a Los Angeles Dodger's baseball hat. Whenever Chung spoke to him, Wang would just say *sit-see,* meaning thanks. It didn't matter what Chung said; Wang would say *sit-see.* Chung and Harold had plenty of time to talk.

"Tell me more about the Mandarin language, why it's so hard to speak." Harold was curious.

Chung smiled and turned toward Harold. "There are many homonyms, more than in English, like the spoken word Ma. "Ma" is mother. "Ma!!" is a complaint. "Ma ah" is a boat anchor. And "Maaaa" is a horse. You must listen carefully. There are several major languages in China: Mandarin in Shanghai, some say the authentic version; Mandarin in Beijing, a dialect that can't be understood in Shanghai; and Cantonese in Guangzhou, to mention three. The thing that has kept China together is the written language – it's the same everywhere. Let me ask you a question about America."

"Okay, Professor Chung. See if you can stump me."

"It's about guns. Do you own one?"

"I own several. I hunt deer in Wisconsin and Elk in Colorado."

"Where do you keep them?"

"At home in a fireproof safe."

"Can you shoot them anytime?"

"At a target range, anytime. Or, out in the country during hunting season, unless it's posted otherwise."

"It's impossible for us to own a gun in China."

"Is there any hunting in China?"

"No, it's not permitted. The communist government will never allow it. They are afraid of the people taking control. Communism needs total control to survive." *Very scary. Thank God for our second amendment,* Harold thought.

"Did you ever read any gun magazines?"

"Yes, in Hong Kong. They are not allowed in China."

It was a bright summer day, a good day for a drive. The countryside was spotted with small villages, some only a couple of miles apart. It was mostly barren land except where there were large government farms. Most trees and bushes had been burned for heat; winters were severe in northern China. When Wang stopped to let the two scientists stretch their legs, Harold noticed an empty field alive with golden-red dragonflies chasing grasshoppers. But that was it for wildlife sightings.

Very few people owned cars, so a town was defined by how far you could walk. A functional bicycle was a valued possession. In fact, old Schwinn bikes from the 1950s were still in use. These small towns were very rural; no electricity, no plumbing. Chung had the driver stop in one he knew.

"What's that boy carrying?" Harold asked, seeing a young boy carrying two large clay jugs suspended on the ends of a pole across his shoulders.

"Urine," Chung said.

"I thought so," Harold replied. "I can smell it. Where does he take it?"

"Away from the village. To a urine dump spot in a field."

"How do they handle fecal matter?"

"They add lime and stir it in pots; use it for fertilizer."

"Who stirs it? Criminals?"

"Good idea, but no; old people stir it," Chung said. Harold was getting an education.

They came to another town about half way to Jixi, somewhat larger. Women were sweeping dirt out from their doorways into the street. Some had dirt floors in their houses. One man was getting his hair cut on the sidewalk, another was welding a broken tea kettle while donkeys passed by him pulling carts filled with potatoes and other root-vegetables.

Some houses and apartments were made from small red bricks, others from wood and thatch; all were old and covered with gray dust from smoldering garbage fires. There was a pervasive sense of a dense population, even without seeing everyone. Many villages had no road access. China and the USA were about the same size in surface area, but China had five times the population and a person could sense it.

In the middle of town there was an open market. Harold was very interested in looking around and Chung walked with him. There were skinny chickens in cages; small pigs tied to cement blocks; goats full of milk; tables with vegetables in neat rows; dried fish on wood racks, looking like large butterflies the way there were cut; a wire rack containing jars of pickled duck eggs with a Donald Duck sticker on each lid; and tables of small plastic bags filled with spices lined up in rows. Most prominent were two tables piled high with peanuts, a rusty scale was between them. Obviously, a staple food in China. Older women maintained the tables and racks, trying to keep everything neat. There was a lingering dampness from rain the night before; Harold and Chung examined the peanut tables.

"Yellow-green on top, red-brown underneath," Harold said to Chung, describing how many of the peanuts were colored.

"I see that too," Chung replied.

"The worst type of mold to have growing on peanuts!" Harold declared, alarmed.

"Not good!" Chung was also very concerned. "That mold produces aflatoxin, a potent immune system depressor. Mostly, we see harmless black mold on peanuts."

"This might be the heart of our problem," Harold declared.

"Some of the peanuts come from Russia, they are shipped long distance by trucks," Chung added.

"We need to take samples back for lab tests," Harold was nervous and sweating. He walked to their taxi parked beyond the market—opened his suitcase and took out a roll of sterile plastic bags and a pair of surgical gloves. Then he told Wang to drive him back to where the peanut tables were and park. It was done mostly with hand signals. Chung waited by the tables.

With the gloves on, Harold carefully took samples. An old woman weighed them and Chung paid her. Then they walked back to the taxi and got in. Chung said something to Wang who replied "*sit-see,*" and they drove away. Harold looked back at the market and shook his head, disgusted and worried.

Near the end of town, a flat-bed truck drove by them with a man chained to a pole in back, standing straight up with two heavy chains locked around him and the pole. The man had a sign around his neck. Harold suspected he was a prisoner. Two men in army camo were in the truck's cab.

"What does the sign say?"

"Two things: one, this man killed another man with a hammer last week and two, this man will be executed tomorrow."

"Wow! Did he have a trial?"

"Yes, yesterday. Two of three judges voted the death penalty. We have fast justice in China. That's why there's such a low murder rate!"

"In America, we do it differently—it's called due process. A jury of twelve citizens would decide his fate."

"Not in China. We have 1.3 billion people. Too many for such a process. A professor of statistics told me if everybody in China walked past you, one-by-one, the line would never end! Do you know why?"

"Because the rate of reproduction would keep extending the line!" Harold answered.

Chung put both thumbs up, "Correct!"

Wang drove on slowly. About ten miles beyond the town, beyond a row of corn planted right to the edge of the road, two boys were flying kites, running and laughing. Their kites soared and dove, often grazing the corn tops. It took skill to keep them from tangling and diving into the corn. One kite had a black dragon on it, the other a Chinese flag. A dragon was chasing China! What did that mean? It was a pleasant summer day now; the air was clear thanks to a mild breeze that had blown the gray haze away. Harold relaxed. Chung wanted to talk more about guns.

When they arrived in Jixi they checked into a hotel for several nights. The city had a population of 400,000 residents and dated back to the Han Dynasty in 200 BC. Its proximity to the Russian border was of interest to Harold. A large freshwater lake, called Xingkai by the Chinese and Khanka by the Russians, was partly in both countries, three quarters of it was in Russia.

Once they had their room keys it was off to tour Russia, a short drive away. Checking their rooms could wait. Chung gave Wang instructions where to go, pointing and using his open hand as a map. Wang nodded.

"One of the most remote border crossings with Russia is just ahead," Chung said to Harold. On the Russian side, there was a small shack with a crossing gate that was open. There was no gate on the China side and no town beyond the gate in Russia, only the lake on the right and a dozen kiosks selling things on the left. Foreigners with passports could get a two-hour visa and visit the kiosks.

Their taxi interrupted the border guard, who was playing cards with himself in the shack; he immediately closed the gate. Harold found this very funny because anyone could walk around the shack or the gate and get in; there were no fences.

Chung organized visas with the Russian border guard. Wang stayed in China with the taxi while Chung and Harold walked fifty yards to the kiosks.

The kiosks were a surprise; some were long tents full of Russian merchandise. Two had fox and martin pelts from Siberia stretched out on racks. One had hot roasted chestnuts, warm beer, and soft drinks for sale, another sold rusty swords. Chung had a beer and a cigarette while Harold drank a warm Orangina soft drink and ate a handful of chestnuts. He bought an extra bag of chestnuts for Wang.

They walked ahead and Harold found a lady selling sets of Matryoshka dolls—eight wooden dolls nested inside each other. The woman opened one set from the first to the last doll. What started as a doll the size of a quart jar, finished with one the size of a raisin. Harold bought three sets. "These are for my lovely daughters." He smiled, thinking of how much he missed them while traveling the world.

"They honor fertility. It means each daughter will have eight children," Chung enlightened Harold.

Harold's eyes widened. "That's twenty-four grandchildren not counting my young son's future contributions…"

"Is this your first time in Russia?" Chung asked as they walked out from the kiosks into barren country.

"Yes, I've been to over fifty countries, but this is the first time in Russia. And by a full fifty yards at that!"

"What do you think of the Russian countryside?" Chung asked while lighting another cigarette. Harold looked out beyond the kiosks and away from the lake into the great Soviet expanse.

"Dry brown dirt with dead weeds and small rocks—looks just like northern China," Harold responded. Chung had a good laugh.

"Come on professor, we're not done with the Kiosk tour," Harold instructed lightheartedly. Chung was just smoking and gazing out. He didn't think there was much more to see.

Back by the kiosks, just beyond the sword seller, a man was sitting on a folding- chair next to a brown suitcase. He was wearing a Russian navy shirt and cap, and drinking Chinese beer.

Harold and Chung could see a large tent at the end of the line of kiosks they hadn't been to yet. As they moved toward it they were stopped by the Russian sailor who shouted: "Ron-ald Reag-an!" mispronouncing the only two English words he knew besides yes and no. He waved for us to come over. He had the suitcase on his lap and was slowly opening it. Harold was first to see inside, raising his eyebrows. Then as Chung looked, the surprise on his face was indescribable. He crushed out his cigarette and put his hands over his ears, his way of showing excitement.

"Guns!" He shouted. The suitcase was full of old Russian army pistols and one shiny Colt-45 revolver. The sailor pulled the revolver out, opened the cylinder to show it was unloaded, then handed it to Harold. With care, Harold re-engaged the cylinder, pulled back on the hammer one notch and spun the cylinder fast to reaffirm it was unloaded, like in a Wild West show. Then he cocked the gun by pulling the hammer all the way back, pointed it at the sun and pulled the trigger, "CLICK." Then, slowly, he handed it to Chung who nervously took hold of the Colt-45. Chung couldn't believe he was holding a gun. "Repeat what I just did with it," Harold insisted. Chung repeated the sequence perfectly; he remembered from the World War II days spent with the Americans.

"My G.I. friends from Texas had Colt-45s," he declared.

At the very end of the row of kiosks was the food tent, stocked full of packaged delicacies from Russia and eastern Europe: jams and jellies from Poland; almonds from Serbia; chocolate from Romania; plum liquor from Bulgaria; vodka—of course—from Russia; and then, last, at the end of the tent, a giant table of peanuts.

"Can you believe it?" Harold exclaimed! "Yellow-green on top, red-brown underneath." More peanuts were infected than those at the Chinese market. Harold's sterile bags were in the taxi—he didn't bring them, never thinking he would need them on a short hike in Siberia. He bought samples and told the Russian merchant to double bag and not use his hands. He had to show the merchant what to do. Harold tried to get more information from him, but the man's English was very bad. When asked where the peanuts came from, he said, "Russkie." When asked how long they had been at the kiosk, he said, "Russkie." They asked the fox-martin pelt seller if he knew where the peanuts came from—he shook his head no. They got the same response from the chestnut and sword sellers. The gun seller told them: "Ron-ald Reag-an."

Harold and Chung walked back to the gate. The young Russian guard had been watching for them and insisted on opening the bags of Russian dolls, peanuts and Wang's chestnuts. Harold objected, but the guard paid no attention to him. He opened the bags, looked inside each one, then gave them back and opened the gate. Harold and Chung walked back to China.

Wang was happy to get the chestnuts; he munched on them on the drive back to Jixi. They stopped on the way to look at Lake Khanka, all 1,600 square miles of it, impressed by the solitude and virgin pine forests. Its long sandy beaches were remarkable, and yet not one of the 1.3 billion Chinese was here, excluding Chung and Wang. This was the first place in China where Harold did not sense the pressure of so many people. There was nothing straight ahead but water, beaches and trees. An oasis of serenity in China. Chung told Harold the dry fish they had seen on racks at the open market were from this lake.

Their hotel in Jixi was much better than the one in Harbin and it was only a three-star! The bed was comfortable, clear water twenty-four hours a day, no sulfur smell, and the toilet flushed! Harold slept well and felt fresh and energized in the morning. The breakfast area at the hotel had a variety of foods. Hong-Kong-style noodle soup was the choice of most Asian guests. Harold had flour puffs sprinkled with sugar and coffee—real coffee! Chung just had tea.

"If this is a three-star, the hotel in Harbin is a one-star," Harold joked. Chung nodded and lit a Marlboro; he felt bad about the hotel in Harbin and would mention it to Mr. Lee during their conference call later in the week. Mr. Lee was aware they were in Jixi and touring; he was not aware they were scrutinizing local markets for mold contamination.

"When we have the conference call, we must be careful how we tell Mr. Lee about the mold. *If we tell him!*" Chung mentioned with trepidation.

"I'm already thinking about that. I could tell him we were touring Lake Khanka and stopped at a local market to buy fruit and noticed moldy peanuts."

"No, don't say that!" Chung said, giving it more thought.

"Why not? It's true. The fact that we're investigating local towns for causes of the disease doesn't have to be said."

"It's implied! This is China; you are assuming they *want* to discover the source of the problem. They might already know it!"

"You mean they just brought me here to help treat existing patients? To make a show out of it by getting the Americans involved."

"That's what I think," Chung said. "They don't want you scaring all the people who eat Russian peanuts. The disease is most likely originating from those who had chickenpox as a child and didn't know not to eat colored peanuts. Business with Russia is important for the Chinese economy," Chung said dejectedly.

"So, what do you recommend we do?" Harold asked.

"We continue our investigation for a few days. Visit more towns close to Russia. Take more samples. Then have a conference call and let Dr. Zhou tell us about the test; what they have seen so far. Details. We tell them we're having a nice time in Jixi touring Lake Khanka. Relaxing." Chung lit another cigarette. "My only pleasure."

"I think I see where you're going! Do you trust Olga?"

"I believe so. We must have a private meeting with her back in Harbin and tell her about the discovery we made. Give her the samples. She will understand why we need to do it this way. She's half Russian."

"The whole thing is just a theory until the peanuts are tested," Harold reminded Chung. "Assuming the tests substantiate our theory, and I'm confident they will, here is a summary of our discovery: Somebody eats a bunch of moldy Russian peanuts that produce a super-toxic aflatoxin that destroys their immune system. If they had chickenpox as a kid the herpes virus is inside them; it takes over and can't be defeated until their immune system is brought back to life! If people who never had chickenpox eat the moldy peanuts, depressing their immune systems, then contact someone with active shingles—they too, can become acutely infected. We're banking on the probiotics to override the effects of the peanuts and reestablish the immune system in both cases.

"Precisely," Chung agreed. "Now, how we get that information out to responsible doctors in China without being chained to a pole in the back of a truck is another matter."

"We're going to need help we can trust!" Dr. Perkins concluded.

They stayed in Jixi three more days and visited five more towns. Out of the five, only two had mold-free peanuts at local markets. Those that had contaminated peanuts—yellow-green on top, red-brown underneath—got them from Russian merchants.

The conference call was set for 2:00 p.m. Mr. Lee organized it and Harold and Chung took it in the lobby of the hotel in Jixi where there was a phone booth with two phones. It would be the three of them and Dr. Zhou.

"Eleven patients are being treated with your probiotics," Olga Zhou confirmed. "After five days, we are already seeing improvements in them! No improvements in the untreated patients. Today, after dinner, we start treating the other eleven with the probiotics." She was being careful what she said.

Olga and Harold had talked on her private phone the day before. He'd recommended she treat the rest of the patients with the probiotics if the improvements continued, and to be careful on the conference call with Mr. Lee not to reveal their peanut theory! Harold, hoping he could trust her, had informed her about it and then briefed Chung who was not on that call.

"Good decision Dr. Zhou!" Harold exclaimed. "This is not meant to be a scientific study; the goal is to cure the patients. Wonderful news. Can you describe the improvements?"

"Significant reduction of rash on the face and arms of three patients; no more discharge from stomach and chest rashes in four patients; all rashes completely gone from four patients; less pain in all eleven." Before she could continue or Harold could talk, Mr. Lee interrupted.

"No more talk on phone, we have meeting when you return Harbin," he ordered. With no choice but to agree, everyone said goodbye and hung up.

"No surprise to me," was Chung's response. Harold was in deep thought.

"Me, neither, but I think Lee was surprised by the fast response with the probiotics and has orders from above to take full control."

"We have to be very careful!" Chung warned.

The next day, Wang got them back to Harbin safe and sound. The drive was uneventful and gave Harold and Chung time for a serious discussion on how they might stop China from importing Russian peanuts. Olga would have to be involved!

"One good thing," Harold remarked, "Lee got us a better hotel." Chung just nodded; he was smoking and thinking. They were in the lobby of a new hotel in Harbin. Mr. Lee was sending a government vehicle to pick them up. They would meet with Dr. Zhou in the hospital conference room at 9:00 a.m.

"We have advanced to government transportation just as I was getting fond of Wang," Harold lamented.

"Where do you have the peanut samples?" Chung asked, not caring about their improved accommodations or the vehicle.

"Locked in my suitcase in the room."

"Good—we'll meet with Dr. Zhou later and discuss testing details," Chung was nervous.

Right on time, a black limousine with government license plates pulled up at the front door.

"Let's go," Chung crushed out his cigarette. When they got to the hospital Mr. Lee and another man were waiting for them.

"This is Dr. Ying," Mr. Lee announced, and introduced him to Dr. Perkins. Ying nodded at Chung, who was surprised to see him. Ying was a doctor at the hospital in Beijing that was part of the University where Chung worked. The four of them walked to the conference room where Dr. Zhou was waiting.

Mr. Lee asked Dr. Perkins to briefly review how A.V. Biotechnology's probiotics help patients infected with viruses, Dr. Ying had not been at the lectures. Harold gave his brief-version lecture in about fifteen-minutes. He drew an immune system diagram on the white board, showing how probiotics interact with it. Dr. Ying, who spoke English, had a question for Dr. Perkins: "How does what appears to be the common shingles virus so effectively depress the immune system in certain people?" Chung looked at Harold, hoping he would be very careful with his answer.

"Frankly, Dr. Ying, I don't know. I'm a biochemist and a medical doctor, not a virologist. Medical science has become very compartmentalized."

Chung smiled, it was a good answer, Dr. Perkins had politician blood in his veins!

"Could some other factors be involved?" Dr. Ying questioned.

"Possibly," Harold said cautiously. Ying did not ask any more questions.

Mr. Lee then asked Dr. Zhou to summarize her experience with the probiotic treatment. She did so adding that two of the newly treated patients were already showing improvements this morning. Dr. Ying asked her questions regarding the patient's backgrounds and medical histories, like those Harold had asked after his lectures. Dr. Zhou looked down, shuffling through her papers—she didn't have the information needed to answer him. "We must change our protocols," she said firmly. Ying knew the protocols she referred to had been in effect for years and it wasn't her responsibility to change them. Mr. Lee adjourned the meeting.

Back in the hospital reception area, the four men stood together talking. Mr. Lee told Chung that Dr. Ying would be replacing him as Dr. Perkins' translator and that his services would no longer be required. He should take the evening train back to Beijing. Harold couldn't believe it!

"You need medical doctor translating now," Mr. Lee explained. Harold was seething inside but trying to stay cool.

"Is new hotel better, Dr. Perkins?" Mr. Lee asked, knowing Perkins didn't like the change to Dr. Ying.

Harold answered curtly, "Yes."

Harold stayed in Harbin another two weeks, in daily contact with Olga Zhou. Eighteen of the twenty-two patients had been released. The remaining four older patients were still in the hospital but out of containment. The other hospital was achieving the same level of success. Dr. Ying was always present at these meetings except once when Harold met with Olga alone. In Ying's absence, he could discuss additional details regarding the peanut contamination theory. She was stunned by the implications and willing to help in any way. They both realized that testing the peanut samples in the USA was an imperative. The presence of aflatoxin had to be confirmed along with immune depression. They both suspected that certain high-ranking officials in the Chinese government were aware of the connection between Russian peanuts and extreme shingles. Peanut imports from Russia had to stop. She would take charge of getting the samples to the USA through friends in Hong Kong. Customs in Beijing would be checking Dr. Perkins closely before his flight home.

Olga had a parting gift for the good doctor; two flower paintings her mother had made. "These are for your home," she said. "I hope I see you again."

"You will! Follow those good vibrations in the meantime and listen carefully to your inner voice!" Harold gave her a big hug.

Dr. Harold Perkins made it home safely, nonstop from Beijing to Detroit with a connection to Minneapolis. His family rejoiced when he walked through the front door! His daughters loved the Russian dolls. His wife hung the flower painting in their bedroom. He didn't bring his son anything from China, but handed him an envelope. In it were tickets to the upcoming Minnesota Vikings—Green Bay Packers game at the Metrodome!

On the flight home, Harold had written Chung a long letter thanking him for his help and guidance. He would keep him informed through a post office box Chung kept in Hong Kong. In the envelope, sent with the letter, he enclosed four-gun magazines.

The peanut samples all tested positive for a new type of aflatoxin that proved to severely depress the immune system in animal studies. Twenty-one of Olga Zhou's patients recovered completely. Only one, an old man with liver disease, didn't make it. Olga's friends in Hong Kong told this story to trustworthy authorities in Beijing and the importation of peanuts from Russia was stopped. Education at the rural village level was initiated and people were taught how to recognize and avoid moldy food.

A.V Biotechnology began selling the new strains of probiotics in China, but sales never reached expectations. A government-owned biotechnology company in Shanghai began producing the same probiotics, not honoring A.V. Biotechnology's patents. Harold Perkins eventually left the company and founded a new probiotic business with a broader product line that helped treat many different diseases.

Postscript:

The author has made many trips to China and understands its multidimensional culture. This story was inspired by true events. The doctor referred to as Olga Zhou became the Chief of Medicine and, among her many duties, was responsible for improving medical protocols.

Author talking with fellow elk hunters

14

My Rookie Hunt in Colorado

Humility or Bust!

Western Colorado, October 2000

It was after lunch when my cousin Ed began playing gin with Pat, the ranch manager, in the front seat of the pickup. I sat in the back seat glassing the hills for elk with binoculars. We were parked at the south edge of the famous "320"—three-hundred-twenty acres of prime elk-feeding lowland in northwestern Colorado. It was hot for October, even at eight thousand feet. No snow anywhere—not even on the distant mountaintops between here and Steamboat Springs. Consequently, few elk were feeding low in the valleys and canyons of the Slater Ranch.

"Pat," I said in a low voice. "Is it okay to crack this window—for a little air?" I had my hand on the truck's sliding window behind me.

"What kind of whisper-voice is that? Keep it down!" Pat hissed back, without looking away from his cards. "No! Keep the window closed or they'll smell us. And keep quiet or they'll hear us."

"Sorry, I didn't realize I was being loud," I whispered back, concentrating on producing something between a whisper and a low voice. "I'll just grin and bear it back here." The afternoon sun was streaking in so I shoved an orange vest up along the back window to block it. I grabbed a sixteen-ounce bottle of Evian water, took a quiet drink, then poured in an ounce of Crown Royal whiskey; just enough to add flavor. This was my first elk hunt.

"Just don't talk and you'll be okay. This ain't some sound-proofed million-dollar RV. It's a frickin' elk-hunting truck!" Pat said in a loud whisper just as he lost a hand and could glare back at me. Ed marked their tally down on a yellow pad and shuffled cards, disregarding the conversation. He was winning.

"Those frickin' elk can hear and smell everything. And there are high canyons north of here full of elk." Pat kept lecturing for my sake. Ed understood all this after fourteen years of hunting with Pat.

"Keep glassing those hills, and watch over by those aspens on the left. A big old bull came out from there last week—right about this time," Pat was pointing left.

"Yes," I whispered, trying to be humble. And sorry I ever mentioned opening the damn window. I took another drink of the whiskey-flavored Evian.

"Did anyone shoot that bull?" Ed asked, obviously paying some attention to Pat's lecture.

"The guy in the back tried; shot right from the truck. God, when I saw the end of that muzzle-brake roving around next to my ear, I bent over and tried to duck under the steering wheel. Too late! *Ka-freaking-boom!* He shot that .300 Winchester magnum next to my ear. It didn't stop ringing for a week!"

"But did he hit the elk?" Ed wanted to know.

"Hell no, he hit the ground under it. Dirt flew up and the elk bolted into the trees before he could shoot again. I was damn mad! I told him not to frickin' shoot again until I covered my ears. The bastard had shot without paying attention to me."

"Was he a rookie?" Ed asked.

"Probably, but I don't know. Those guys in that group last week didn't say much about anything. I think he was a dirt-bag lawyer from out east."

"Well, that would explain it. At least my cousin isn't a dirt-bag lawyer. Right, cousin?" Ed looked at me.

"Right," I acknowledged in a very low voice. "I'm a dirt-bag biochemist."

"Say again, didn't hear you?" Ed asked me, grinning like a child. Pat glared back to see if I would take the bait—no way. I kept quiet, hiding a smile.

"Just don't screw up if I get you a shot." Pat instructed.

"Right," I muttered. Pat was doing a good job of what I'd been warned to expect from him on our first outing. It was fortunate that I had rechecked the sighting on my Winchester 7mm last week. It shot low until I adjusted the scope up four clicks.

Ed shuffled the cards and was grinning at Pat. Ed Fallin was my only cousin on my mother's side. Two years younger than I, he liked joking around with a polished sort of sarcastic humor. He was smart and a good hunter.

The card-playing and blocking the sun from scorching my neck continued...

It was now 4:30 p.m. and billions of the sun's photons still penetrated the rear window as the gin game continued silently. Nobody said anything for almost an hour. I could feel it—the sense that everything was more critical now than earlier. When my watch beeped twice at 5:00 p.m. I got an end-of-the-world glare from Pat. He finger-slashed his neck and pointed to my watch. I got the message and deactivated the alarm.

I kept glassing the hills. Thankful I brought the Leitz binoculars instead of the Nikons; they were kinder to my eyes after hours of use and didn't give me a headache. Forget that they were heavier—what does heavy mean when sitting in a truck? Little perfections make a difference. I often had to re-learn this.

"See anything at all?" Pat whispered.

"No, just two mule deer about thirty minutes ago—two does." I replied quietly then put the binoculars down and took a handkerchief out of my pocket and wiped sweat off my neck. The sun, angled lower now, was still an annoyance. This was not how I expected the elk hunt to be. I figured there would be more tracking and hiking around—more action.

"Damn, I wish it would snow. Snow will bring them elk right down into this valley. They come down that draw over there. I've seen thousands of them come down when it snows—it's magic. Snow gets them feeding low and this is the best fricking low spot on the entire ranch," Pat said in a voice louder than my watch alarm. It was one of those excuses guides often used during slow times. I've heard many variations of it from Wisconsin musky guides; they liked snow too if it came with the first hard frost. A quick cooling triggered fish to feed just as it got elk to come down into the valleys.

I went back to serious glassing while Ed and Pat kept playing gin. Everybody was silent again. It was only Day One of four days of hunting and I was rethinking my decision to do this! But I'm a learner; these four days would be a test for me. Ed had warned it would be different than action-packed tarpon fishing in the Florida Keys—something we both enjoyed.

I rubbed an ounce of condensate off the back window with the cuff of my shirt and finished the last of the flavored Evian water. One ounce of Crown in sixteen ounces of water was only for flavor—too weak to soothe any nerves. Looking north with the binoculars, on a high ridge, I saw three elk.

"Look north, on the high ridge!" I said quietly. Pat and Ed grabbed their binoculars and focused on the elk in seconds.

"Nice bull with two cows. Three golden silhouettes on the horizon—at least two miles away. Did you sight-in that 7mm Winchester for two miles?" Ed asked. My rifle had a scope that could be zoomed from three to nine-power. But he was just kidding; 10,560 feet was a bit out of range. Four hundred yards was my personal maximum, but I was most confident under three hundred.

"Yes, but I'll have to aim five feet high," I replied. Ed grinned like a teenager now.

We watched the elk move across the ridge, big silhouettes considering the distance.

"They're almost in Wyoming," Pat blurted. Pat was a tough cowboy, not much more description was necessary. Tall and rough cut, he was in his late forties and had been guiding for elk over twenty years. He knew every tree and sage bush in the thirty-thousand acres we could hunt.

"How many points on the bull?" I asked.

"Can't tell for sure—maybe five-by-five," Ed said while glassing them. In Wisconsin deer hunting jargon that meant a ten-pointer, five on each antler.

"Stanley, hand me the spotting scope." Ed pointed to his Swarovski 20x60 spotting scope in the back seat. He wasn't too quiet about it either. What happened to the whispering drills? Pat said nothing. I handed the scope to Ed and he rolled down his window enough to fasten it to the top edge. He now had a sixty-power telescope aimed at the elk.

"Four-by-five," he said when his scope came into focus. All three of us watched the elk move across the ridge at a variety of magnifications. They moved slowly and deliberately down the ridge until disappearing behind a distant tree line.

At 5:30 p.m. without any warning Pat said, "Let's go!" In a moment, he and Ed were out of the truck and heading toward the fence line, all set to hunt. Ed had his .338 magnum elephant gun ready, fleece-camo jacket zipped, and his new Filson hat snug on his head.

"Holly Jesus!" I said out loud. I was totally blindsided! My gear was all over the back seat, jacket, hat, gloves, gun, ammo, fanny pack... In two minutes—record time for me—I had everything all together and tumbled out of the truck with it. Disheveled and disoriented, I unconsciously slammed the door shut. I knew instantly it was a major mistake. "Damn," I said. I made a gun with my hand and pointed to my head to signal my mistake, then headed behind the truck to urinate.

"No! No! No!" Pat loud-whispered as he came running over. I was already in full stream and there was no possibility of stopping.

"I'm behind the truck and we're downwind," I said in a hopeless effort to find some logic he would buy. No such luck. Pat threw handfuls of brown dirt on the urine and glared at me. A glare that spelled out: "stupid rookie."

"Sorry," I said. "When you gotta go, you gotta go..."

"You get my permission before you urinate out here, understand?"

"Yes Sir," I replied, knowing not to say any more.

"I would have dug you a hole," Pat said. "But it's too late. I hope to hell those elk don't smell that urine."

"I hope not, too—they're a good mile away," I mumbled, and threw a symbolic handful of dirt on the wet spot.

Pat and I walked together to the fence line where Ed was standing and just grinning. He didn't have to say anything, his grin said it all: *You rookie!*

When we got to the fence Pat said to me, "Put three cartridges in the magazine, but don't chamber one until I tell you." I nodded and took three 180-grain Federal Trophy Bonded cartridges out of the ammo band on my jacket. I quietly opened the bolt on the Winchester Model 70 and inserted them into the magazine. Then, while holding down the top cartridge to prevent it from chambering, I quietly closed the bolt firmly. The Model 70 was now loaded but not chambered.

"Good." Pat mouthed the word.

Good, I thought to myself. *Wow, an embryo of a compliment.*

Pat held the barbed-wire fence apart enough for Ed and me to climb through it. Once through, we held it open for him. And then we were hunting—finally elk hunting.

Pat moved ahead rapidly, Ed right behind him, both dodging sagebrush. It was interesting how the sage bushes spaced themselves apart uniformly, leaving room for prairie grass to grow into elk feed in the gaps. An infinity of sagebrush stretched ahead of us. Following Ed, I had to double step to keep up with him—and he'd had hip replacement surgery two years before!

I moved thorough the brush *zip-zap, zip-zap,* enjoying my new denim jeans which were comfortable. When bent over to stay down, it was impossible to be quiet. But I was developing a rhythm and it felt good. We were at an altitude of 8,500 feet! Maybe all those antioxidants I'd been taking for the last three years were really helping.

Pat stopped near a patch of oak brush and glared at me. *What now*? He was staring at my pants and waving me to come over to him.

"Those frickin pants—where the hell did you get those pants?" Pat demanded when we were face-to-face.

"They're brown Wrangler jeans, bought them for this hunt; two pair," I said.

"Can't you hear them zipping and zapping through the sagebrush? Why do you think Ed and I are wearing this soft-fleece camo, because it looks like trees? Hell no, because it's quiet in the sage brush. Understand? Don't zip-zap!" Pat ordered.

Ed pointed to his camo-pants and kicked at the sagebrush; there was no sound. "Quiet pants."

"They were *not* on your list," referring to the list of required clothes and gear he had sent me before the hunt. Of the twelve hunters in our group, I was the only Rookie. Everybody else had been on this hunt many times. And ranch manager Pat, had told Ed he would break me in on Day One. This was Day One.

"Sorry; I'll go into Baggs, Wyoming tomorrow and buy quiet pants. For now, it's stay with these or drop down to my jockey shorts," I responded to Pat in an undertone.

"Spare us! Just be quiet and high-step the sage! Let's move," Pat whisper-barked his commands. I knew from experience how a fraternity initiation felt; Pat had taken that experience to another level.

We walked at a good pace through the sagebrush, and as I followed behind I thought about the money I'd paid for this hunt. For getting maligned, abused, embarrassed, denigrated, brow-beaten, and cussed at in a whisper-voice. "Nobody talks to me like this in my business. I own my business. I sign the checks. I'm the boss." But then, I thought: "What the hell, why not? Why not pay for it and, maybe, just maybe, get an elk in the process." It was certainly humbling and gave me pause.

Pat motioned for me to get between him and Ed. I sidestepped several sage bushes and arrived in place with a minimum of denim-zipping and zapping. "Follow me close," he commanded.

We moved ahead again and I tried my best to be quiet while keeping up with Pat. Ed stayed on my heels. I was thankful for the light-weight La Crosse boots I'd bought before the trip; my Wisconsin deer-hunting boots would have been too bulky and heavy for this country. *Little perfections are important,* I thought to myself, *too bad I screwed up on the pants…*

"Keep low from here on," Pat motioned with his hands. Then he stopped and got down on his knees; I instantly did the same becoming his mirror image. He was glassing a small clearing between two patches of oak brush where, miraculously, a small herd of elk had appeared. Both Ed and I had our binoculars on them. We sat down quietly in the sagebrush like soldiers and watched the elk. It was 6:30 pm and dusk was near—we had about an hour left to hunt.

"Don't move," Pat whispered, cupping his hands. "They can't see you if you don't move." He pulled a small bottle of odorless soap solution out of a long pocket on his pants and squirted it into the air about two feet above the sagebrush. This would test the wind direction: tiny marble-size bubbles swarmed above the sage and got caught in the light breeze that blew them to our right, parallel to the elk. We were not upwind from the animals, which was good; had the bubbles blown toward them they would have picked up our scent.

We watched them quietly without moving. There were three cows and two calves but no bull in sight. Fifteen minutes passed, and no bull appeared. Pat blew into a large U-shaped elk call that imitated a bull—a competitor! Would this bring a bull out? He blew it again. The calves perked but that was it. The cows were indifferent to the sound. No bull came out. Would Pat insist that I shoot a cow? He wouldn't, I thought. But, what if he did? I would have to shoot; they were easily in range at 120 yards. The meat would be excellent. No, he wouldn't do that to me on the first day. He knew I wanted a bull elk.

Pat grabbed my jacket by the bird pocket in back and gave it a pull. I immediately looked at him. He motioned for me to follow him, asserting himself like John Wayne in an old western movie. Ed had already figured out whatever Pat was thinking. And then we ran—north through heavy sage—no longer concerned about the five elk we had been watching. I stayed behind Pat. Ed stayed on my heels. In about ten minutes we reached a span of aspen trees that blocked our view east; we could no longer see back to the elk group. I was out of breath. The sun was almost down and the shadows were long, the sage was dark now and difficult to run through.

We ran on, at eight-thousand feet, into the approaching darkness. Pat was truly poetry-in-motion moving through the sage. I followed him, but not quite so poetically. It was harder to get air now. *I must get into better shape if I decide to do this next year,* I thought.

Pat paused for a moment to glass ahead, looking through the trees. When he noticed me glassing in the same direction he pulled me to him. "Damnit! Let me do the glassing; you watch me from here on!" I gave him the scuba divers okay sign with finger and thumb, wondering if this was a major or a minor screw-up. He glared again at my pants as we moved on, reminding me they were a major mistake.

Ahead, not far, the aspens ended and we could see out to the east again. It dawned on me how dark it had become; the sun was down and all the long shadows had disappeared into that gray dusk that precedes darkness. I recalled how bright it was the day I sighted-in the 7mm Winchester at the target range, but that was not this reality—this darkness was. Pat crouched next to a tree while I stayed back a few yards. *Mistake!* "Get the hell over here," he lipped the words without making a sound. I was obviously too far out from cover. I quickly crawled over to him.

"Hug these fricking trees," Pat muttered. "Become one of them!" I moved next to a quakey tree immediately to Pat's right. "Chamber a cartridge now!" He silently mouthed the words. I quietly pulled the bolt back allowing a cartridge from the magazine to enter ahead of the bolt face and then quietly closed the bolt on it, moving it into the chamber. I pulled the safety back, putting it on "safe"—ready to fire now when I moved it forward (off safe).

Pat glassed east and then looked back at Ed. I didn't move, keeping my eyes on Pat. *I could really learn to dislike this man,* I thought. I cautiously glanced at Ed behind me who was opening and closing his right hand, spreading his fingers wide—signaling a five-by-five bull. I turned my head instantly and looked east.

"Shoot that frickin' elk," Pat pointed to an animal standing out in a meadow, 150 yards away. All I could see was a large, dull, yellowish oval.

"*What frickin' elk?*" I couldn't see it, so I raised my binoculars. Pat, right next to me, pushed the binoculars down. "With your gun!" he hissed. I raised the 7mm and noticed the Leopold scope was zoomed to nine-power. I quickly turned it back to five-power so I could hold the gun steady and get more light to come through the scope.

I had to move the gun barrel around to find the elk in the scope. Pat watched, deeply concerned when he saw the muzzle-brake of the barrel moving around aimlessly. *Damn Rookie,* I knew whet Pat was thinking. He didn't know I was trying to find the elk in the scope. Then I saw the antlers, a nice five-by-five bull, facing north, broadside to me. My thoughts raced. It was dark looking through the scope; unfamiliar—reality, not practice. I had to make do with it. I moved my head farther back. Heart pounding, I pushed the safety forward, taking it off, ready to fire. The animal was motionless, but for how long? In my mind's eye I disregarded the head, neck, and tail, and divided what was left both vertically and horizontally into four equal sections. I held on the spot where the imaginary lines crossed—the cross-hair spot—and then aimed slightly forward of it. This was the shot that hunting magazines told you to take, the shot that disabled the shoulder and then hit into the vitals bringing the animal down and killing it quickly. But if I hit high the bullet would hit into dense muscle and be non-lethal. A wounded bull could run a long way in the dark. I moved my aim down an inch. Took a deep breath. Held it. Right index finger on the trigger, ready to squeeze it…

"Don't screw up," Pat said at the last moment—I lost my breath. *What kind of advice was that at such a super critical time!* I tried to disregard his comment and concentrated on re-scoping the spot. Ready again.

"God help me if I miss," I said to myself. "Forget about it. How can I? If I miss I'll be the joke at camp tonight. If I wound the animal and it runs off in the darkness, it would be worse than missing. I won't miss—I'm a good shot with this rifle. Screw the darkness. Shoot the elk," I told myself. I took another breath, held it, and squeezed easy: *Ka-Ra-Boom!* The 7mm detonated.

"You frickin' missed!" Pat shouted!

"I hit that elk, Pat! I hit him good. I saw him jump and limp east."

Ed was nodding his head. "Yes, he did!" We all headed east in the gray dusk, moving fast. Ahead of us—beyond where the elk had been shot—was a trail of blood that lead into a thick forest of aspens. I had worries: if my aim was off, this animal was wounded and moving—in the dark, in the thick brush. My flashlight was back in the truck, in the fanny pack that I didn't bring along, forgetting it during the two-minute drill. "Damn," I said to myself. My wife always told me my best gear would be somewhere else when I needed it. She was right.

We entered the woods. Strangely, it seemed to be brighter! The sun was down but clouds in the west had cleared. We moved fast over logs and dead wood and brush piles following the blood. I was tired but not feeling it. Adrenaline was flowing. Then, directly ahead there it was: A trophy bull elk lying motionless, sixty yards from where I shot it—*with one shot! I was euphoric. . .*

It's hard to explain the inner satisfaction a hunter feels at the end of a successful hunt. The positive effect of such an experience is medicine for the soul. It was for me. It taught me that small details count and how to find grace under pressure! This didn't really sink in until several months later when Pat's words of instruction and critique still rang true. Even his last second command to not "screw up" caused me to refocus the scope which guided the bullet to exactly the right spot.

I needed the help of a professional guide on this first elk hunt. Sure, a lot of it was initiation, bombastic rhetoric, exaggeration—the price of admission. So what part of Pat's act helped me get the elk? Fact is, as I considered it in retrospect, it all helped. I needed mental conditioning to have a good chance of success and Pat gave it to me: Discipline gotten from tough coaching using the right verbs in that special order. But in the end, I still had to do it myself!

That night, after dinner, they all beat me at poker. It was good not to win at everything that day.

Postscript:

Some people don't agree that hunting should be allowed—that it is cruel. Nature is cruel and man is part of nature. Man has been hunting forever to fulfill his protein requirements. But today, it must be done ethically and regulated properly. Elk meat is exceptionally lean and has no wild taste. I took some of the meat from this kill home to Minneapolis and donated the rest to local families in Baggs, Wyoming where the economy is depressed. Everything was professionally butchered and frozen at my expense. I've been on eight elk hunts with Ed and Pat since this Rookie Hunt and got an elk each time.

The elk herds in the western United States are substantial. States like Colorado and Wyoming dedicate licensing fees to herd management. Driving home from this hunt I had to stop on Interstate 80, just east of Rawlins, Wyoming, for over an hour to allow a large elk herd to cross the highway. One-by-one they were heading south to Colorado.

Sumatran tiger

15

Green Indonesia

From Giant Bugs to Comedian Orangutans

Java, Indonesia 1996

Two boys played with large black beetles. The females were four inches long and the males even larger. When a male approached a female, she unfolded her hard wings to expose soft wings underneath, then moved them rapidly, slowly gaining enough lift to rise straight up like a helicopter and hit the patio's tin roof. The roof was a full stop. Instantly, the beetle fell straight down on the floor, usually landing upside down. Then, moving all six legs, she would try to right herself. Males didn't fly often but fought continuously with each other, often resulting in one or both upside down. Sometimes three would fight—an upended male was vulnerable. The boys watched the beetles intently.

I referred to them as junior entomologists. They had small rattan boxes for transporting their pet beetles, and somehow, they knew theirs from all the wild ones when it was time to go home.

"They are Goliath beetles," Professor Sumendra said. "Some are over five inches."

"What do they eat?" I asked, watching the boys watching the beetles.

"Tree sap; they're mostly vegetarians."

We were outside at a seafood restaurant in Surabaya, eating Indonesian fried rice that was spicy enough to keep flies off! A fresh breeze coming off the Java Sea cooled the humidity. Surprising us, a female Goliath landed on our table, upside down. I nudged her from behind and flipped her over. She walked around in a circle, confused by what had happened.

Pick her up," the professor said, "she won't bite." I picked her up from behind, her six legs squirming, and set her on the sandy floor. After she walked off, one of the boys held a large male up to my face, giggling. Its mandibles were an inch from my nose. The other boy and the waiter laughed. So did the professor.

None of the beetles wanted anything to do with the spicy fried rice. After the boys left with their pets, the other beetles thinned out, probably heading back to their daylight hideouts.

There was nothing fancy about the restaurant. The professor and I stayed awhile after eating, talking science and drinking cold tea without ice. In Indonesia, ice was made from tap water that couldn't be trusted. Tea was too, but the water had been boiled! We spent the night in Surabaya on the island of Java.

Professor Trisno Sumendra was a wise man, one of the best biologists I've ever known. His specialty was aquatic microbiology, but he knew every aspect of biology—from bacteria to blue whales. He was a thin man in his mid-fifties, born in China, and had perfectly disheveled black hair and penetrating green eyes. I'd met him at an aquaculture conference in Singapore five years ago. Being scientists with common interests, it was easy to become friends. He lived in Jakarta and spoke Indonesian, Mandarin, and English.

We had started the trip in Bali at a marine science conference, and after three days, took the ferry across to Java. We were heading west to Bogor for another conference. It was a long drive, seven hundred kilometers, so we hired a car and driver for the trip.

Our driver's name was Ada. He didn't talk much, but, speaking in Indonesian, he did point out sights he knew the professor could explain.

"Ada says the road is good here but will get bumpy soon," the professor interpreted, sitting in the back. "There will be fruit stands ahead where we can stop."

We stopped at one of the larger stands that had a selection of tropical fruits. We bought rambutans and mangosteens, two of my favorites. The rambutans looked like red, hairy golf balls. When twisted they opened revealing a white nugget that tasted like a tangy grape. The mangosteen, called the "Queen of Fruits," was plum-sized and reddish purple. When squeezed from the bottom, the rind split exposing six or more white segments, like a tangerine, but with a strawberry-peach flavor touched with vanilla. Good tropical snacks.

About two hours out of Surabaya we encountered monkeys, lots of them. They were blocking the road. "These are long-tailed Macaques," the professor said. "Common here."

We stopped and Ada signaled us to close the windows. The Macaques were occupied with various activities: two were copulating, one was eating a mango, two were picking fleas off each other, and others were self-grooming and body-shaking. Unlike in a zoo, these monkeys had total freedom and they knew it. One big male, obviously the leader, stood in front of the troop, staring us down. We blew the horn but none of them moved. Ada inched forward and hit the horn again. The big male made hooting sounds and waved his arms, mocking us. Then he pounded on the car.

"Give me that bag of rambutans," the professor said. I handed it to him and he opened the back window and started throwing them behind the car. Immediately, the two copulating monkeys disengaged and ran after the rambutans, then the mango eater followed with the groomers. This allowed us to move forward slowly, disregarding the few that didn't move. The leader, arms waving, alternating grunting with hooting, was going crazy. We moved ahead while I took pictures of him.

These monkeys had done this before; it wasn't their first road block.

We continued the drive with the professor identifying various tropical trees in the surrounding hills. The wide umbrella-acacia trees were easy to spot; sandalwood groves delightful to smell, giving off a cedar-lilac aroma; and durian trees with their armored, odorous fruit—edible once I developed a taste for it. It took some effort!

"Is it true durians are aphrodisiacs?" I questioned the professor.

"Yes, many say it is, but it must be very ripe. Young couples are told to leave it outside for at least two nights after picking it. Longer is better. When it tastes like garlic-flavored vanilla custard, it's ready; if skunky, it's spoiled." He explained. Then he told Ada this in Indonesian to see if he agreed. Ada nodded and smiled, saying something.

"What did he say?" I asked.

He said he has eight kids, and his wife won't allow him to eat durian anymore!" I looked at Ada and grinned. He grinned back and drove a little faster.

Everything was remarkably green! Volcanoes were behind the hills on our left. Many kilometers went by as snakes occasionally crossed the road. Some were big, but I couldn't identify them. The professor was dozing, apparently immune to the bumpy road. I had to roll up a tee shirt and put it between the car seat and my lower back, then tried out some preschool Indonesian on Ada as we passed Java's green hills and volcanoes.

"Ada wants to know if we should stop for the night," the professor said.

"I'd say yes, it's hard to see on this highway at night." We had driven into the dark, which came early in the tropics. As good as the car was for a rental in Indonesia, the headlights both pointed left, obscuring the view to the right.

"Is it possible in this part of Java to have elephants running around? Or one of those Javan rhinos?" I asked the professor.

"Elephants yes, but rhinos are very rare here—sixty was the last count on Java. But there are nine national parks running the length of Java from the Bali ferry to the Straights of Sunda. And they have no fences," he explained.

"We don't need a bull elephant storming out from the right." We were going ninety kilometers an hour. Even though we had planned to make it to Bogor, good sense told us to stop.

"The next city is Bandung, we'll find a hotel there," the professor was hopeful.

It was easier said than done. The upcoming conference in Bogor, one hundred kilometers away, had become popular, and hotel rooms in Bandung were full. We drove through the city and on the west side—just before the jungle started again—we found an old, musty motel with two rooms available. Ada slept outside in a hammock, the accepted practice for drivers.

The rooms were bad; humid, and unclean. I took the bed covers off the bed and sprayed under it with bug spray—forty-percent Deet. I went into the bathroom and surprised a large blue mouse in the bathtub. It had Mickey Mouse ears and was the size of a chipmunk, jumping up the sides of the tub then sliding back, not able to get a grip. I looked around and grabbed an old wire waste basket from under the sink and put it over the mouse. Now what to do? There was a rubber mat by the door; I grabbed it and pushed it under the mouse, keeping the basket on top. Using two hands, one under the mat and one on top of the basket, I went outside and released the critter. It scampered away; I felt happy for it. Now to get some sleep. I curled up in the center of the bed in my shorts, no covers, and thought about Christmas in Minneapolis. A cold, white one!

When I awoke, it was raining and water was running in under the door. I took the one towel there was, rolled it up, and tried to block the water. I grabbed my duffel bag off the floor and put it on the bed. I opened the window and looked out; Ada was sitting in the car, out of the rain. Nothing else seemed to be going on except rain. I opened the duffel to take out a couple of mangosteens to eat. The professor had only thrown rambutans at the monkeys. I reached into the bag and two, giant, four-inch cockroaches ran out, over my arm, onto the floor and under the bed.

"Cucarachas!" I shouted, brushing my arms with my hands. These guys were larger than those in the Amazon—long-legged and whiskey brown! I turned the duffel over and shook it, all the stuff fell on the bed along with mangosteen rinds and stems. No edible fruit segments were left uneaten! "Wow! Those bugs ate everything." Then I realized I was talking to myself. I shook out my pants and shirt then put them on; they had been on a hook by the door. I knocked my tennis shoes together upside down. Nothing ran out. I saved the rinds and stems to show the professor…

"Look at these, Dr. Sumendra. Not a speck of fruit left!"

"It's not surprising; bugs rule in Southeast Asia. On the island of Sulawesi, the natives bury their dead in trees. Out in the open. The bugs eat all the tissue, skin, hair, anything organic, leaving only bones. Enterprising young natives sell the perfect skeletons to doctors and hospitals around the world."

"Amazing." I was still in disbelief of the super roaches.

Back on the road, the trip to Bogor was uneventful except for driving over a large dead snake that even the professor didn't recognize.

Our conference was at the Bogor Agricultural University. It was overbooked, but somehow, they made room for everybody. Because I was with "The Professor" we got seats up front. The presentations on controlling the microbiology in aquaculture ponds were pertinent to my business.

"You can call me Mr. Trisno, or just Trisno," the professor said. "It will signal that we are friends, not just colleagues."

"Okay, Mr. Trisno, but I might forget sometimes; to me you are "The Professor."

That night we had reservations at one of the dormitories. It was hot, clammy and smelled of Lysol. I had to reinvent myself again. My dad would have said, "It's all in your head." Maybe so, but at 2:00 a.m. the smell of the phenolic germicide was very real and I was wet with sweat. I dried off with a towel, took six milligrams of melatonin, and went back to sleep.

We had a full next day at the conference, but there was time in the afternoon to visit the Bogor Botanical Gardens. It was home for thousands of tropical plant species, including the remarkable Fantasy Flower in bloom; the largest flower in the world measuring a meter in diameter. The professor had been to these gardens many times and knew exactly what to show me in the short time we had. Beyond the gardens, dominating the horizon, was Mount Salak an active volcano.

"How open is your schedule next week?" The professor asked me.

"Open," I said. "I go back to Minneapolis a week from Saturday. What do you have in mind?"

"Sumatra," He answered.

"Tell me more, I'm interested." Part of this business trip was meant to be vacation. I had thought about snorkeling in the Thousand Islands Marine Park out from Jakarta but had no firm plans.

"Two things: First, I have a friend doing tiger research at an outpost camp in Way Kambas National Park. I have arranged to visit him. Second, there is an important aquatic microbiology conference at Lake Toba that will interest you. And the best news: The Indonesian government will pay our expenses!"

"Let's go! Thanks for the invitation. I haven't been to Sumatra; it would be great to see it—and tigers, too!"

"I'm pleased to hear that. I promise the accommodations will be better than the last two nights. We will hire a different car and driver tomorrow and take the ferry to Sumatra, across the Straights of Sunda. Tonight, we stay in Bogor at an air-conditioned hotel, compliments of the Indonesian Government!"

Boarding the ferry was a spectacle. Lots of eco-tourists, local youth, government officials, Chinese tour groups, and some Russians were crowding on board, mostly going over without a vehicle. Even our new driver, Hasan, was excited. The professor and I went up to the top deck, above the cars, where most of the people were. Everybody was looking out and seemed anxious to be going to Sumatra.

The water was mostly calm with long, lazy swells, the temperature tropical. Out to the southeast was the volcano Krakatoa, famous for its earth-changing eruption in 1883 when it blew itself apart. It produced eleven cubic miles of ash that changed the world's weather. The following year, 1884, was called "the year without summer." Ash had blocked much of the sun that year.

It was a clear weather day on the Straits of Sunda. Trisno and I absorbed the sunshine on the two-hour trip to Sumatra.

Hasan was in the car with the engine running before we docked in Lampung. The professor and I got into the car after it was off the ferry. I was excited to meet the "The Tiger Man," Dr. Robert Weaver, who would be waiting for us at a hotel close by. Hasan drove us straight to the hotel.

"Robert! Greetings my friend," the professor said with a big smile, giving him the traditional Indonesian loose handshake, lasting ten seconds or more. Both were happy to see each other.

"Trisno, it's great to see you!" Robert responded, still shaking hands.

"Please meet Mr. Stanley, my biochemist friend from Minneapolis, Trisno said. I think you know the place."

"Minneapolis! What a coincidence. I went to graduate school at the U of M," Robert said. "Pleasure to meet you, Stanley."

We shook hands American style. "You can call me Stan."

"Robert is on a U.S. government research grant. He's studying our tigers," Trisno smiled as he spoke. As I mentioned on our Java drive, we call him 'Tiger Man' at the university in Jakarta."

"I'm not sure I've earned that title yet," Robert humbly replied.

"Let's discuss tigers while Hasan drives us to Way Kambas," Trisno suggested.

Way Kambas National Park wasn't far, about seventy-five kilometers directly north. One hundred fifty kilometers southwest was Barisan Selatin National Park. So, you didn't have to go far from the ferry to be in thick jungle, in or near one of the parks. While Hasan drove, Robert briefed us on Sumatran tigers.

"There are five national parks in Sumatra and eight nature reserves. Tigers are found in most of them. They're completely gone from Bali and Java. The Sumatran tiger is not as large as the Siberian, but takes no second seat as a powerful predator. One tiger can cover a territory of fifty square kilometers. Its favorite foods are wild pigs and deer, but it will eat most small animals including fish and tortoises. Like lions in Africa, it causes fear in many of the local tribes; its roar is quite fearsome. There are about five hundred tigers in Sumatra, which are protected by law, but there is still poaching. Both the pelt and penis are sold at high prices on the international market. The penis is eaten in China as a delicacy and can be found in some Jakarta restaurants.

"Ecotourists want to see tigers, and it's not a guaranteed safe venture, so the government allows armed guards to trek along. Some of the daytime guards turn into poachers at night, using government rifles. My job is to study the tigers—their habits and reproduction—to assure they will not become extinct. You will see how I monitor them with trail cameras. But a government guard will be with us…we have no choice."

"Wow," I said, "it's complicated."

"True, but we scientists, including Trisno's team in Jakarta, are pushing for better controls."

"Yes," Trisno agreed. "And money from ecotourism is helping the push."

When we got to Way Kambas we stopped at a clearing near the Sumatran coast where there was a headquarters building and a large, open gazebo that was elevated off the ground. It had stairs on one side and a fire pit in the center surrounded by wooden benches. No one was around.

Robert and Trisno headed to the building, while Hasan and I stayed at the gazebo. Looking at the edge of the jungle, Hasan pointed to a large bird standing on a tree branch.

"A great hornbill," I remarked. Hasan nodded. It had a brilliant yellow head and large bill with a black ring enclosing its eye; the bill had an extension on top that resembled a hat. As we looked at it, it moved to face us, then started chuckling and barking. It didn't sound like a happy greeting. When I moved toward the car to get binoculars, it took off with its white-tipped wings and tail spread wide. It flew over us toward the Java Sea just beyond.

"Good sighting," I said. "Big bird!" Its wingspan was close to two meters.

Hasan nodded. He knew what I said without understanding the words. He spread his arms out, flapping them, to imitate the bird. I laughed at his imitation and gave him a thumbs-up.

Robert and Trisno were in the headquarters building which, on closer inspection, had an army truck parked behind it. Hasan and I walked around the gazebo, at least forty meters, looking for more birds. *Where are all the ecotourists?* I wondered, looking puzzled. "Where is anybody?" I put my arms out, palms up.

Hasan just shrugged his shoulders, guessing at what I said.

Robert and Trisno came out of the building with two men wearing military camo. One of them was holding a folder containing papers. The older soldier asked me in English for my passport, which I had in my front pocket. I handed him the passport. He looked at the photo page, looked at me, then flipped through the visa pages. Then he studied one of the pages in his folder.

"You travel a lot," he said.

"Yes," I answered. "I travel on business that involves studying animals." Trisno had told me to say this if asked; no need to add they were mostly microscopic. Still animals.

The soldier handed my papers back and told Trisno in Indonesian that it was too late to walk to Dr. Weaver's research facility; that we should do it tomorrow when a guard could be with us. Robert tried to tell him we could still make it before dark.

Trisno grabbed Robert's arm while shaking his head no. "I'll explain later."

"You can make yourselves comfortable in the gazebo." The older soldier said. "We will supply blankets and mosquito netting, and will bring out some fried rice. We cook it hot."

"Okay," Trisno said in English. "Thank you." The two soldiers went back into the building.

"What's going on?" Robert asked.

"Problems with some Brazilian tourists yesterday," Trisno answered with concern. "There was a fight and one got stabbed, hurt pretty bad. She's in the hospital in Lampung. He told me this when you were in the restroom. They closed this section of the park but knew we were on the way. I had confirmed our arrival from the hotel in Lampung." The army knew about Trisno's honored position at the university in Jakarta and that the government was paying for our visit.

The three of us walked down to the shore to get some exercise. There were birds everywhere. We talked more about tigers, the zoology department at the university in Jakarta, and about the walk through the jungle tomorrow. Robert informed Trisno of some necessary preparations for the next day: socks pulled up over pant legs; long-sleeved shirts and hats sprayed with Deet; and everyone with two water bottles and salt pills.

"I think they have the fried rice ready; I can smell it," Trisno remarked. "Sorry about our accommodations tonight."

"There's nothing you could do about it. No apology required," I told him.

"I had put clean sheets on the two army bunks in my 'guest room.' Sounds like you won't be using them," Robert said, knowing we had to leave tomorrow afternoon. "Let's go eat."

The Soldier's Indonesian fried rice, *Nasi Goreng,* was surprisingly good. The rice—dark brown from frying it with *Kecap manis,* a thick sweet soy sauce—was fortified with onions, peppers, fresh scallops and a touch of garlic; a complete meal.

The morning came with discomfort. The semicircular benches in the gazebo were wide enough that we could put two together, cover them with a blanket, and lie curled up on top. The mosquito netting was another story: it kept hitting me in the nose and tickling my feet when I shifted around. It made the humidity and heat worse. Breakfast was bran muffins with strawberry jam washed down with instant coffee. The two soldiers had brought out a kettle of boiling water and three cups. I made the coffee.

Trisno apologized again for the accommodations; we were just thankful one of the five hundred tigers didn't stop by.

It was a four-mile walk to Robert's facility. There was no way to drive it, not even in an ATV. We followed a narrow game trail through the jungle, vines growing over sections of it—we had to walk single file most of the time. The guard walked in front of us carrying an AK-47. He wouldn't have to be very accurate with it; just point in the general direction of a charging tiger and pull the trigger. Snakes and spiders were my real concern.

The guard turned to Trisno and told him in Indonesian that we should talk more; the louder the better. Robert agreed. Robert and I talked about fishing in Minnesota while Trisno sang a song in Mandarin. After playing "follow the guard" for an hour, we came to an open area with a small lagoon. The trail went around the lagoon in both directions. The guard pivoted around looking at everything; no predators in sight.

Just beyond the clearing was another clearing without a lagoon. Here, thousands of insects, sounding like circular saws cutting plywood, were "singing" in the trees. The noise was astounding.

"Tropical cicadas," Trisno commented.

"Hold still a moment," I said to the three men. I took out a military whistle that I always carried in the bush and showed it to Robert and Trisno; they looked puzzled. The guard had no reaction to it. I put the whistle to my lips and with cicada-bugs sawing away at maximum decibels, I blew it as hard as I could. Two seconds later, total quiet. The insects had quit. "It was an evolutionary moment for them!"

"How about that!" Robert said. "My entomology buddies would be captivated." The guard just scratched his head. As we walked on, back on the narrow trail, the insects started up again. It was my only jungle trick—learned it as an Eagle Scout.

Halfway to Robert's research facility we stopped to take a break. I was drenched with sweat and my legs felt heavy, made worse by knowing we had to go back the same way later today! Trisno had kept up behind me while Robert and the guard led the way. It had been slow going in areas where vines crossed the trail. The Number One Rule was: "Don't trip." No large cats or elephants had tried to attack us, but it was essential to avoid the tarantulas patrolling the vines. They were the size of a man's hand, brown with black legs, and had six eyes. They were not venomous enough to kill you but their bite would spoil your day.

"Don't put your hands any place you can't see," Robert instructed. It was tempting to use hanging vines for leverage, like Tarzan. "Don't do it." This was Rule Number Two.

It took another two hours to get to Robert's research facility. A "shack in the jungle" would have been a more accurate description. It was a wooden building with three rooms, about the size of a two-car garage. He had electric lights and a radio connected to twelve-volt batteries that recharged by solar; a cistern for water collection with gravity delivery to a water filter; canned and freeze-dried food everywhere; lots of spaghetti and meat balls, freeze dried ham and eggs; a propane stove; a dozen books on tigers; and a five-gallon bucket with a toilet seat.

"All the comforts of home," Robert joked.

"How did you get all this stuff in here?" I asked him.

"With help from the government, all of it got walked in. Ladies with baskets on their heads carried food and small stuff; men carried the bigger things tied to bamboo poles."

"I'm amazed at the simplicity and desolation of this compared to my university lab in Jakarta." Trisno observed. "It takes a dedicated zoologist to do this."

"I am that," Robert said humbly. "Let's have lunch—you guys must be starved! Then I'll show you some tiger photos and take you out to one of my trail camera locations." He opened two cans each of red sockeye salmon, mushroom soup, new potatoes, and sweet corn. They all got cooked together in a large frying pan on the propane stove. For drinking, he reconstituted Tang in filtered rain water. Lunch was served.

It was better than I expected; the only thing missing was a cold beer! Robert handed me a large can of fruit cocktail to open for dessert on his way into the "guest room." Shortly, he carried out several photo albums.

"These were all taken with trail cameras," he explained. "I have twelve trail cams out within a three-kilometer radius. I get a lot of exercise. Check them most days. Bait them with liver paste, pork or deer meat. Locals walk-in the meat and help set the bait."

There was one trail camera a hundred meters away that we went out to see. It was mounted on a tree facing a small cleared area, just off a game trail. The bait was nailed to a stump about four meters from the camera tree. All cameras had flash units and were water resistant with awnings above them to deflect sun and rain. They were all motion-activated to take photos whenever a large creature moved into the focal zone.

There were some exceptional photos in the albums. Some were blurred or only showed half an animal, but there were many perfect tiger shots with the full animal in focus. Bird and snake photos were relegated to the back of the book; one of the hornbills looked familiar.

"I can identify each tiger in most of the photos–their stripes act like fingerprints. No two are the same. There are at least six different tigers visiting the cameras—four females and two males. These are the ones that revisit. There may have been two others, but they were hard to identify due to blurring."

"Aren't this many tigers unusual, considering their low density on Sumatra?" Trisno asked.

"Yes, it is. Sumatra is a big island, 473,000 square kilometers. My twenty-eight square kilometers divides into the total 17,000 times! Taking just twenty percent of Sumatra as tiger habitat, there should be over 3,000 tigers if you extrapolate my numbers. There are three possibilities for what I've observed so far: one, the five hundred animal estimate is wrong – too low, which is what I hope; two, what we have in Way Kambas is a fluke of nature, more tigers than the average due to optimized habitat or better poaching control; or three, my providing easy meals of tasty bait has attracted them disproportionally. I need to get to the bottom of this before I leave."

"A conundrum," Trisno said. I agreed.

I was looking again at the photos. One was exceptionally clear. "That's Sam," Robert said. "The larger of the two males."

"Do all six have names?" I asked.

"Yup, Lizzy is my favorite female. I believe Sam mates with all four females. Joey, the smaller male, is trying to get in on the action. He better be careful or Sam will kill him. Lizzy had a litter of seven last year. Only two survived, best I can tell. They followed her twice to the cameras then disappeared. The shots of the cubs were mostly blurry—hard to get them to sit still for the camera!"

"What are the most important things that can be done to increase their numbers?" I asked.

Robert was about to answer, but Trisno beat him to it. "Get more private funding from Europe and the USA. Use it to protect the habitat, hire more trustworthy wardens, dissuade rich Chinese from eating the you-know-what, and get the military out of it."

"That's exactly right," Robert confirmed. "We are losing habitat to logging that serves the toilet paper industry of Indonesia—over two hundred million people. Poachers kill over fifty tigers a year. Fewer tigers means thousands of dollars more for a pelt!

The guard had been nudging Trisno and pointing to the trail back. We needed to get to the car by 6:30 p.m. at the latest. We said goodbye to Robert with long Indonesian handshakes and a big thank you, and got ready to leave. We wished him well in solving the conundrum.

"Robert, I have one more question for you. How many tigers have you, personally, seen in the two years you've been here?"

"One," he said. "It was crossing the highway last year on our way back to Lampung. I was in a taxi and it was about fifty meters ahead of us." I concluded that one guard was enough for our jungle trek.

We got to the car just before dark. It was an uneventful walk back except for the guard letting me shoot the AK-47 at a dead tree. I had often wondered how an automatic military rifle would shoot. I aimed low and held the trigger back for twenty-five shots. It was loud and powerful. The tree came down. It was fun—didn't kick as much as I expected. Automatic rifles absorb most of the recoil.

Hasan was waiting for us with the car. We drove back to Lampung and found a suitable hotel with a swimming pool and good restaurant. The large pool was clear and cool; a swim before dinner was very welcome!

At dinner, we overheard some young trekkers speaking to the waiter about Way Kambas. "Is it open?" They asked. "Not yet," the waiter said. "Why not?" "Government says tigers are around more than usual…"

"Well, which was it, a stabbing or tigers that closed the park?" I asked Trisno.

"I think you know the answer, tigers are usually the default excuse!" He replied. *Considering Robert's conundrum, I wasn't so sure.*

I slept well. It's amazing how much difference a little walk in the jungle and an operating air conditioner can make!

For breakfast, Trisno and I had omelets prepared in front us by a pleasant, young Muslim girl wearing a white *dupatta* over her hotel uniform. It was a reminder to me that Indonesia was the largest Muslim country with over 180 million Muslim citizens. A long way from Mecca.

Hasan was waiting for us after breakfast, we had asked him to join us but he had eaten across the street at a roadside food-stand with other taxi drivers—a steamed mixture of white, yellow and brown rice called *Urap.*

It was going to be a long drive to Lake Toba. The road was not the best, and it wound through many small towns and villages, more than on Java. Local people dressed in colorful clothes, particularly the women. They carried groceries home in baskets on their heads. Chickens ran wild and were community property. We frequently passed open markets; lamb and goat carcasses hung from racks, drying in the sun. Durian, jack fruit, rambutans, and mangosteens were neatly displayed, kept organized by women and older children. Roosters crowed throughout the day.

The road mostly followed the south shore of the island with the Indian Ocean off to the left. Truck traffic was less than on Java. Hasan drove well. Kilometers bumped by. Hungry for lunch, Trisno told Hasan to stop at a tourist restaurant he knew on the east side of Padang.

Two large orangutans were putting on a show outside the restaurant. I had to look twice to believe it! They were big, dressed in blue and red boxer shorts over cinnamon brown hairy legs, standing up and shaking hands with tourists.

"These are our pets," a tall man said. "Their names are Elmer and Fud." They were over five feet tall and had name tags around their necks. Elmer was smoking a cigar. Fud was drinking a can of coke. Unbelievable. They were hairy people.

"Shake hands with them," the tall man encouraged. "Give them some money." I pulled out a U.S. five-dollar bill and handed it to Elmer. He put the cigar between his lips and grabbed the money, showing it to the tall man, then put it in a flowerpot on a table. Fud immediately finished his coke, tipping the can high with one hand, then reaching out to me with just an open hand.

"He wants money too," the tall man said proudly. Trisno, who had just been watching the ordeal, gave him a five-hundred rupiah note. He grabbed it, showed it to the tall man, smirked, then threw it on the ground. It was only worth a few cents.

"He likes U.S. money," the tall man said. I was captivated; I had to play their game! I had some U.S. singles and took five out of my pocket and gave them to Fud. His eyes opened wide, and I believe he smiled, happy to show the money to the tall man who nodded. Then the bills went into the flowerpot containing a lot of other money, mostly Euros and U.S. dollars.

Then, the long-armed orangutans, excited now, began arm-swinging and screaming joyfully. It was unworldly. I've been fortunate to have seen many disarming, fantastic things around the world; this one certainly made the Top Ten List.

Then Trisno spoke to the tall man. "This is not legal. These animals are fully protected."

"We have special permit from police," the man answered. Of course, this meant the police got some of the money. The law of the jungle…

Trisno signaled Hasan to pull up the car and we headed out to find a different restaurant. I looked back to see Elmer puffing on his cigar, and Fud drinking another Coke.

We had a good meal in a Chinese restaurant in Padang, then drove on. Lake Toba was our destination; we still had a long way to go.

We were killing snakes on the road in the dark. Big ones! Hasan stopped and let professor Sumendra identify a few, providing they were dead. Road snakes had become an unintended nature study for me. The big ones went bump in the night—one almost tipped our taxi! They ranged in diameter from a garden hose to a fire hose. According to Hassan some were even larger. He told Trisno that he had seen one that was fifteen meters long and a meter wide in central Sumatra a few years ago. It had choked on a large deer. It was a reticulated python which is considered the world's largest snake, but nobody verified the dimensions of this monster. It rotted alongside a jungle road and gradually disappeared thanks mostly to millions of carnivorous ants. It made me think about our walk to Dr. Weaver's research shack and how taking along a big gun really wasn't as unnecessary as I had thought.

Trisno had translated Hasan's story for me. "I'm not surprised. I believe him," Trisno said, confident. "It's just too bad our zoology department didn't get word of it. They would have been here fast for a snake a meter wide!

"It's hard for me to imagine. If the dimensions are true, that snake would have been the length of a double-decker tourist bus and wider than the diameter of a telephone pole!" It gave me pause…

We arrived at Lake Toba late, taking longer than we expected, but Hasan did a good job of driving safely in the dark, snakes notwithstanding. The conference was in Parapat, a small town in northern Sumatra on the edge of Lake Toba. Trisno had made reservations at the Atsari Hotel on the lake, a popular spot for conferences and European tourists. Finally, we had a first-class hotel. Both Trisno and I slept well.

"The conference starts tomorrow," Trisno said at breakfast. "Today we can visit Lake Toba."

It was a magnificent day at three thousand feet—the elevation of the hotel and the lake. What a difference altitude makes in the tropics; we were treated to a cool breeze off the lake as the waiter filled our cups with strong Indonesian coffee. We toasted the day.

"Nothing better than a coffee toast," Trisno said. He didn't drink alcohol.

"Most of my fishing buddies in Minnesota would disagree," I said. Trisno smiled.

I looked over Trisno's shoulder and saw that a sharply dressed concierge was looking at us. I waved at him and he came over.

"Do you speak English?" I asked him.

"Of course," he said proudly. "And French, German, and Indonesian."

"Great," I said. "Can you tell Professor Sumendra and myself about Lake Toba? I've read a few things about it." Trisno just let me be myself. He was smiling, knowing I was giving him a break.

"Well, let's start with the fact that it's the largest volcanic lake in the world, and when it erupted 77,000 thousand years ago, give or take a thousand years, it changed life on the planet. Most humans were killed and temperatures dropped worldwide due to tremendous amounts of ash. Should I go on?"

"Please," I was impressed by his knowledge.

"It has an average depth of 1,666 feet and a large island in the middle called Samosir Island. Lake Toba sits in the largest volcanic caldera known; underneath this lake is the world's largest super-volcano."

"Are you worried it might erupt again?" I asked him.

"It did in 1987, along the southern shore. Small eruption, it didn't do much damage. The earth- changing eruption 77,000 years ago was the largest explosion on planet earth in twenty-five million years. Krakatoa was nothing by comparison."

Trisno clapped. "Couldn't have said it better myself!"

I thanked the concierge for the information and looked at Trisno. "What's the plan for the day, boss?"

"Well, Stan, I think we should take a cruise on Lake Toba and stop at a native Batak village. I have made a reservation."

"I'm ready." I said excitedly.

The cruise boat was small and mostly open with a canvas top covering half of it. Trisno and I sat in the back on deck chairs looking at our hotel. It rains often here but today was sunny and the water deep blue, sort of mystical. The sun enhanced the brilliance of everything green.

There were ten other visitors and two operators on the boat. The lake was calm as we headed into it. Our hotel was located between the north shore of Samosir Island and the mainland in a narrows area with open water several miles ahead. We had to go out to the open water to get around the island. We were headed for the south shore of Samosir island where there were several Batak villages, some more traditional than others. I took my shirt off, put my feet up on the transom, and started producing vitamin D. It was a smooth cruise.

"Look at the fish pens," Trisno pointed out as we came into the dock at the Batak village.

"They're made of wood," I remarked. We had seen aluminum pens in use near the hotel. "This might be the birthplace of pen aquaculture."

"Maybe for freshwater," Trisno said. "They catch local fish for consumption. There are many species of small fish in Lake Toba."

The village looked inviting, I was anxious to look around.

"This is a traditional Batak village with authentic houses and no electricity or running water," Trisno explained, as we began walking the ramp to shore.

"Robert would be at home here," I joked.

A local reception party greeted us. We walked to the center of the village where we were surrounded by houses straight out of *National Geographic Magazine.* The distinctive roofs, curled up on each end, looked like the bows on old sailing ships. The houses were tall and A-shaped when viewed from the front. The village was small, and not filled with dozens of shops like others, only two that we could see. In one, a woman was weaving a table cloth with golden thread and colorful beads. It was exceptional.

"How much is that one in U.S. dollars?" I asked, pointing to a finished table cloth that would look great on our dining room table. One of the reception guides spoke to her.

"She says ten dollars," the guide interpreted.

"How long does it take her to weave one?" I asked the guide. He spoke to the women again.

"Four days for one that size," he said.

"I'm going to buy that one." I pointed to it again. I paid her in U.S. singles while the guide rolled it up and tied string around it. The woman smiled.

Trisno had been talking to a different reception guide outside while I was in the shop. "The Batak people are good-looking and smart," Trisno said. "But the young ones are breaking loose from their roots." This was the concern of the guide he had been speaking with.

"It's happening all over the world," I added. "The problem is finding good jobs for them."

"Yes, it's not a big problem in self-sufficient tribal life, like here, but becomes one when these circumstances change." Trisno pointed out, looking at the village.

"Do these natives use drugs?" I asked him.

"Magic mushrooms, hallucinogenic ones," Trisno answered. "They grow all over Indonesia's 17,000 islands."

"Any government controls on them?" I asked.

"None that are enforced," he said. "Like the poaching of Robert's tigers, there is very little enforcement."

"It's a problem for civilization," I said. "The more restless the young become with nothing to do, the more mushrooms they eat. In other countries, it's different narcotic plants, or toxic drugs like in America..."

Twelve of the Bataks had organized in front of our group, ready to do some dancing. Both men and women were wearing black cloth wraps, with long woven dress scarves across their shoulders and backs, and down their chests. The scarves were narrow versions of the table cloth I bought. The men wore woven conical hats; the women, flower hats. It started with all of them holding their arms out, palms up, and chanting an ancient melody. It moved the soul! There was intrinsic sincerity in these people. I said a prayer that their world wouldn't change.

At the end of the conference, there was a closing ceremony and dinner on the hotel veranda. Fifty-seven cubic miles of fresh water was in front of us, the mystical Lake Toba.

Sumatra's tigers were out in the jungle, how many still in question. Reticulated pythons patrolled the roads. At least two of its orangutans smoked cigars and drank cokes. Nobody knew how many brilliant hornbills there were or how many Goliath beetles were pets for young boys, or how many monkeys chased rambutans on Java... Indonesia is one of our planets natural gems. Everywhere I looked, it was brilliant green.

Postscript:

I have been fortunate to have visited Indonesia often. This story was from one of the early trips. Elmer and Fud are actual names of real orangutans. Once my company's probiotic (beneficial bacteria) business developed in aquaculture—prawn farms in Indonesia—I had to recruit additional technical help from our Minnesota headquarters. Some of them held up well, others not so much. When you travel to places like this you need to let adventure trump discomfort. If you're someone that can't do that, this story hopefully put you there in comfort.

Aberdeen Harbor

16

Murder in Hong Kong

Blood in the Wonton Soup

Prologue

If I had to pick a city—just one—to best illustrate humanity on our planet, it would have to be Hong Kong. It runs like a blockbuster movie that encompasses a large spectrum of human activities and circumstances; from modern marvels and lavish luxury to traditionalism and poverty. But it leaves a huge middle ground that allows the majority to thrive.

The Hong Kong area, including Kowloon and the New Territories, was returned to China at midnight on June 30, 1997 after 156 years of British rule. It was a peaceful transfer of sovereignty! The Chinese had agreed to manage Hong Kong as a Special Administrative Region (SAR), allowing the people special privileges for at least fifty years. It would be kept separate from mainland China and remain a free trade zone with a capitalist lifestyle, private property ownership, and freedom of speech. "One country-two systems" was what they called it in Beijing. Margaret Thatcher had bargained hard to get this!

Hong Kong SAR, May 1998

"Over here, partner!" Tom Wong's voice reverberated. An airport taxi had dropped me off at the Peninsula Hotel in Kowloon and Tom was standing in the lobby, waving.

"Dr. Tom!" I responded with a smile. "You haven't changed in six months!" I had been to Hong Kong in November.

"Neither have you, Stan! How was your flight from Singapore?"

"Uneventful. As they all should be!" We had talked on the phone for an hour before my flight, so no "hello" or "how are you" was required. We man-hugged and slapped each other on the back. Tom was born in Guangzhou (old Canton) but grew up in California; he lived in Hong Kong now with his wife, Jill. He was my age, tall, with alert brown eyes and short black hair—a smart guy I'd known for twenty years since graduate school. He had a PhD in Food Science and a wise business acumen.

"Get checked in, there's a lot happening since we talked this morning!" He started pulling my suitcase as we walked and talked. "Prawn farmers across South China want to talk to us; I spoke with several big aquafarms while you were napping six miles above the South China Sea. I told them of our successes with probiotics in Taiwan—they want to work with us!"

"That's exciting news, Dr. Wong! Music to my ears."

Everything was bright and white in the immense lobby where a dozen large columns towered to the ceiling. Areca palms in antique bronze-planters stood as guards, one at each column. This grand, historic hotel at the end of the Kowloon peninsula was only a ten-minute walk from the quays where passengers disembarked from ocean liners, and equally close to the Star Ferry's terminal. The area was one of the action centers in Hong Kong!

I checked in at the desk and got my room key—a real key, not a plastic card—and went up to drop off my suitcase and take a quick peek out the window at Victoria Harbor. A flotilla of cargo ships, tour boats and ferries were either going to or coming from Hong Kong Island, the other half of the city. Wooden nineteenth-century sampans competed with ocean liners for open water. I'd seen this view before; it was never boring.

When I got back to the lobby, Dr. Tom was charged up like the Energizer Rabbit—boiling over with ideas. Our plans to expand our aquatic probiotic business in prawn farming in South Asia had become more complex. We went directly to the hotel bar and picked up where our phone conversation had ended. I ordered each of us a pint of Guinness; it had to be five o'clock somewhere.

"God, Save the Queen!" I knocked pints with Tom.

"And Hong Kong!" Tom added. "Next month will be the one-year anniversary under Chinese control."

"How's the level of apprehension—any change since I was here in November?"

"About the same—the tourists can't tell much difference from before the transfer; most of the apprehension is in the business community."

The bartender had made a "good pour"—the iconic beer's smooth, milky head perfectly complemented the toasted wheat flavor of the dark beer underneath. Its perfectness depended on the pouring technique—a good head was essential. We toasted the bartender.

With Guinness in hand, we got back to talking business. Our success using probiotics on prawn farms in Taiwan—more prawns with less pollution—had been spectacular. We had planned to utilize our experience in Taiwan as a model for prawn farms in China, with intentions to run the business from Hong Kong. But that was before Hong Kong had switched ownership, which now presented a dilemma: nothing angered the communists in Beijing more than the independence of Taiwan. Businesses that attempted to connect Taiwan to other countries using Hong Kong as a hub were, let's say, closely scrutinized.

Just before Tom could update me on our progress, three businessmen arrived and sat down across from us at the bar. Since it was a travel day, I was in shorts and a Green Bay Packers tee shirt; Tom was dressed like a tourist too. The businessmen each ordered a pint of Guinness. Not knowing them from Adam, I just smiled. But they sure activated Tom.

"To three Chinese copy cats!" Tom toasted them, holding his pint high. All three were dressed in tailor made suits and had Asian faces. The stout man who looked like Oddjob in the movie

Goldfinger took off his hat and pretended to throw it at Tom—like in the movie. Tom ducked and they both laughed. They knew each other and had been through this routine before. The stout man then explained in Mandarin to the other two men who Tom Wong was…

Bo, the stout man, was a business attorney in Hong Kong. He specialized in helping businesses bridge the difference between Common Law under Britain's rule versus Basic Law under Chinese rule. Basic Law had been negotiated between the British and Chinese preceding Hong Kong's transfer of authority on July 1, 1997. It spelled out the freedoms Hong Kong (SAR) citizens would retain under capitalism compared to the more severe restrictions Chinese citizens had under socialism. So Basic Law defined the "one country-two systems" in an agreement signed by both the British and the Chinese. But there were exceptions allowed! And Beijing could amend the agreement when necessary. The concern that it might metamorphize into rigid socialism over time presented a real probability.

Bo explained this to his two clients from Shanghai who didn't speak English. Tom and I discussed our situation with Bo. It was possible he could help us. Tom would arrange courier delivery of our marketing plan and technical literature to Bo's office. After reviewing them he would let us know if he could be of help. We all shook hands and let Bo get back to his Shanghai clients. Smiling to myself as we walked out of the bar I couldn't get over Bo's likeness to Oddjob—I was a big James Bond fan.

"What a coincidence," Tom said. "I know Bo from China Club meetings but didn't know he specialized in Hong Kong's transition issues."

"There are no coincidences!" I reminded Tom.

We got into the taxi line in front of the hotel. Tom had his favorite Cantonese restaurant in Kowloon scheduled for lunch.

"No surprises this time. Like those boiled sea-slugs you ordered us last time for an appetizer!" I chided. Tom was a serious guy most of the time but could turn comic in a microsecond.

"What do you mean? Those were fresh sea cucumbers. Mucho deliciousness!" Tom had been well-Americanized during his California years.

"They tasted like a fisherman's rubber glove soaked in garlic juice," reminding him of my previous assessment. I'd taken just one bite out of a half-cooked slug that day; chewed it for five minutes then spit it out. We volleyed like this with each other frequently—it burned off excess energy.

"Okay, no surprises this time." Tom chuckled in Mandarin. You could take Tom out of China but you couldn't take China out of Tom! He seriously enjoyed those awful creatures. I had to be on my toes whenever we were around food.

"Will Jill be joining us?" I hoped she would.

"She'll be there."

"Super!" I knew she would put the brakes on his food surprises, at least for her and me. Tom had met Jill during his California days in the 1970s; they'd married and had two boys who designed computers in Silicon Valley. Jill, like Tom, was also born in China and grew up in California. They'd both changed their first names when they got to America at the suggestion of an immigration official. Changpu became Tom and Dongmei became Jill. If Tom started to get too serious or goofy, all I had to do to straighten him out was call him Dr. Changpu.

As usual the restaurant was crowded and noisy, with a plethora of servers in dark blue uniforms dashing around. Some were stretching noodle dough into noodles with lots of drama; one was showing a live octopus to a table of people before boiling it, proving it was fresh; another was stir-frying skinned eels—black ones—on a propane-fired cart. Their equipment and utensils clanged in a strange cadence within the restaurant's symphony of Cantonese and Mandarin voices. Tom could speak both languages, including the Shanghai dialect of Mandarin.

"Authentic Cantonese food!" Jill exclaimed while reading the menu. "Tom loves this place." Her green eyes and light brown hair hid some of her Chinese heritage.

"How about some crab eggrolls for starters—they're excellent here!" Tom suggested.

"Sounds civilized to me," I replied. A waiter filled each of our ceramic cups with green tea, responding to a nod from Jill, then patiently waited for the rest of our order.

"I suggest we order bamboo chicken. The chicken is mildly curried then stuffed into bamboo shoots and roasted in a charcoal fire. It's quite good, not greasy." Jill had eaten it before.

"It's fine with me—you know I eat anything," Tom responded. "I would have opted for grilled snake but…"

"Tom, quit it!" Jill gave him a stern look. Snake meat was dry and tasted like reptiles smell—Tom would drown it in spicy soy sauce to partly civilize it.

"Bamboo chicken sounds good to me," I was quick to say. "Turmeric in the curry boosts the immune system."

"And…" Jill paused for a moment looking up at the waiter. "An order of tiger prawns stir-fried in olive oil and dribbled with coconut sauce." Tom and I smiled.

"We did a good job of setting her up, didn't we?" Tom said to me, teasing his wife.

"We would have ordered prawns if you hadn't!" I admitted. Jill shook her finger at both of us.

By the time the crab eggrolls arrived we were hungry—one bite confirmed they were delicious. The other food followed. It would all have pleased the Queen of England—but she didn't run things anymore!

Looking around at the many tables of people, I noticed that two men from different tables had been staring at us off and on. They looked away when I looked at them. I was accustomed to this in rural China where Americans were a rarity, but not in Hong Kong.

"Let's do some tourist things on Stanley's first day. Like take the Star Ferry to Hong Kong Island and the tram to Victoria Peak," Jill suggested. "You guys can talk your heads off about big shrimp while I take in the sights."

"That's an easy sale," I said, looking at Tom who was looking for a taxi. "Sure," he said. "I've never been there." Arguably, Victoria Peak was the most stunning sight in Hong Kong; I'd been there twice.

We boarded the famous Star Ferry to take us across Victoria Harbor; it connected Kowloon and the New Territories on the mainland to Hong Kong Island. The exorbitant fare was two Hong Kong dollars per person (26 cents, U.S.); the price hadn't changed in years. It was a big diesel-powered passenger ferry with two decks; the best view with the least diesel vapor was on the upper deck. Shipping and transport boats were everywhere in every size with an amazing variety of horns—from low growls to high pitch squeaks. It was the most dramatic ten-minute boat ride anybody could take. The three of us stood together near the bow, dwarfed by the rows of skyscrapers directly ahead. Hong Kong was built on hills which enhanced its dramatic scenery.

"Did you notice the looks we were getting from those two men in the restaurant?" I asked Tom.

"Yes, I sure did! We call them 'Beijing Eyes.' The communists in Beijing have 'eyes' everywhere. Many in the party did not agree with the freedoms that were preserved after the return of Hong Kong. The 'one country-two systems' approach was popular in Hong Kong but not in China."

I started imagining that several passengers were watching me. *When does a brief glance become a watchful look?* Tom was indifferent to all the commotion and wanted to keep talking; he was in his serious mode.

I reminded Tom that Jian Chang from Taiwan was coming to meet us tomorrow. He was flying to Hong Kong from Kuala Lumpur using a Malaysian passport. Our successes in Taiwan had been catalyzed by his indefatigable efforts. "He wants to expand our business into Malaysia and the Philippines!" Tom nodded and seemed anxious to see him again.

When the ferry docked on Hong Kong Island the passengers—tourists and locals—rushed off like stampeding cattle. We did the sensible thing and stayed on the ferry until most of the others were off.

Jill was in front of us and she moved quickly off the ferry to get in the taxi queue. Tom and I followed her. There were about a dozen people ahead of us.

"What's Beijing's main concern?" I asked Tom as I saw a tall man looking at us from the front of the queue. My question was rhetorical, I knew the answer but needed his confirmation.

"They have many concerns but Taiwan is number one," Tom answered. "This is where we must be careful using our experience in Taiwan to sell the aquaculture industry in China. It was not a problem when Hong Kong could participate as a British Colony. Now, under China, it's a potential problem and we don't know what the consequences might be."

The Pearl River Delta (PRD) was gigantic—it surrounded the Hong Kong area with over fifty million people and miles of brackish water. The potential for prawn aquaculture was huge! Done right, using our probiotic technology, it could provide megatons of protein for China's 1.2 billion people.

"Hong Kong is a mighty hub for business in Asia with its location, logistics, banking, and western thinking-executives. We both know this," I reaffirmed, then saw the tall man get in a taxi and look back at me—it was a stare, not just a glance. It gave me a strange feeling. I had thought I was immune to paranoia; never felt it after an IRA bombing in Belfast or at the North Korean border in Panmunjom, but did here in civilized Hong Kong—strange!

"Showing the Taiwanese data in China is one thing; selling probiotics to both Taiwan and China from Hong Kong is a cat of a different color," Tom said.

"They eat cats in China," I responded, trying to buy time to think about our dilemma. I could talk about one thing while thinking about others. It sounds crazy but it stimulated creativity when clouds of dissimilar thoughts collided in my mind—the challenge was to find patches of blue.

"There are strict laws against eating cats in Hong Kong!" Tom assured me.

"I've seen it in Guangzhou: a pickup truck hauling a large cage of yelping dogs to a butcher along with dozens of cats in a separate cage." It was a vivid recollection for me…

"Not here in Hong Kong," Tom affirmed. "But they do eat dog meat in China."

We both paused for a few seconds. "Would we be willing to give up the business in Taiwan and sell only to China?" Tom asked me, getting to the heart of our dilemma.

"Let me cogitate on that. Taiwan is a bird in the hand bringing in revenue. China is only a potential right now, albeit huge. Jian Chang might have some ideas, he's had other situations like this with China. Our meeting with him tomorrow is important." I could see the tram terminal up ahead.

"We have to figure a way to do both without getting shot!" Tom whispered so Jill wouldn't hear; she was sitting in the front seat of the cab. It was a hot, humid day in May—some altitude would be welcome.

"We've arrived at the tram station," Jill declared. "Tom's first time up to Victoria Peak—after living in Hong Kong for eight years!"

I paid the taxi fare and got out with Tom. Jill was already out and moving fast to the ticket queue. Moving quickly to get in queues was essential in Hong Kong.

Tom and I queued up for the tram while Jill waited to buy the tickets. Up to ten thousand people ride the tram daily. It's a steep funicular railway that rises four-hundred meters in seven minutes. If you don't sit down, the twenty-seven-degree angle will have you leaning like a skier doing the Matterhorn. The three of us sat on the right side for the best views.

From Victoria Peak, the view was a wow! At 575 meters (1,888 feet) we were looking over seven thousand skyscrapers divided by a big horseshoe of seawater called Victoria Harbor. This was the heart of Hong Kong SAR, as it was now officially designated.

"Isn't it marvelous, Tom?" Jill said, smiling happily. "Your first time!"

"It is, indeed. I can see past Kowloon, halfway to China!"

The Bank of China towered below us—three-hundred meters high. Its stunning blue glass architecture with dominant triangular patterns had been approved by a Feng Shui Master. It owned the skyline and promoted a positive flow of energy (qi).

Two men on roller skates were swerving through the crowd near us, slowing down then speeding up—turning their heads, looking at people.

Jill yelled "Look out!" Tom was facing me with his back to the skaters. They whizzed by him inches away. A teenage girl on one knee taking pictures almost got run over.

I heard a tourist shout, "Who are those guys?" They were tall and had head phones connected to MP-3 players stuck in headbands. Both were wearing gold Rolex watches.

"They didn't look Chinese," I mentioned to Jill.

"Russians," Tom surmised; they didn't fit the Chinese mold. "The watches are fakes sold at the Temple Street Market. Too much shine and glitter for real gold!"

"It appeared they were scanning the crowd," I noted. "Maybe 'Beijing Eyes' on the move!"

"It's possible," Tom agreed.

Jill wanted to take the one-hour stroll around the peak. Tom and I were happy to do that—the crowd was too dense this close to the tram stop.

Tom was lucky to have Jill; she watched over him diligently. She was an editor for the Hong Kong Daily News and trilingual like her husband. Her only sadness was not seeing their boys often enough; but they were coming in August and she was anxious for that.

We walked the steep terrain slowly, taking in the sights.

The tram ride down was much faster—almost like Space Mountain at Disneyland. Two older ladies had to hang onto each other—tightly. My kids would have loved it!

I walked in the general direction of the pier where the Star Ferry docked; didn't need a taxi. Tom and Jill walked to their apartment in Sheung Wan just west of the Central District on Hong Kong Island. I planned to make some phone calls from my hotel and change clothes—then meet them in Kowloon's "Wonton Soup Alley" at 7:00 p.m.

The spectrum of activities you see walking the side streets of Hong Kong are quite amazing; it's what makes it my Number One city to best illustrate humanity.

I meandered along taking an indirect route, surviving the heat and humidity quite well. I witnessed a sample of everyday life in Hong Kong: An older lady pedaling a bicycle had a poodle strapped into a baby seat on the bike's fender, a man in a brown suit pushed a coatrack of men's suits across a busy street—motorbikes had to swerve to not hit him. I passed a massage parlor where a big woman was sitting on a plastic chair on the sidewalk having her hair colored bright red. She winked at me. Two Arab men shrouded in white and wearing turbans walked ahead of a clown who had a lion on a leash—presumably from a circus act. Further on, young boys had ignited a long string of firecrackers suspended from a stairway where old men engulfed in the smoke played a dice game I didn't know. Amidst these everyday occurrences, sitting at a lone table dressed in an expensive black suit was a businessman calmly drinking hot tea. He lowered his sunglasses and looked at me…

It was 6:00 p.m. when I got back to the Peninsula hotel. The Star Ferry was a twenty-minute ride this time due to traffic—boat traffic. I had an hour before meeting Tom and Jill for a classic Kowloon dinner: wonton soup.

Wonton Soup Alley had many outdoor food stands featuring different varieties of wonton soup. Tom's favorite place had clean outdoor tables in a small courtyard. There was a nice breeze coming off Victoria Harbor, and strangely, the area reminded me of Key West. The three of us sat down and looked at the menu. I already knew what Tom would do.

"Don't need this menu," Tom declared and signaled with the hang loose sign, his thumb and little finger up—the number six in China. The waiter, who knew him, understood. Jill shook her head no, and put up five fingers. The waiter smiled, he knew what she meant and so did I—five bowls of Tom's favorite wonton soup. The bowls were small, so it was common to order two per person. Jill was fine with one.

Tom's recipe: Shiitake mushroom broth full of springy rice noodles dusted with chopped Asian greens and topped with five fat wonton dumplings filled with ground pork and baby prawns. A meal in a bowl (or two).

The courtyard tables were full now; we got there at just the right time. Most of the people were Chinese but there were a few Indians and Europeans—men and women. From what I could see, most were eating some variety of wonton soup including two large men sitting two tables away from us. They were having a serious conversation in Mandarin—business, I presumed.

"They're talking about Taiwan!" Tom said to me in a low voice. I nodded. Sitting at the table between us and the two men, an older couple was quietly eating their soup.

Neither of the two large men paid any attention to other people, and only one was eating his wonton soup. The face on the man who was not eating had turned red and he was violently shaking his head "NO." The man eating was insistent about what he was demanding and raised his voice. The red-faced man wouldn't concede. He kept saying, "*Bu Dui! Bu Dui!*" meaning "Not okay." The man eating swallowed a mouthful of wontons and took a gulp of broth from his soup bowl, then bellowed his command again in an even louder voice. The red-faced man raised his right hand and made a tight fist with it, the sign for *zero* in China and repeated loudly, "Bu Dui!" The man eating, clicked his chopsticks and stuffed two more wontons into his mouth—then crumpled his napkin into a ball and threw it on the floor. He kept his hateful glare as he stood up and moved back from the table. A tall man on roller skates had been skating in the alley parallel to the courtyard. When he saw the napkin on the ground and the big man standing, he turned sharply and jumped over the curb that separated the courtyard from the alley.

Dah Boom-Boom-Boom! Dah Boom-Boom-Boom! The skater pulled the trigger six times on the 9mm pistol. The red-faced man stood up, pushing down on the table with both hands, and looked at the big man who was still glaring. Blood was shooting from his chest in several places. Each stream pumped in spurts that shot out at least two feet before hitting the table. Then the red-faced man, red-chested as well, dropped into his chair sitting straight up—and died!

Right after the first volley of three shots, I had pushed our table over and pulled Jill down next to me. Tom had jumped on top of us both. Between the two of us we completely covered Jill.

Strangely, it was quiet. Then a few muffled screams erupted as people saw the blood on the table. The dead man was sitting, leaning back in his chair, eyes open, staring out.

"Jill! Tom! Are you guys all right?" I shouted as I wiggled out from between them.

"We're alive!" Tom shouted. Jill was crying and madly checking Tom for bullet holes.

The skater was gone after he'd pulled the trigger. The other big man just walked away. There was a buzz now, mostly in Cantonese.

The older couple that had been sitting between us and the two men were still sitting at their table. The man was shaking, his left hand kept hitting the underside of the table. The woman was trying to wipe blood off their table with a single napkin. She needed more napkins.

"Most of the people thought it was fireworks!" Tom translated the buzz. Many were now standing around the dead man who was still sitting up—there was blood in his wonton soup.

Nobody waited around for the police to show up. We paid our bill in cash and left. I didn't feel good about doing that, but Tom wisely pulled Jill and me away. This was the first time I had witnessed a murder—it was sickening.

"My God! An actual murder!" Jill exclaimed, her face wet from tears. It was like her mind had just caught up with what had happened; "And he wore a gold Rolex!"

"Who did?" I asked her.

"The skater," she said. "Like the two men on Victoria Peak!"

"Did you see his face?" Tom asked, holding her hand.

"He wore a black headband and sunglasses. He was tall and thin. When you both were on top of me I could still see with one eye."

Tom held her hand tightly as we walked away. It was not an easy walk. Emotion raged in me; sorrow for the man who died and hate for the skater and the other big man who set it up. Tom was stone-faced, thinking.

"I'll file an anonymous report with the police; I'm quite sure it was a 'transition killing'—probably an assassination. The two men were arguing over some business connection with Taiwan. If we wait for the police we could be detained for days—we were only one table away from the murder scene. We're not tourists; Jill and I were born in China, grew up in the U.S. that supports Taiwan, and now we live in Hong Kong and just started using information from Taiwan to promote products in China. Not good," Tom concluded.

"Not an innocuous combination," I mumbled. Jill was nervous now and so was I. This could have been us, shot full of 9mm bullets! Tom had just explained what we had known. But the enthusiasm created by our spectacular results with aquatic probiotics had neutralized our caution. This murder had changed that!

Then I remembered the meeting with Jian… "Jesus. Jian Chang will be here early tomorrow!" His company was my largest customer in Asia and he planned to share his expansion strategy with us!

"We're just asking for trouble if we meet with him here. Even if he uses a Malaysian passport, the computers will know he's Taiwanese," Tom pointed out.

"And it's no secret that his company is based in Taipei," I added. "I'll call him when we get to the hotel."

When we arrived in the lobby of the Peninsula Hotel, a young Chinese lady was playing Chopin's Piano Solo on a Steinway grand piano. It echoed wonderfully in the spaciousness. What a disconnect from what we had just experienced! We walked over and watched her play. Jill was in tears; her one tissue was soaking wet.

I left Tom and Jill with the music, hoping it would help sooth their hearts and souls, and used one of the hotel phones to call Jian in Malaysia.

"Did I wake you up?" I asked when Jian answered the phone.

"Mister Stanley, my good friend, you can wake me up anytime! But I was awake reading about your probiotic trials with prawns in Australia."

"Our man Adam Rody is doing a good job down there," I confirmed. "Did you see the article in the NT-News from Darwin? He's getting twenty percent more prawns with ten percent less feed!"

"Amazing results, just like we get in Taiwan—and as a bonus we control pollution!" Jian was excited. "I'll show you tomorrow how we can expand into Southeast Asia. Will Dr. Wong be with us?"

"Yes, in fact we're together now." I knew Jian would start right in on business but I had to change the subject. "Jian, I must tell you what happened tonight! A little over an hour ago." I described the murder we witnessed. He was silent for a full minute.

"Tell me that again! I think you are trying to get even for all the jokes I've pulled on you." He got me once with a "photo" of a prawn the size of an alligator. I had believed it for a few moments, before realizing Photoshop had arrived in Taiwan.

"I'm not kidding," I said to my largest Asian customer. There was another long pause.

"Macau!" He declared. "I'll change my ticket. We need to meet in Macau, not Hong Kong."

"Okay," I said. "Hang on Jian. Tom!" I shouted out. He was still standing with Jill by the piano player. He came running over.

"Say hello to Jian." I handed him the phone. Tom had met Jian once in Bangkok with me. They talked on the phone in Cantonese for about five minutes then Tom gave me the phone back.

"Macau," Jian insisted. "Get there before noon. I'll meet you in the lobby of the Lisboa Hotel! And, be sure to eat breakfast with a security guard at the Peninsula Hotel in the morning."

"That's not a joke, I presume."

"No joke; feeding the world is serious business. Big business! We're going to do that. See you before noon." Jian was on the same energy scale as Tom and me—mega-joules.

I turned the TV on when I woke up, the Chinese national anthem, March of the Volunteers, was playing as Hong Kong's

Channel Four started its day of programming. That would be the most obvious change a returning tourist would recognize—gone was the playing of God Save the Queen. I jumped up and looked at my watch. Phew! It was only 6:00 a.m. I showered and went downstairs to eat a veggie omelet accompanied by a glass of mangosteen juice, trying to ignore the nightmare I'd had of being shot repeatedly with a 9mm pistol. Then I called Tom at home.

"I'm up," he answered. "We're booked on the Turbojet to Macau at 9:00 a.m.—I'll meet you at the Sheung Wan ferry terminal at 8:00 a.m. It's a fast one-hour boat ride to Macau."

"Understood. See you then." I had time to take a swim in one of the hotel's pools. Anything to get my mind off tall men skating fast wearing Rolexes.

The Turbojet was a nice surprise. We sat up front in carpeted, air-conditioned comfort—totally enclosed so we couldn't be blown off into the South China Sea. We were served *lychee* nuts and *mangosteens*—fruits, in English—as we cruised powerfully.

Macau was located on the south coast of China, forty miles west of Hong Kong—across the South China Sea. Under Portuguese control since 1887, it was scheduled to return to China in 1999. Macau occupies nine square miles with a population of 650,000; compared to Hong Kong's one-thousand square miles and 6.5 million people. But Macau was rich and wild—the world's gambling and prostitution center for the rich and famous. But there were dangers here, too: Both "Beijing Eyes" and gambling inspectors tended to have short lifespans. Nevertheless, it was a good place to have secret business meetings. Historically, the Hotel Lisboa, surrounded by casinos and "massage parlors," was the place to meet.

We arrived at the hotel an hour before Jian. Tom had arranged a small meeting room with a white board, bottled water and snacks. It also had a balcony facing a construction zone where the Macau Tower was being built.

"I forgot to tell you; Bo called me this morning," Tom mentioned. "He offered to take us on a tour of Aberdeen Harbor in his cabin cruiser—if it's not too late when we get back."

"Jian has to fly to Taiwan after our meeting, so that should work. Does Bo know about the murder?"

"I explained it to him in detail. He said there was a brief mention of a shooting in Kowloon in the morning paper. He sounded very concerned…"

Jian didn't knock; he barged into the meeting room with his hair on fire. He was not your typical Asian businessman. Jian was a little older and about the same stature as Tom; clean shaven, tan, with slightly graying hair but a rounder face.

"Greetings, gentlemen!" Jian said, smiling big. "I almost didn't make the flight from Kuala Lumpur—traffic in Malaysia is as bad as Taiwan! Some guy with a truck full of ducks hit a telephone pole and the ducks scattered everywhere. They stopped traffic for almost an hour! Jian grabbed some of the snacks and a bottle of water. With his hands full he greeted me with a shoulder bump, then smiled at Tom, put down the water, and shook his hand. "Dr. Wong, it's great to see you again!"

"That goes both ways Jian. Welcome to Macau!"

"Ah, Macau! I've never seen it; just inside its many meeting rooms." He scanned the ceiling and looked under the table for bugs—the electronic type. "The construction noise is good, but let's not talk too loud. Tell me once again the details of the murder."

I let Tom go first, then added what I saw. Jian had a serious face now.

"How is your wife doing?" he asked Tom.

"Amazingly well, at least this morning," Tom replied. "Chopin calmed her down."

"That's very good to hear!" Jian said sincerely. "This was not an uncommon event, gentlemen! Similar assassinations have been going on since Hong Kong's transfer back to China. Most don't even make a blip in the news. Did you hear many police sirens as you walked back to the Peninsula Hotel?"

"I didn't hear any," I said. Tom shook his head.

"That's a telltale sign of an assassination—the police move slowly," Jian explained. "Let me tell you what I found out this morning: The man killed was a Taiwanese bank executive connected to the banking industry in Taiwan and Hong Kong. The other man was a government banker from Beijing who insisted upon imposing strict controls and taxes on transactions between Hong Kong and Taiwan. They couldn't resolve the matter, so the Beijing banker signaled for the assassin to settle it. When the police finally arrived, there was only the dead man and two waiters!"

There must be "Taiwanese Eyes" in Hong Kong also, I thought. *Otherwise, how would Jian know this so fast?* "One country—two systems, but with exceptions!" I exclaimed. "We've got to be damn cautious and smart!"

We switched to discussing our business dilemma. Two hours went by. We examined every possible angle of how to bake our cake and eat it too—and not get shot! How could we sell our probiotics in China using data from Taiwan and Hong Kong as our business headquarters? That was the sixty-four-million-dollar question—coincidentally close to the size of our market potential! We delved into the rewards versus the dangers. Given that the transition of Hong Kong to China hadn't celebrated its first birthday yet, we agreed it would be wise to allow it to mature. I decided to put a hold on selling probiotics to China and not use Hong Kong as a hub for the business. Macau was not an option since it would be transferred back to China in less than two years.

Jian's company in Taiwan would remain our hub in Southeast Asia for now. Tom was not happy about the decision, but he understood. I had to take the bull by the horns on this one. Avoiding danger trumped opportunity.

Tom agreed to help Jian develop the business in the Philippines and Malaysia and give Hong Kong (SAR) time to settle down. Any trips to Taiwan would be arranged through Macau. Jian used the white board and a map of Southeast Asia to illustrate where and how he and Tom would approach the new opportunities. I was in full agreement, impressed with Jian's plan and Tom's willingness to work with him. It had been a good meeting! They could enjoy eating sea cucumbers together.

It didn't appear the construction workers had made much progress on the Macau Tower during our three-hour meeting. The three of us took the same taxi from the hotel Lisboa, first dropping Jian off at the airport for his flight to Taipei then Tom and me at the Turbojet dock for the torpedo ride back to Hong

Kong. No time for the casinos in Macau—we had enough gambling going on!

It was 6:00 p.m. when Bo drove up in his Mercedes to pick me up at the Peninsula Hotel. I'd been to Aberdeen once years ago and was looking forward to a repeat as well as the chance to get to know Bo. Tom and Jill passed on the tour and planned to meet us at the Shum Wan Pier in Aberdeen at 8:00 p.m.—from there we would go to dinner at Jumbo, the famous floating restaurant.

The Aberdeen district on the south side of Hong Kong Island is sequestered from the masses by a naturally-protected harbor. It's where thousands of boat people live on hundreds of junks, large and small. A water-city originally populated by fishermen now supported a wide diversity of humanity.

Bo's mate drove the Chris Craft 36 up to the dock. When I saw the stern of the boat I laughed out loud! The beautiful wooden cruiser was named *Oddjob.* Bo put a captain's cap on, one with that classic scrambled-egg design on the brim. Then he took it off and pretended to throw it at me, laughing. In the movie *Goldfinger,* Oddjob's top hat had a razor-sharp steel rim that made it a weapon. Bo was a double for Oddjob; it contrasted with his business persona but he loved the attention it created. There were two distinct sides to this man's personality—much the same as with Dr. Tom.

Bo took over the controls on the cruiser and gave me a five-star tour of Aberdeen harbor. There were junks so large they could house extended families and some so small that three people were a crowd. Some people rarely, if ever, went ashore! They used smaller sampans to visit other junks—a unique lifestyle to be sure.

Bo drove the thirty-six-foot cruiser right into the myriad of junks. He waved at the people, many waved back.

"The younger kids always wave back," He told me. I was waving to everybody now too. Old men repairing fishing nets paid no attention, but the kids sure did.

It was dinner time. Men were frying fish on the decks of the junks while women hung clothes out to dry. Young kids fished with bamboo poles and worms. One boy was peeing off the bow of a junk, tweaking my memories of the bronze statue of a boy doing the same thing in Brussels.

"How do they handle the sewage?" I asked Bo. There was some odor, but not as bad as I recalled.

"They are told to contain it; some do, some don't. They need your probiotics!"

"*Another future market,*" I thought.

We meandered through the maze of junks and sampans—which covered a large portion of the harbor. I had a chance to explain what Tom, Jian, and I discussed in Macau and asked Bo whether I had overreacted by postponing our business in China.

Bo had studied the information the courier had delivered. He steered the cabin cruiser carefully through one of the boat city's main "streets" while thinking about my question. "You absolutely made the right decision," he said, emphatically. "Your probiotics will help feed the world and protect the oceans from overfishing and pollution; the data from Taiwan is un-disputably positive! But there is too much risk to bringing your probiotics into China right now—the whole idea of running Hong Kong as a Special Administrative Region (SAR) is new to Beijing. We need to give it time to stabilize." His advice made me feel much better.

We picked up Tom and Jill on time and Bo gave the controls back to the mate, who took us to the floating restaurant. It was a city-block long, four decks, multiple pagoda-style upcurving roofs, and lit up like an athletic stadium with JUMBO spelled out in giant neon letters. And jumbo it was—it could have competed with an aircraft carrier for size.

Tom and Jill had been here several times; Bo was instantly recognized. I kept looking around at it all. *Dazzling* would be the one word to describe it.

Bo asked if we would share a bottle of *Dom Perignon* with him. "I love its taste!" He said bashfully.

"It's the world's best vintage champagne—how could we say no?" I replied. Tom and Jill agreed. All Bo had to do was raise his right hand and it got delivered in a silver bucket of ice.

Hmm, I thought, *this is no mirage—this man is authentic; a trustable risk!* I had experienced other people like Bo in my travels; they seemed to pop up just at the right time!

"Tom, remember when I emailed you about the membership dues for China Club, that they seemed expensive?" I asked him.

"Yes, I remember."

"Delete that email!" That got a strong laugh from Bo, it's where he met Tom. It was obvious he was going to help us—my inner voice was signaling positive vibrations.

When we all had our glasses filled with the famous champagne—Bo proposed a toast to feeding the world! "How did you know that was our vision?" Tom asked him.

"Because I know Bond—James Bond!"

I laughed so hard I spewed fifty dollars of *Dom Perignon* onto the floor.

We kept the levity going for a while longer. Jill was totally relaxed and enjoying it. We all were. Then the discussion turned serious.

Bo took over—"I have reviewed your successes with prawns in Taiwan and Australia and with salmon in Chili. They are remarkable. I'm convinced that probiotics, your formulas, can supercharge aquaculture and take a giant step toward feeding the world and reducing pollution. It was no coincidence that we met in the bar. Without sounding too spiritual, I can tell you *The Source* was involved." Bo took a drink of *Dom Perignon*—a real drink, not a sip. Then he put his right hand up and another bottle quickly appeared.

Bo continued, "Mr. Randolf, you have two very special colonels in Tom and Jian but you must be the general. I have no ambition of taking control of your company. It took a murder in Hong Kong to refocus you! For that, the man with the red face did not die in vain. But now you know the dangers that exist. Listen to me—I want to help you feed the world and reduce pollution. I agree with the decision you made today; don't waste your energy worrying about it. There are several avenues to get your probiotics into China when the time is right. In the meantime, I'll have your back!"

Again, Jill had tears in her eyes, but these were happy tears. She stood up and gave each of us a hug and kiss on the cheek. When she sat back down, the head chef brought in our appetizer: a platter of luscious baby prawns anointed with coconut sauce and key limes. "*Bon Appetit,*" he declared.

Postscript:

Well, well, well . . . I had kept this story secret for many years. It was in my notebooks and diaries stored in a musty, old, wooden filing cabinet. In fact, it's the last of seventeen stories I actually wrote for this book. I was afraid to tell it back when it happened. It kind of felt the same way when writing "Frozen in Peru" (in More Adventures of a World-Traveling Scientist). I didn't want anybody—friends or associates—to get hurt by erroneous association with people in the story.

The business of using probiotics in prawn aquaculture has developed in Southeast Asia. But I no longer own the company that produced the probiotic microbes referred to in the story. My contacts tell me that the well-managed aquafarms in Thailand, Indonesia, and Malaysia are culturing probiotics on-site with good success and great economy; when inoculated into shrimp (prawn) ponds the result is more shrimp with less feed and pollution. Shrimp are literally bathed in trillions of microbes —some good, some bad. Probiotics keep the good microbes in control. More details of how this is done is touched on in "Frozen in Peru."

Old Town Square

17

Cobblestones in Prague

A Spontaneous "Secret Service" Assignment!

Prague, Czechoslovakia, January 1991

We were two hours out of Munich on the night-train to Prague when the Gulf War broke out. While Bagdad was being blasted with cruise missiles and smart bombs, the intense shrill of our train's horn penetrated the German night. We had mostly a smooth ride until the train slowed before making a screeching stop in Regensburg. Our car was close to empty except for three couchettes; Ludwig and I had been dozing in one when three hard knocks rattled our door. I opened it and two German border agents walked in—one was talking on a VHF radio.

"*Reisepass!*" The other agent demanded. Ludwig fumbled for his passport in his jacket, while I pulled mine from a front pocket on my jeans. The agent examined Ludwig's first, then mine, then back to Ludwig's. I looked like an American tourist—Ludwig didn't. Both agents spoke to him in German for several minutes before returning our passports back and walking out.

"What was that all about?" I asked Ludwig, puzzled. We were about halfway to the Czechoslovakian border. Germany was in the European Union; there was no reason for mid-country passport checks in 1991!

"You're at war with Iraq!" Ludwig declared, looking at me with deep concern.

"You're kidding, right?" I was stunned. Just what we needed—a war in the Middle East.

"It's called 'Operation Desert Storm.' It's happening right now! Live on TV," Ludwig elaborated. "Agents are checking all trains; they wanted to know if you were in the military. I told him we worked together in the agricultural business."

"Now we have something serious to think about," I responded, "besides the freezing temperatures." It was cold in the couchette and freezing outside.

"There will be another check in Schwandorf before we leave Germany. It reminds me of when I was ten years old and the Nazis constantly checked everybody for everything. Now I'm sixty and don't like being checked any more than I did then," Ludwig elaborated. Most Americans have no idea what it feels like to potentially lose—in an instant—all rights and freedoms you thought you had! Ludwig Guenther remembered World War II well.

There were helicopters with spotlights shining on the train when we stopped in Schwandorf. Here the inspection was more intense. Two UN soldiers in blue helmets armed with nine-millimeter handguns did the checking which included Ludwig's briefcase and my backpack. They confiscated my Swiss Army knife! I let them take it, knowing that if I argued they might detain us in a broom closet somewhere—wisdom prevailed! The UN soldiers grilled Ludwig awhile longer, then left.

It was a cold January night and we had at least another four hours to go. It was eerie! The smell of oil on wet pavement combined with the shrill of the train's horn reminded me of World War II movies. If I imagined hard enough, *I could hear tanks and halftracks grinding on the road that ran alongside the tracks.* We both dozed after crossing into Czechoslovakia.

When the horn sounded, we woke up to a surprise—there was no stopping for a passport check in Pilsen, the first major town beyond the border, and we were still two hours southwest of Prague.

"They probably haven't heard about the war yet," Ludwig commented. "Things are disorganized in Czechoslovakia these days. They have many loose cobblestones to trip on."

'And no blue helmets helping them!" I injected. The UN was not looked upon favorably in Bohemia.

It had been just over a year since the Velvet Revolution had forced communism out of business—the entire leadership of the Czech communist party resigned in November of 1989 and was replaced peacefully with a democratic government. But the change to a parliamentary republic with capitalism was not a slam-dunk. It required political evolution, which in turn brought some confusion and disorganization.

Communism demands a single political party that governs all aspects of people's lives; a forced monoculture that eliminates individual rights and freedoms. Democracy involves having opposing parties that alternate leadership and protect society from totalitarianism. I didn't get a true feeing of this difference on my first trip to Czechoslovakia; it was a student tour and we were bussed around to selected spots with little time to explore and talk to people. Full-throttled communism was in control but I didn't feel it so much. Now that democracy had "won," it would be interesting to discover how people felt compared to before.

We arrived at the Hlavni Nadrazi train station at 6:40 a.m. It hadn't been the smoothest or most uneventful train ride in my travels but we were here in Prague, "Praha" in Czech. It was just a ten-minute walk to our hotel in Wenceslas Square. Neither of us had slept well on the train, so after checking in we decided an early morning nap would be a good idea. I noticed it wasn't as cold here as in Germany.

"How about a late breakfast at 10:00 a.m.?" I asked Ludwig.

"Downstairs?" he responded sluggishly, I could see he needed a few hours rest.

"Yup," I said. "Let's meet at the breakfast buffet." Ludwig nodded and went into his room next door to mine.

My room was clean and comfortable—big compared to the one in Munich. There were pictures of Prague's Gothic castles and cathedrals on the walls; a sunrise over the Old Charles Bridge hung above the bed. I sat on the bed, turned on CNN, and watched the war for an hour. Our Lockheed F-117 Nighthawks were destroying Bagdad—six aircraft carrier groups were involved in the attack. I fell asleep and woke up two hours later with the TV still on and the war going strong.

Downstairs I found the breakfast buffet on the second floor of the large nineteenth century hotel—quite exquisite. It was 9:30 a.m. and a cup of hot coffee revived me enough so I could read the USA Today newspaper while waiting for Ludwig.

"Well Doctor Guenther, did you get some rest?" I asked Ludwig when he walked into the restaurant. He was short and stout with white hair and wore thin-rimmed glasses. Add a white beard and he could have doubled for Santa Claus. His smiles and chuckles added to the likeness. A doctor of veterinary medicine surrounded by an aura of goodwill.

He and I were business partners working in the E.U. to improve silage preservation with probiotic microbes. Good-quality silage—cow food—meant good-quality milk! And more of it! Ludwig was an old-school veterinarian and, with my background in microbiology and biochemistry, we complemented each other well.

"I slept lightly—a brandy would have helped deepen my nap." Ludwig yawned.

"All right Winston, we can make that happen tonight." He did look a little like Churchill, too, who always had a brandy at bedtime. "What's the plan for today?" I asked him. I knew we had business meetings with farm cooperatives tomorrow—those that were reorganizing after throwing the communists out.

Ludwig laughed at the Churchill analogy but turned serious with any mention of communism. "Farmers were enemies of the state under communism," he told me. "During the Stalinization of Czech farms in the 1950s and 1960's single farms were restricted to fifty hectares and forced to form collectives. They were told what and how much to plant. Prices were set by the government and there was no competition for one farm to excel over another. Food shortages were common," Ludwig explained. "I could say more about it, but let's have a nice day in old Prague walking around, watching people. Their country is going through a life-changing transition."

"Good plan!" I agreed. We walked out of the hotel onto Wenceslas Square where there were celebrations going on. The square was a wide boulevard that ran for almost a kilometer with bars, restaurants, shops, and apartments on both sides. It was the nucleus of the Velvet Revolution the year before. A remarkable, peaceful transfer of power from communism to democracy; exactly the opposite from the 1968 Prague Spring when the Soviet military brought in two-hundred thousand troops and two thousand tanks to quell a similar effort.

"November of 1989 was a historic month!" Ludwig declared, fully awake and energized now. "The Berlin wall came down on the ninth and the Velvet Revolution started here on the seventeenth."

Vaclav Havel, the first democratically elected president in forty-one years, was scheduled to make an appearance in Wenceslas Square later in the day. Jubilant crowds of people were jingling their keys in celebration—just like in November of 1989. Beyond the hotel entrance we saw posters on stands depicting Russian Matryoshka dolls wearing military belts. The dolls were in a long line that faded away. Not a subtle hint! Another poster read: "CCCP GO HOME." And another showed Karl Marx admitting he was wrong. Many posters displayed Havel as their hero. Most of the Russian military had left, but their support personnel and deserters were still hanging around. It was obvious they weren't welcome.

Christmas decorations were still out on the boulevard. Chimes, bells, and people shaking keys kept Christmas alive into mid-January. Ludwig was looking around at all the people and flashing his Santa Claus smile. Many spoke German, so he conversed with them, anxious to hear their opinions about the new government.

A well-dressed man wearing a dark blue overcoat and expensive shoes told Ludwig that nobody had smiled or had fun like this under communism. Key-jingling and laughing people were everywhere now. Ludwig nodded his head in agreement as the stranger continued: "People did not talk in public under communism. They walked fast to their destination with heads down. More than four together was considered an assembly, which was illegal. Travel was by *permit only* and very expensive. Newspapers and magazines had to *explicitly agree* with Marxist-Leninist doctrine or they were shut down. Everyone was frightened of the Secret Police." The well-dressed man had a confident smile while stating his critique. Ludwig never got his name.

"It's not uncommon to be interrupted on the street by political sermons these days. The change is dramatic!" Ludwig remarked. My political education was ramping up fast!

We saw a crowd of people outside a large tent next to the equestrian statue of Saint Wenceslas at the southeast end of the boulevard. We walked over to investigate. On the way, I heard an English lady yell to someone: "Meet me by the horse's tail!" It was a common expression in Prague and there was no ambiguity about it—Wenceslas' bronze horse had the largest tail in Prague. There was a general euphoria emanating from these people; they were seeking fun and happiness in their new world. I was happy to see so many happy!

Inside the tent with propane heaters blowing, six barbers were shaving the beards off heavily-bearded men as more bearded men elbowed their way through the crowd to get into the tent for a shave. It was a spectacle! There was a small mountain of black hair around each chair. The barbers were having fun yelling to each other as they happily labored. People watching were jingling their keys.

"What's going on?" I asked Ludwig.

"It's called ritual barbering," He remarked, pausing, leaving me up in the air.

"Okay, Doctor Guenther, more detail please." I gave him a stern look.

"It's been going on since the Soviet army left. Ritual barbering! These men being shaved made a promise—twenty-three years ago—not to shave until the Soviet army left Czechoslovakia," Ludwig chuckled. I was deeply moved by this impassioned protest.

It took us about forty-five minutes to walk to the Old Town Square from the horse's tail. The day had warmed and was now more refreshing than cold. This was the beginning of Old Prague and a transition into the past.

The towering two-spired Tyn Church stood out to the east beyond the square which housed the Town Hall and its famous clock. The twelfth-century Saint Nicholas church, with its copper-green dome and spires, was just north of the Town Hall. The sun was melting snow on the red-tiled roofs of many buildings. Since there were more than a few rain gutters missing, we had to watch for miniature waterfalls. Locals were easy to spot; they all wore long overcoats and carried umbrellas.

Multi-colored eighteenth-century buildings crowded together around and beyond the square; a plethora of rectangular windows defined the buildings and cobblestone streets were everywhere. Some of the imbedded bricks were loose, so we had to pay attention as we walked. Ludwig had already tripped twice due to his flat-soled business shoes. I insisted we stop and buy him a pair of athletic shoes like mine. He shook his head no. I nodded yes and bought them for him anyway.

"Cobblestones can be stubborn things, both literally and figuratively," Doctor Guenther professed, releasing his Santa smile. "Thanks for the shoes. They look funny but feel good!" They were white Nike's.

We saw activity around the six-hundred-year old astronomical clock—still marching its little statues around every hour on the hour while keeping perfect time. Most of the people watching were tourists. Chimes and church bells added to the hourly entertainment. Behind it, the Old Town Square glistened after the rain when the sun peeked out.

The Old Charles Bridge was a five-block walk from the clock. We stopped at a kiosk for a mug of hot coffee before going across the famous bridge—drinking it while sitting on plastic chairs under a propane heater.

"I'm not sure what disrupts the ambience more—my white shoes or the white plastic chairs," Ludwig lamented while swinging his feet.

"Definitely the chairs!" I assured him.

Some kids on skate boards blurred past us, clacking on the cobblestones then jumping onto the flat surface of the Charles Bridge where they swerved around pedestrians.

"They seem to handle the cobblestones better than I did," Ludwig joked, smiling at his new shoes and the young boys having fun. "This would not have been allowed under communism—there was little approved fun; and *only* activities that were approved were allowed." Once again, old memories from East Germany haunted Ludwig.

The Charles Bridge crossed the Vltava River and was guarded by the spirits of thirty Baroque statues of saints and noblemen, and three medieval towers. The view, with the Prague Castle high on a hill beyond the river, easily became a postcard memory.

The statutes and towers were stained with coal tar from ages of heating and cooking with coal fires—indelible ash-gray stains that couldn't be washed off. That old-world smell of coal burning in a damp environment hadn't left Prague—coal heating was still in use—adding to the medieval atmosphere enveloping us in the oldness. About halfway across the bridge we stopped to admire the Vltava River and its many bridges.

"The river runs southeast from here and then turns north and goes across Bohemia—it joins the Elbe River in Melnik," Ludwig explained. I studied the river, looking at it from both ends of the Charles Bridge. But then my thoughts changed! I started thinking again about the challenges Czechoslovakia was undergoing—*it must be like suddenly turning on the lights in a room that had been dark for forty-two years. The collective group-think and dark monoculture has departed!* The Gulf War also crossed my mind with its profound significance. There was much to think about on this fourteenth-century medieval bridge. I noticed Ludwig was checking his watch.

"Ludwig, how will the younger generations adjust to democracy and the free market competition it creates? They have lived their entire lives under communism?

"The new society has to undo years of brain washing! Under communism school is easy—everybody gets a passing grade. Menial work and security are provided for the others. Every day is the same. Some people adjust to a government that controls every aspect of their lives," Ludwig explained. "There has to be a plan to correct these misunderstandings—one that convinces the younger generations to climb aboard and ride in the new direction."

"Yes, but seeing is believing!" I replied. "Such a plan must teach which guideposts to watch for, so successes of the new government are made obvious. For example, monitoring how promotions change in the workplace should be one. Do they become based on ability and results rather than party affiliation? Are bribes largely eliminated? Are food shortages prevented? Are less expensive goods produced—like better skateboards at a lower price? And the big one: medical care! Can an average person get the same quality care as a government bureaucrat? Positive improvements must guide the transition."

Ludwig thought for a while, then answered me. "You raise a poignant concern. There will always be a communist element in society. But many who lean in that direction are not incontrovertible. Your idea of a plan that highlights guideposts is vital. It's predicted that before the end of the year there will be over twenty political parties in Czechoslovakia! Constructive coalitions will be essential to assuring success of the democratic process. It will be a challenge once the euphoria wears off."

The Charles Bridge was only for pedestrians. Our walk across it ended when we entered an arched gateway in one of the towers. Leaving the Old Town Quarter behind on the opposite side of the river, we had arrived in the Lesser Quarter in the domain of the magnificent Prague Castle.

Coming out of the gateway, cobblestones started again and the road slanted downhill. Two older women with canes had to take it slowly. The street narrowed and filled with shops and cafes, including one for stamp collectors. Ludwig collected stamps so we stopped; he found some colorful commemorative stamps celebrating the rebirth of democracy and the free market in Czechoslovakia. He bought some and so did I; another way to remember this historic event.

Ludwig checked his watch again. "There is an old friend who I want you to meet—the time is right. He will be down by the river where geese congregate—a place with benches that tourists don't know about." Ludwig was wearing his Santa Claus smile.

I followed him off the road and down a path through thick bushes and leafless trees until we came out by the river and the benches. An older man wearing a yellow rain jacket was feeding geese; seven completely white geese circled him. Ludwig put his finger to his lips and we sat down quietly.

"He's hand-feeding them," Ludwig noted. The man held a brown paper bag filled with corn and had spilled some on the ground. But the geese only wanted it from his hand, honking in excitement. When all the corn was gone from the bag, the geese ate the spilled corn. This is when the man looked at us. I could see him squinting at Ludwig like he might know him. Ludwig laughed and the man laughed, clapping his hands. "*Du hast mich gefunden*," The man said loudly.

"Yes, I have found you, Pavel!" Ludwig exclaimed. He looked amazingly like Ludwig but a little taller. They could pass for brothers!

They greeted each other and spoke in German for a couple minutes, then both looked at me and Ludwig made the introduction. Pavel was a retired, large- animal veterinarian who had known Ludwig for years.

"I'm very pleased to meet you, Mr. Randolf," Pavel said in English. "Ludwig told me I must speak English! It has been awhile, I may need him to translate some words."

"Thank you—it's always a pleasure to meet a friend of a friend." I felt a tug on my coat and turned around and saw the geese were behind me. One was nudging me.

"Don't worry, they are my pets. They want more corn." Pavel picked up an old lunch box that was on the ground next to our bench. It was full of whole kernel corn. He refilled the brown paper bag and gave it to me. "Go feed them, act like a tourist," Pavel suggested.

While I was feeding the geese, Ludwig explained to Pavel our business relationship and how, as a biochemist, I complemented his knowledge as a veterinarian. Ludwig and Pavel had communicated by mail but hadn't seen each other in over three years.

"First time in Praha?" Pavel asked me.

"Second time; first time was on a student tour many years ago," I replied. "My paternal grandparents came from Bratislava."

"In Slovakia! An important agricultural region in Czechoslovakia," Pavel added.

For a winter day, it was now sunny and pleasant. Pavel sat between Ludwig and myself. An American, a Czech, and a German—a scientist and two veterinarians—sitting on a bench on the bank of the Vltava.

The three of us got into a remarkable conversation. We discussed a variety of subjects from farm science and the Gulf War to the transition of Czechoslovakia into democracy. We talked for over an hour with no awareness of time. The sunshine felt wonderful; Ludwig and I unbuttoned our coats. We were discussing the government transition when Pavel asked if we were hungry. It had been awhile since our late breakfast so Ludwig and I were ready to eat something.

"I would like to buy lunch for us at a good Czech restaurant," Ludwig offered.

"Thank you for that generous offer, Ludwig, but let's go to my cottage and have some *kolaches*. It's close, we can walk," Pavel insisted. "I am so happy you're here, Ludwig and to meet you, Mr. Randolf. It tells me sanity is finally returning to our country after forty-two years." Pavel's English was perfect, he didn't need any translator.

The three of us stood up, stretched, and looked to our right. The geese were over at the foot of the Charles Bridge, and a lady was feeding them. Pavel told us they had been endangered under communism.

"If the command economy didn't keep their trucks in good working order, or the farmers from drinking too much, meat deliveries often got delayed. Since very few people had freezers to store meat, they had to shop every day. Fat geese were an easy target for night poachers," Pavel elaborated. Ludwig shook his head as it brought back old memories. The Third Reich had many threads of communism woven into it—threads the

Gestapo enforced! I was getting more education. We walked together in the direction of Pavel's cottage.

"We are in the Mala Strana district of Prague or 'The Little Side of the River.' We intentionally confuse tourists by also calling it the Lesser Town or Lesser Quarter, or even the Little Quarter. Take your pick. It's quaint, charming, and picturesque. A town that clusters in the foothills below the famous Prague Castle," Pavel was proud to say.

"You forgot to tell Stan that Mala Strana is filled with sixteenth-century burgher houses with arched doorways, frescos and carvings. Some even have statues of saints with swords," Ludwig teased.

"That was covered by 'quaint and charming.'" Pavel grinned.

"You can see the Prague Castle," Pavel pointed up. "Exactly one month after the 1989 revolution, Vaclav Havel, a playwright, walked down the center isle of Vladislav Hall in that famous castle and recited the oath that transformed him into the president of the NEW Czechoslovakia—December 29, 1989."

"I missed most of Mala Strana on my first trip to Prague," I mentioned as we kept walking. I was happy to see it now without the restrictions of an *approved tour*.

Pavel opened the door to his modest cottage just off Vlasska Street. His home was a square blue building with a red tile roof—two stories. It was joined on both sides by two similar cottages, one yellow and one white.

Inside, everything was clean and immaculate. "Let me show you my humble home," Pavel said proudly. He showed us his new carpeting and leather chairs in the freshly painted living room. In the kitchen, recently retiled, he was insistent we look through a high window to see the Prague Castle. Ludwig used a stool; I could see it on my tip toes. The blue-tiled bathroom with its large bathtub was his pride and joy. His bedroom's new oak dresser was his latest investment; he opened several drawers until he found a U.S. Marines tee shirt that had been given to him. He held it out using Churchill's two-finger "V" for victory sign while pointing in the direction of Bagdad. Ludwig and I were impressed.

"It wasn't like this under communism!" Pavel asserted. "I repaired, retiled and painted last winter, after Havel became president."

"Did the communist government prevent people from remodeling and improving their homes?" I asked him.

"No, they didn't. There was no private property ownership under communism. The government owned all the cottages and apartments and inspected them often. So, they were happy to let people remodel and paint. If you got things looking too good, they could make you move into an old cottage in disrepair and give your remodeled one to an up-and-coming bureaucrat—a communist of course. There were many inspectors. That's how communists created jobs and kept track of everything. I'm not exaggerating!" Pavel assured us. "I kept *my* cottage looking okay but not like now. I would put a dead mouse in a trap in the hallway and a plunger in the toilet. That worked several times with inspectors provided I gave them some money too. It was not a friendly world!"

"First-level inspectors inspected second-level inspectors who inspected lower- level inspectors who inspected people like Pavel," Ludwig chuckled at the irony. "If you had enough Francs or Marks you could bribe them—you were always breaking some nonsensical law and not knowing it! Same under socialism, which is communism in its childhood." There were always loose cobblestones under any form of Marxism," Ludwig reminded us.

"I live here alone," Pavel informed us. "My wife died four years ago." He pointed to her picture on the wall leading upstairs. "Before the Velvet Revolution—if I got word an Inspector was checking cottages and apartments in the area—I would ask a neighbor lady from a big family to come over and pretend she was my wife. If an inspector discovered I lived alone, he could force me to board several people."

"It was Lenin who determined a person was entitled to only *nine square meters* of living space!" Ludwig reminded us. My education continued.

"The UN *still* has a plan for that!" I added.

"Let me show you upstairs." Ludwig and I followed Pavel up a narrow stairway and into a large room. There were color photos all over the walls, mostly of animals and nature scenes.

Easels with paintings in various stages of completion were everywhere; two had white geese eating out of a man's hand. An old leather couch in one corner had a pillow and a blanket on it. A rotating fan in the middle of the room created air movement for drying the paintings.

I could smell both oil and acrylic paint. His paintings were remarkable; they looked like photographs! Ludwig was examining one showing several lions on a beach somewhere. I admired one showing a herd of Cape buffalo in a rainstorm in Africa. Pavel was silent, allowing us to look.

"I don't paint just one at a time; I alternate and move around, giving each one a few dabs of paint. They're selling well in Old Town now—there were few tourists and no real money under communism. Good income from selling paintings this year paid for my new furniture."

"Your cottage is marvelous, and this room is crazy beautiful," I complimented him. There were so many things we took for granted in the USA!

"Let's go downstairs and eat some food," Pavel said. "I made fresh sausage kolaches this morning, I think you'll both like them!"

We followed Pavel downstairs and into the kitchen. He opened the refrigerator and brought out a plate with a dozen kolaches on it. They looked like German hotdogs; the bun completely encircled the sausage so it couldn't fall out. He heated them in the oven. They produced an appetizing aroma, like sausage frying in a donut shop, instantly reminding me I was hungry.

Pavel's kolaches were made with sweet pastry dough and spicy pork sausage. The dough absorbed juices from the sausage and produced a unique taste. "Dip them in my secret sauce and eat three of four of them," Pavel recommended. He put the pan of warm Kolaches in the center of the table and a small bowl of his sauce in front of each of us.

"*Guten Appetit,*" Ludwig said as he took his first bite. I followed. The soft dough synergized perfectly with the sausage—not too sweet, not too spicy. After taking three bites without sauce, I dipped the remainder of my first kolache in Pavel's sauce. It looked like caramel pudding but had a pleasing sweet-onion taste with a touch of chili pepper. All my future bites were dipped.

Ludwig and I were into our second kolache when Pavel brought out three bottles of a good Czech Pilsner. He hadn't eaten yet; he was warming another surprise—homemade sauerkraut containing diced red beets.

"Prost," Ludwig said looking Pavel in the eye, then took a drink. "*Gutes bier!* Like in *München.*"

"Cheers," I said, looking them both in the eye. "Good beer! Like in Milwaukee!"

I asked Pavel if he had a radio. "Of course," he answered, sounding curious. He opened a kitchen cabinet where there was a portable radio. When he turned it on it was tuned to a station playing accordion music. It reminded me of my uncles playing accordions at family picnics. Pavel started tapping his foot to the polka song that was playing. But it wasn't music I was interested in.

Ludwig took over for me; we both figured Pavel was distracted and didn't have the Gulf War in mind. "Can you tune to a news channel?" Ludwig asked. Pavel hit his forehead with the heel of his hand—understanding now—then moved the radio from the cabinet to the table, pulled up the antenna, and tuned to *CRo-1, Radiozurnal,* a station for news and information. Two male voices speaking in Czech were discussing Operation Desert Storm. Pavel translated for us: "The attack was a response that followed Iraq's invasion of Kuwait. The two commentators are discussing satellite-guided smart bombs from U.S. stealth bombers. They are listing all the targets that have been hit: military installations, electric power plants, water works, palaces, bridges, dams, airports, and more…"

"More war!" Ludwig exclaimed. Pavel was shaking his head in disgust.

"Sounds like it might be over soon, hopefully—this is still day one!" I didn't want to see another Vietnam.

"*Hoffentlich!*" Ludwig exclaimed, translating "hopefully" into German. He anticipated German soldiers would become involved.

Pavel spoke to Ludwig in German for a couple minutes then asked me if I would like to visit the Prague Castle. "Certainly," I replied. "The same one in your kitchen window?" I joked.

"Same one!" Pavel smiled.

"You only see a small part of it from that window. Some say it's the world's largest castle complex." Pavel loved the Prague Castle.

"Mozart and Beethoven walked its marble pathways; there were no cobblestones to disturb chord progressions in their heads." Ludwig said, he thrived on their music like many Germans his age.

"Just pure music from *The Source,*" I remarked in awe.

Pavel stood up and looked at us. "Keep eating. I need to change from my geese- feeding clothes before we go." He excused himself and went into the bedroom.

While Pavel was changing, Ludwig told me this was my chance to find out even more about how life was under communism in Czechoslovakia—Pavel had experienced it firsthand. I was pleased we could have more time with him.

"I don't believe there is a professor of sociology in America who has heard what you and Pavel have told me about communism. Not even a conservative one, if there is such a person. Unbelievable!"

"There's more you haven't heard yet!" Ludwig said.

We headed out on Vlasska Street to Nerudova Road then uphill to the castle. We walked together with me in the middle. I was anxious to ask Pavel more questions.

"Pavel, can you tell me what school was like during communist rule?"

"Let's start with a three-word summary: It was horrible!" He replied.

"*Schrecklich*!" Ludwig translated "horrible" into German.

"Communist Ideology was stressed. It permeated everything. Only books that supported the Marxist-Leninist view were allowed! Every student was forced to read and reread The Communist Manifesto and other books by Marx and Lenin. Nobody was permitted to discuss their opinions on issues. In fact, open discussions were discouraged and many words were disallowed—words like democracy, Individualism, excellence, profitable, superior. Students that were found with western newspapers or magazines were severely punished," Pavel explained as we walked. It was easy to tell the question motivated him.

"It was the same in East Germany!" Ludwig interjected firmly. "East Germany was controlled by Soviet socialism to an even greater extent. Walls and barbed wire had to be used to keep people in!" I tried to imagine that in America.

"What about the secret police, were they the inspectors you mentioned?" I asked Pavel.

"No! They were separate. Like the Nazi Gestapo during World War II," Pavel stressed. "The secret police became very active after the Soviets crushed the 'Prague Spring' revolution in 1968. In 1972 one of our neighbors was put in jail for reading *Time Magazine* when the secret police broke into his house. Another neighbor was jailed for listening to Radio-Free Europe. I was spared because I kept their horses healthy. Horses were still the best transportation to use when looking for people hiding or assembling in groups in alleys and parks."

Directly ahead of us loomed the Prague Castle. Truly a large complex; we would need a full day to take it all in.

"Look at it," Pavel exclaimed. "I see it every morning when having my coffee."

"While reading *Time Magazine*?" I asked him.

"No, *Playboy*!" he answered, grinning at me.

Ludwig had a good laugh. "If the secret police were still around they would steal it and tell you they'd be back in a month for the next issue!"

Pavel went on to explain about the castle: "The Prague Castle is a huge, walled-in complex of buildings, many dating over a thousand years old. Directly in front of us is the magnificent Saint Vitus Cathedral. Beyond it, the palace—then apartments, churches, museums, and a convent."

We walked and talked as we meandered through the castle grounds. *Maybe this is where Mozart got the inspiration for his Requiem. Or, The Marriage of Figaro,* I pondered.

We returned to Pavel's apartment after our walk and he made us each a hot toddy—Czech version—for our trek back to the hotel. We thanked him for his hospitality and sharing his wisdom. The time we spent with Pavel was special. I told him he should consider speaking at universities in the USA; many needed to hear about his experiences.

At the Charles Bridge, Ludwig and I looked back at the castle and about where Pavel's cottage was, behind buildings on the left. The weather had cooled after sunset but the brisk air didn't bother us. When we got to the Old Town Square and its famous clock it was almost 9:00 p.m. We stopped to watch the Czech version of Munich's Glockenspiel.

Ludwig found another German man to talk to who was also watching the rotating figurines on the clock. Ludwig looked concerned after talking to him.

"Is there a problem?" I asked Ludwig.

"Some Russian men were starting fights in Wenceslas Square. He told me we should be careful."

Now more alert and cautious, we walked back to the southeast end of Wenceslas Square, coming out in front of the National Museum and the equestrian statue of Saint Wenceslas. Ludwig chuckled, pointing at the horse's tail. The tent where the ritual shaving celebration had taken place was torn apart and pulled down, lying in a pile in front of the bronze horse. Fires burned in rusty steel drums on an adjacent street connecting to Wenceslas Boulevard. We heard men shouting and saw six men, three wearing jackets embroidered with bold C.C.C.P. letters; two of the other three looked to be dressed in security guard uniforms. C.C.C.P. was the acronym for the Soviet Union commonly branded on all their Olympic athletes uniforms, but many Russians wore it.

Looking across the boulevard we saw three more men in shabby gray coats, talking and smoking cigarettes while looking at the ground. Wenceslas Square had morphed from this morning, no longer alive with tourists and happy Czechs. It seemed cold and desolate, like it must have appeared under communism. Glancing down the adjacent street again we could see that the six men had started fighting. Those wearing the C.C.C.P. jackets were throwing burning posters of Vaclav Havel at the guards who were defending themselves with batons.

"Crazy Russians fighting with Czech security guards," Ludwig said. "Not good."

"These must be the Soviet strays that haven't left yet," I commented. Suddenly one of the Russians landed a hard punch to the face of the man who wasn't a guard—then the Russian grabbed something from him.

"He's got his briefcase!" Ludwig exclaimed. The Russian started running toward us, holding the briefcase shut with two hands. Papers stuck out from under the top of it, which apparently was not shut tight.

"*Nech Taho Muze!*" One of the guards shouted and started to chase the Russian.

"*Stop That Man!*" Ludwig shouted, translating. The guard chasing the man couldn't move very fast. He shouted again "*Nech Taho Muze!*" I could see looking back that the three men in the shabby gray coats had moved to the center meridian of the boulevard coming in our direction! The running Russian turned toward them. My mind was racing. *Could I do something?* Ludwig looked at me and shouted, "*Go Trip Him!*" I ripped off my coat and took off without a second thought, running fast toward the Russian at an angle that would put me in front of him. Holding the briefcase with two hands seemed to slow him down. I ran faster until I was even with him, then surged forward, twisting toward him and kicking my right leg high in front of him. He tripped and tumbled over me as our legs tangled. The jolt spun me around and off balance. My mind hung on the sight of four bold, capital letters—C.C.C.P.—staring me in the face just before getting an elbow in the jaw and spinning around. The next instant I was falling backwards—hitting the pavement hard then sliding on gravel.

The Russian vaulted forward as the briefcase opened and flew out of his hands. He landed on his stomach, spread out flat with papers flying everywhere. The security guard arrived and jumped on the stunned Russian—quickly cuffing his hands and duct-taping his ankles together. When the other security guard arrived, talking on his radio, he immediately started picking up the papers.

I stood up and assessed my condition: both elbows were skinned, my left jaw was sore, and my jeans were ripped in the seat. Otherwise, I was all right. Lucky. I looked around and signaled Ludwig I was okay. I felt strange; I wasn't hurting much. The fall had knocked the wind out of me which took about ten seconds to get back. That part was scary, but I had experienced it before in high school wrestling after being slammed on a mat. I was very glad the security guards had been behind me.

Ludwig was helping the guard who was picking up the briefcase papers.

When I had first moved to stand up, I saw the three men in gray coats throw their cigarettes away and quickly move to get off the boulevard and out of Wenceslas Square. I surmised they were the intended recipients of the briefcase. The other two Russians and the man who lost the briefcase were nowhere in sight. Ludwig brought my coat to me and I put it on.

The cuffed and taped Russian was squirming and shouting profanities in several languages. The first guard quickly taped his mouth shut and kicked him in the ribs. This encouraged the Russian to make elephant-mating sounds through the tape but stopped his squirming. The apparently-important papers were scattered everywhere. I joined Ludwig and the guards—we were all picking up papers now, including photographs of men and women.

Once the papers were back in the briefcase, we stopped to catch our breaths. Ludwig pulled the back of my coat up and checked me out. "How's my bum doing?" I asked him. "Quite well," he reported, "just a few gravel stripes and a little blood—but you'll be needing another pair of jeans!"

Shortly we heard the loud *Dee-Dee, Dee-Dee, Dee-Dee!* alarms of several police cars with their blue lights flashing. We didn't know what to expect!

After an hour of dialogue with several police officers, and showing them our passports, driver's licenses, and hotel keys, they eased up on us. Fortunately, two of them spoke German, so Ludwig did most of the explaining. Both security guards kept nodding while Ludwig spoke. The police sergeant in charge made me drop my pants and moon him as part of the inspection, apparently to check the validity of our testimonies! *I can assure you this wasn't on my Bucket List!* After seeing the stripes bloodied by the boulevard's gravel and my rough, red elbows, the sergeant was convinced I'd done what I said. One of the other officers made a drawing in his notebook of my bare butt with red gravel streaks, which looked like something Picasso would have scratched out on a bad day. Neither Ludwig nor I could keep from laughing; that contagious type of laughter that makes your eyes water. The two guards and the some of the police laughed too.

The sergeant called the hotel manager to confirm we were registered and talked with him for a few minutes. Possibly checking for the two missing Russians and the guy who lost the brief case. Finally, he permitted us to go to our hotel, telling us to expect a Case Inspector in the morning. Knowing that many of the old-guard employees from the communist era were still employed, I wondered: *Would this inspector be one that had inspected Pavel's neighbors, or be from the ex-secret police?* Retraining of public employees was another guidepost that should be monitored during the transition. Now I had a personal connection!

When we got to the hotel, Ludwig enlightened me: He told me he'd read some of the papers when he helped the guards collect them. They detailed a specific government plan to improve the transition from communism to democracy for all the people of Czechoslovakia, even staunch nonbelievers—a plan that would maximize individual freedoms without compromising security. Key individuals critical to the plan's success were named and photo-identified. It was easy now for me to understand what had happened: Ludwig and I had been part of a failed Soviet spy operation.

At breakfast the next morning I was hailed as a hero. The hotel manager had the head chef bake me a cake showing an American tackling a Russian. Then the staff all sang a song celebrating their recent revolution while jingling keys. For the finale' they gave me a new pair of jeans in my size. I was honored.

No Case Inspector came to the hotel to further question us. We spent an additional night in Prague to be sure there would be no complications. The following morning, we asked the hotel manager to call the police and ask them if they required any additional information from us; that we were checking out and leaving. After a long delay, a police captain came on the phone and told the hotel manager the case was closed.

Ludwig and I worked together for several more days in Czechoslovakia before returning to Munich, Germany. We would come back to Prague as new business opportunities developed—there was an awakening occurring in agricultural biotechnology. Improving silage quality for dairy cows was just the beginning; there were many new potentials for probiotics. Those beneficial bacteria were here to stay!

More political changes were on the horizon as well, we could sense it. Not a return to communism certainly, but better understandings on how to operate democracy and free markets within the confines of numerous political parties. New challenges would come forth in the evolving world. New cobblestones! But the *Prague Effect* would always be strong and stabilizing. Once you've been there, as the old proverb says: "Prague will never leave you."

Postscript:

The man I called Ludwig, sadly, is no longer with us. The residual effects of communism were obvious in various countries during this period, even in ones not ruled under the Soviet Bloc during the Cold War. It amazed me how so many people could be sold by dogmatic rulers who replaced proven facts with corrupted versions. The answer was that many people didn't care; they were satisfied with living under a lower-class system where most everybody was a loser except for a handful of ruling elitists. This is the intrinsic self-destruct feature of communism—eventually winners reappear in large numbers.

To You, My Readers and My World Family,

I hope you enjoyed your trip around the world. I tried my best to put you in the drama and the action. Some of the stories happened on business trips, others on vacations. You probably figured that out by now.

I have been fortunate to have had the opportunity to experience the events revealed in these stories in their unique and exotic locations. What you believe and take away is up to you. I can attest to the accuracy of those parts where I was directly involved, but cannot guarantee the validity of information obtained from others, then used herein; although I believe it all to be true or I wouldn't have included it. Vetting such information is always an author's greatest challenge when writing true stories.

Some of society's most troubling problems surfaced in several of the stories; both subtle and not so subtle messages were revealed. Whether you choose to get involved and participate at some level in solving humanity's intractable problems, as I have, is your choice. There are organizations looking for your help—let your soul voice guide the way.

Sincerely,

Stanley Randolf

P.S. See photo gallery of Stanley's adventures at:
adventuresofaworldtravelingscientist.com

Questions for Group Discussion

1. Which story was your favorite story in this book and why?

2. What did you find the most thought-provoking of the discussions within the stories?

3. Which adventure would you like to have had with Stanley and why?

4. Where do you picture yourself in the action most? How does it make you feel to be in the middle of that particular adventure?

5. If you had a free ticket to anywhere in the world, where would you go and what would you do?

6. What kinds of issues or perspectives on life came up for you in any one story in this book?

7. What is your personal perspective on the issue you chose?

8. How would you change any of the problems you read about?

Questions for Group Discussion